D0936288

WARCRAFT

BONDS OF BROTHERHOOD

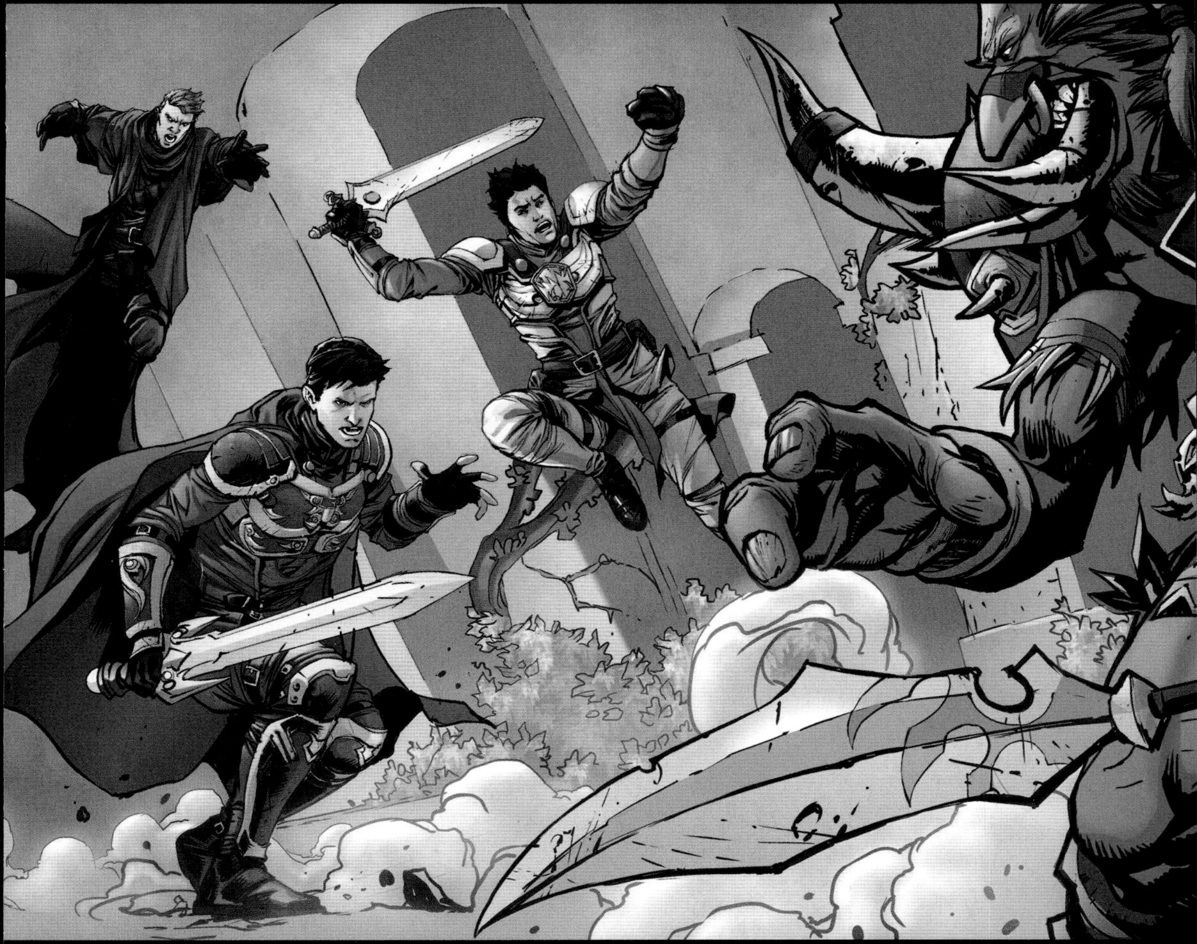

STORY BY **CHRIS METZEN** WRITTEN BY **PAUL CORNELL**

ART BY **MAT BROOME • MICHAEL O'HARE • EDDIE NUNEZ**
ROY ALLAN MARTINEZ • ALE GARZA • MIKE BOWDEN

INKS BY **SEAN PARSONS** COLORS BY **WENDY BROOME • GUY MAJOR • CARRIE STRACHAN**

LETTERING BY **A LARGER WORLD STUDIOS**

STORY CONSULTANT **JAMES WAUGH** PUBLISHING & EDITORIAL CONSULTANT **ROB SIMPSON**

COVER BY **KEVIN TONG** BOOK DESIGN BY **JOHN J. HILL**

EDITED BY **ROBERT NAPTON**

THOMAS TULL Chairman and Chief Executive Officer

MARY PARENT Vice Chairman of Worldwide Production   **MARTY WILLHITE** Chief Operating Officer & General Counsel

EMILY CASTEL Chief Marketing Officer   **BARNABY LEGG** VP, Theatrical Strategy

MIKE ROSS SVP, Business & Legal Affairs   **DANIEL FEINBERG** VP, Corporate Counsel

LEGENDARY COMICS

BOB SCHRECK Senior Vice President, Editor-in-Chief   **ROBERT NAPTON** VP, Editorial Director

DAVID SADOVE Publishing Operations Coordinator   **GREG TUMBARELLO** Editor

SPECIAL THANKS

JON JASHNI • DUNCAN JONES • JILLIAN SHARE • REBECCA ROVEN • ALEX GARTNER • STUART FENEGAN

DIPESH PATEL • BARNABY LEGG • MANSI PATEL • ADAM COCKERTON • ETHAN STEARNS • BAYAN LAIRD

JENNIFER STEWART • KARL ALTSTAETTER • MATT BEECHER • MATT BURNS • BYRON PARNELL

• •

Published by **LEGENDARY COMICS** 2900 West Alameda Ave Suite 1500 Burbank, CA 91505

© 2016 Legendary Comics, LLC. All Rights Reserved. The WARCRAFT name, logo and characters are trademarks of Blizzard Entertainment, Inc. Used with permission. Published by Legendary Comics, 2900 W Alameda Ave, Ste 1500 Burbank CA 91505. No portion of this publication may be reproduced or transmitted in any form or by any means, whether now known or hereafter invented, without the express written permission of the copyright owners, except where permitted by law. This is a fictional work that includes references to true events and real people. No similarity between any of the names, characters, persons and/or institutions in this publication and those of any existing or pre-existing person or institution is intended, and any similarity that may exist is purely coincidental. Legendary Comics and the Knot Logo are the trademarks of Legend Pictures, LLC. Blizzard Entertainment and the Blizzard Logo are trademarks of Blizzard Entertainment, Inc. Printed in the United States. Printed at Quad/Graphics Versailles. First Printing: April 2016

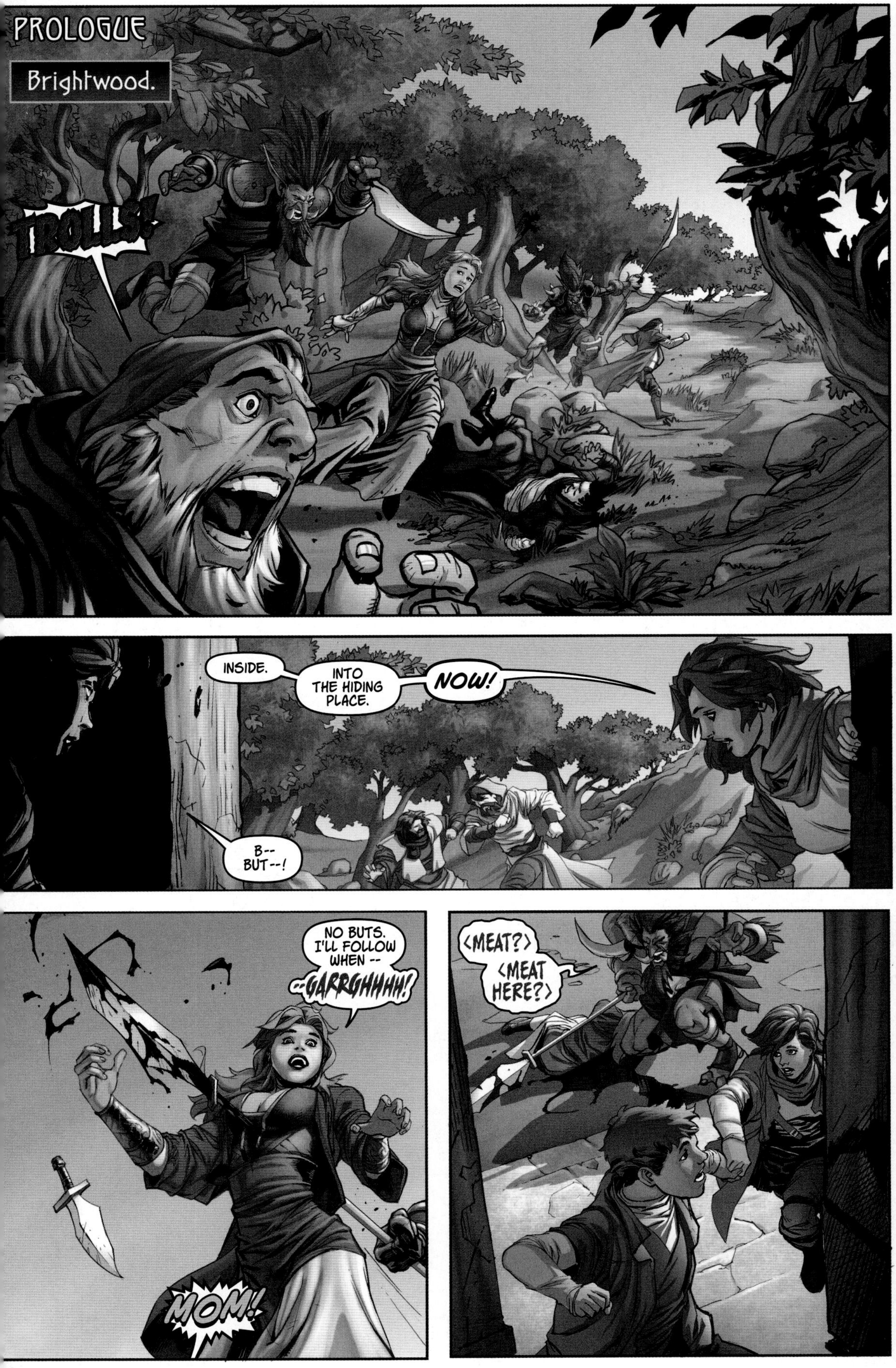
PROLOGUE
Brightwood.
TROLLS!
INSIDE.
INTO THE HIDING PLACE.
NOW!
B-- BUT--!
NO BUTS. I'LL FOLLOW WHEN --
--GARRGHHHH!
MOM!
<MEAT?>
<MEAT HERE?>

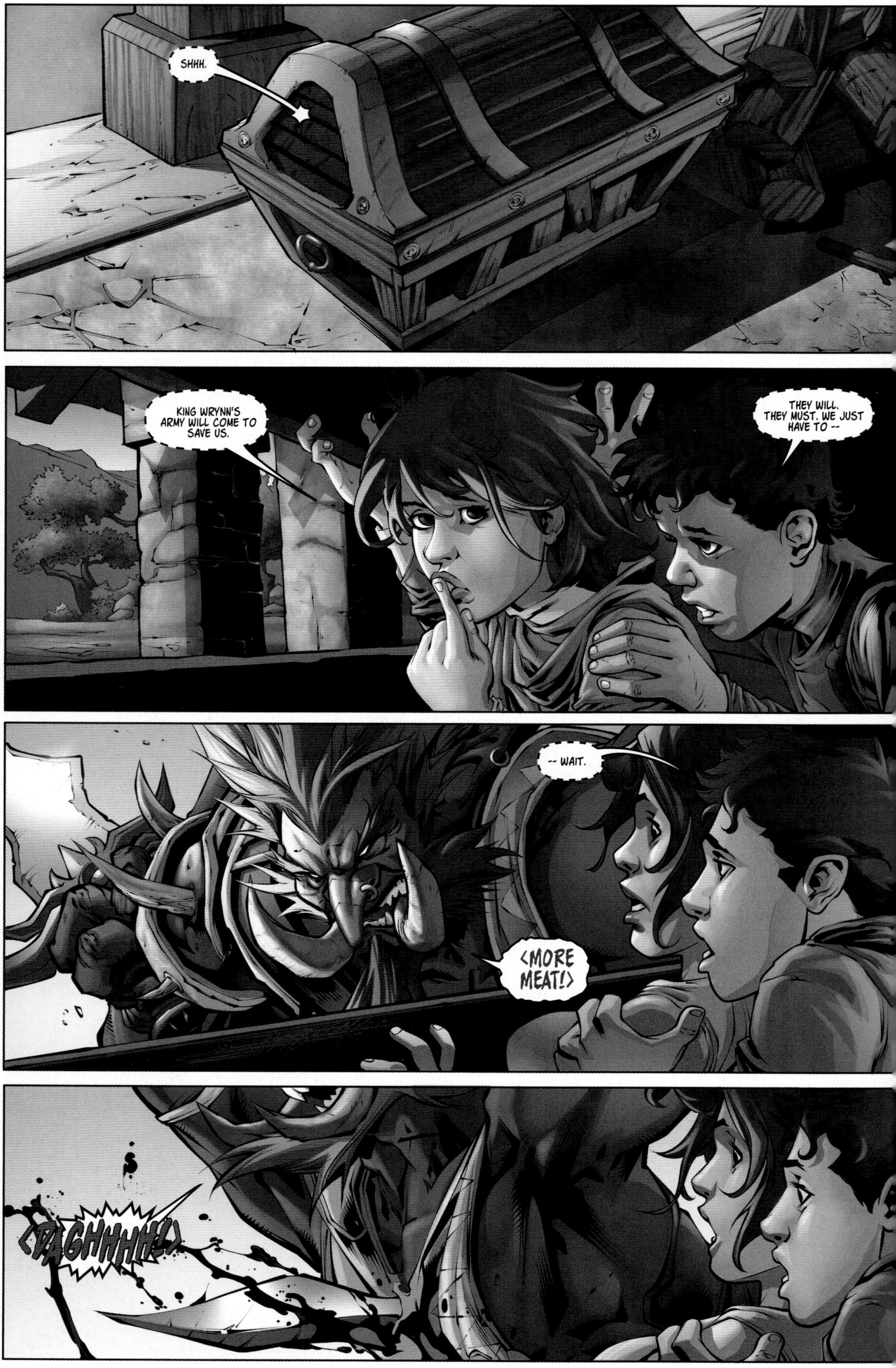
SHHH.
KING WRYNN'S ARMY WILL COME TO SAVE US.
THEY WILL. THEY MUST. WE JUST HAVE TO --
-- WAIT.
<MORE MEAT!>
<DAGHHHH!>

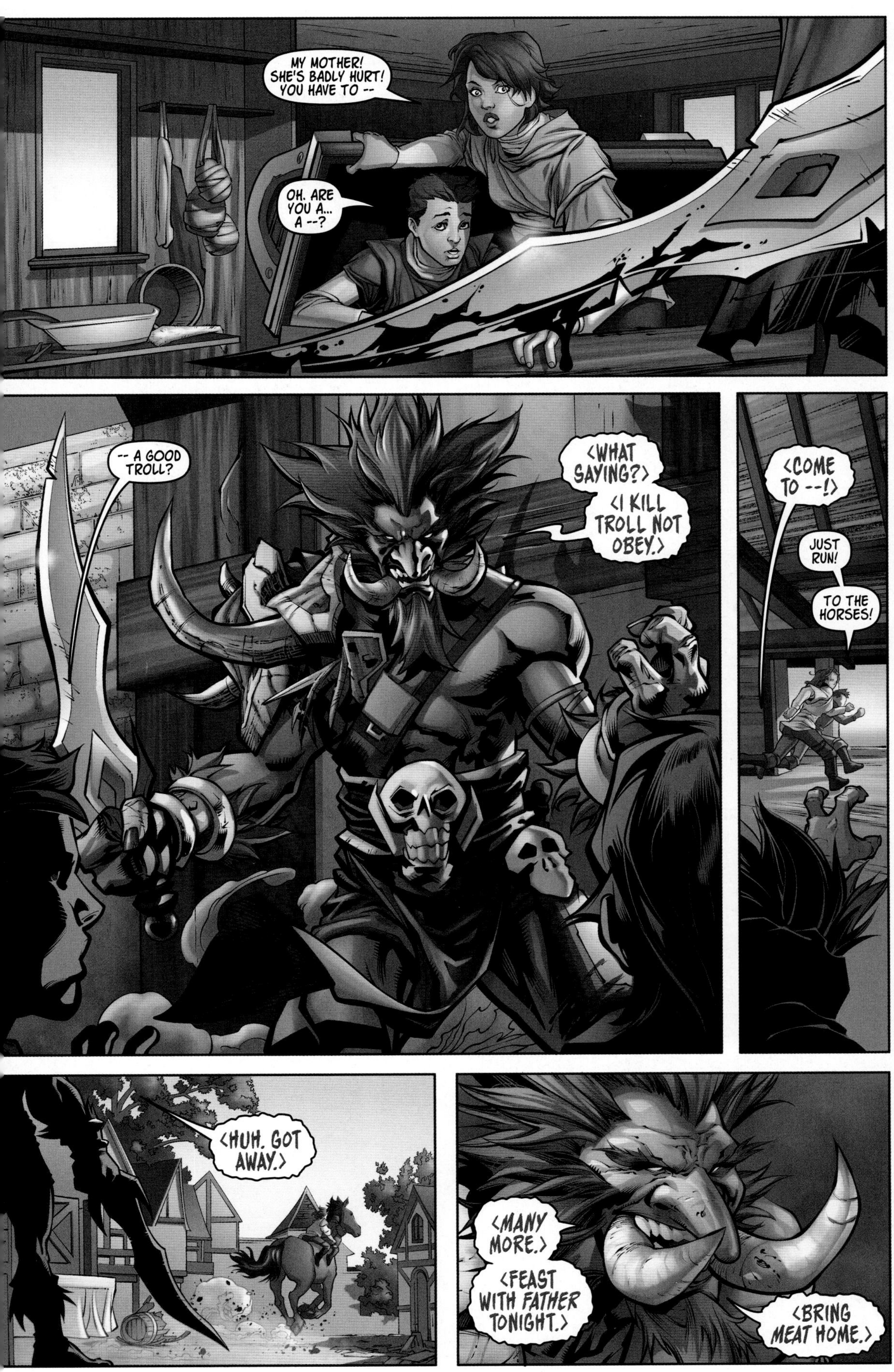
MY MOTHER! SHE'S BADLY HURT! YOU HAVE TO --
OH. ARE YOU A... A --?
-- A GOOD TROLL?
<WHAT SAYING?>
<I KILL TROLL NOT OBEY.>
<COME TO --!>
JUST RUN!
TO THE HORSES!
<HUH. GOT AWAY.>
<MANY MORE.>
<FEAST WITH FATHER TONIGHT.>
<BRING MEAT HOME.>

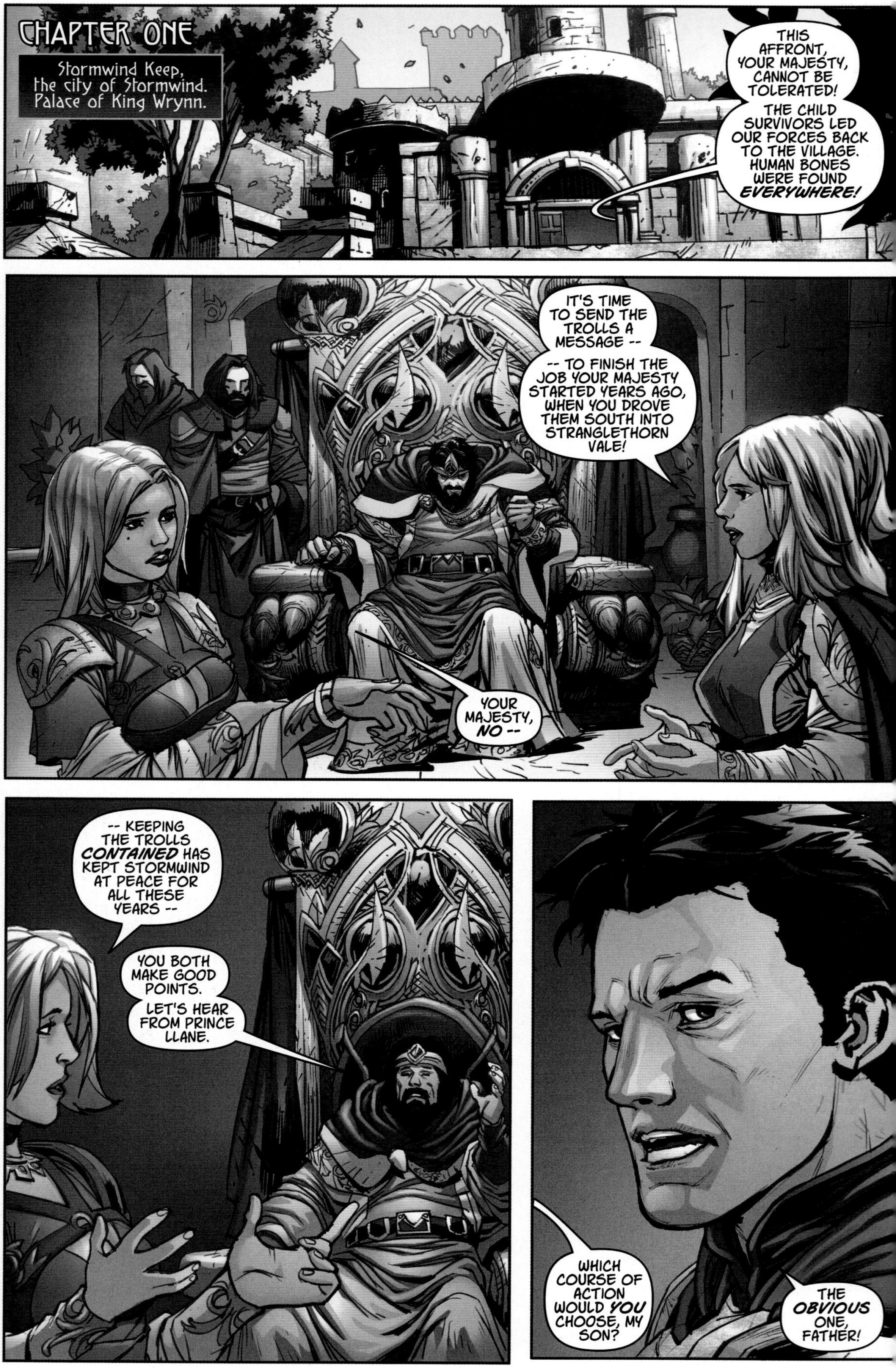

CHAPTER ONE
Stormwind Keep, the city of Stormwind. Palace of King Wrynn.
THIS AFFRONT, YOUR MAJESTY, CANNOT BE TOLERATED!
THE CHILD SURVIVORS LED OUR FORCES BACK TO THE VILLAGE. HUMAN BONES WERE FOUND EVERYWHERE!
IT'S TIME TO SEND THE TROLLS A MESSAGE --
-- TO FINISH THE JOB YOUR MAJESTY STARTED YEARS AGO, WHEN YOU DROVE THEM SOUTH INTO STRANGLETHORN VALE!
YOUR MAJESTY, NO --
-- KEEPING THE TROLLS CONTAINED HAS KEPT STORMWIND AT PEACE FOR ALL THESE YEARS --
YOU BOTH MAKE GOOD POINTS.
LET'S HEAR FROM PRINCE LLANE.
WHICH COURSE OF ACTION WOULD YOU CHOOSE, MY SON?
THE OBVIOUS ONE, FATHER!

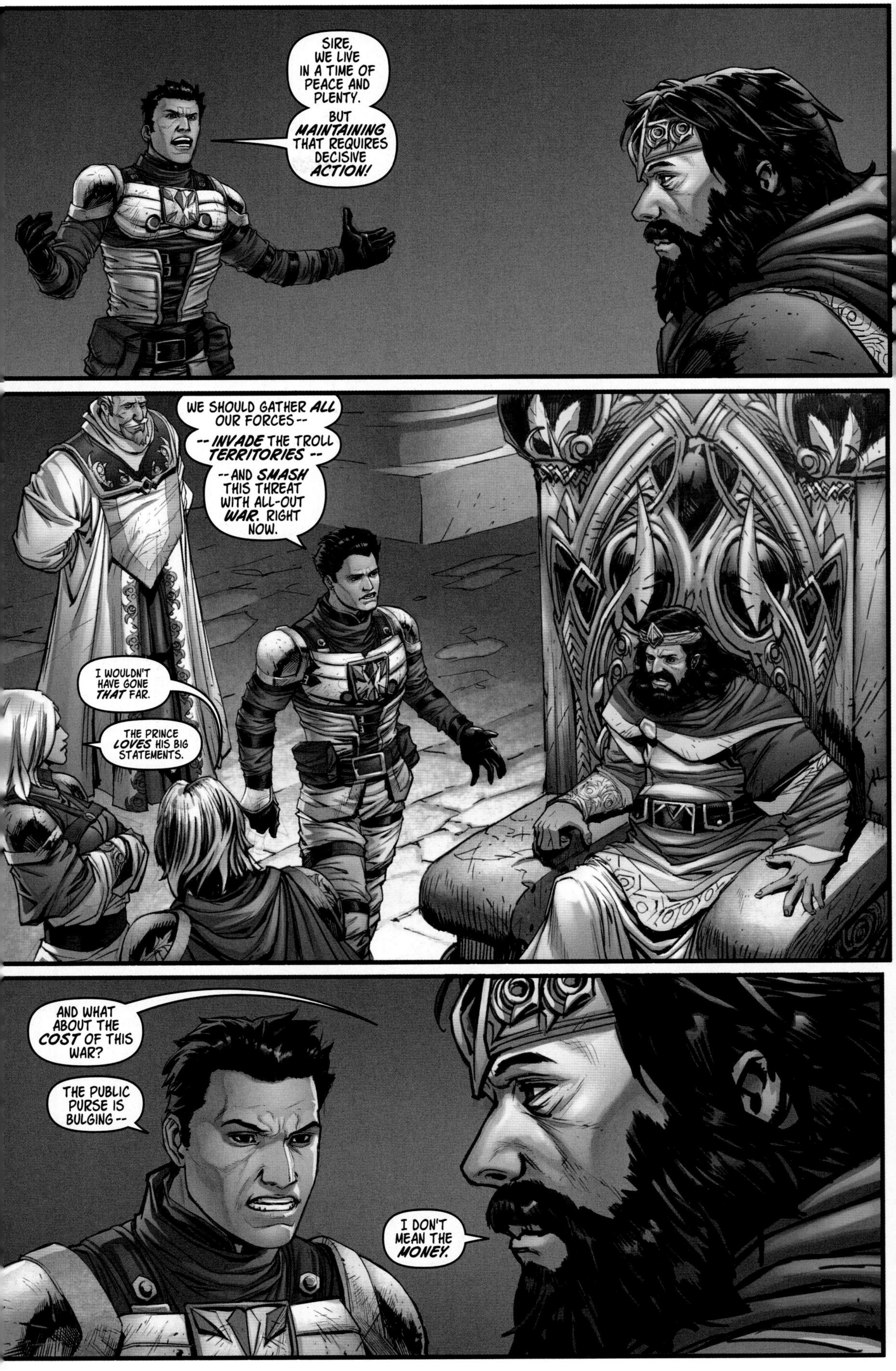
SIRE, WE LIVE IN A TIME OF PEACE AND PLENTY.
BUT MAINTAINING THAT REQUIRES DECISIVE ACTION!
WE SHOULD GATHER ALL OUR FORCES--
--INVADE THE TROLL TERRITORIES--
--AND SMASH THIS THREAT WITH ALL-OUT WAR. RIGHT NOW.
I WOULDN'T HAVE GONE THAT FAR.
THE PRINCE LOVES HIS BIG STATEMENTS.
AND WHAT ABOUT THE COST OF THIS WAR?
THE PUBLIC PURSE IS BULGING--
I DON'T MEAN THE MONEY.

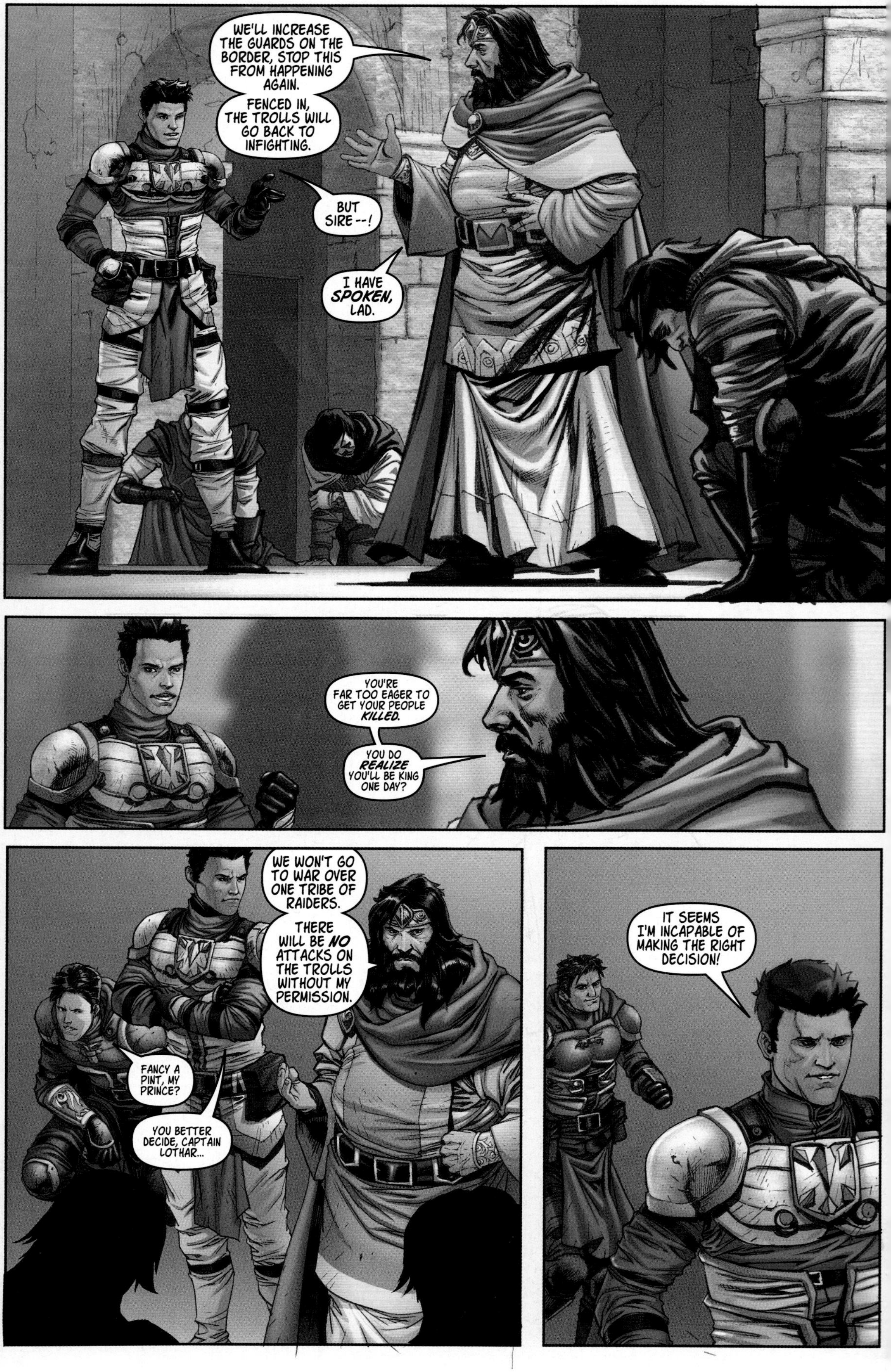
WE'LL INCREASE THE GUARDS ON THE BORDER, STOP THIS FROM HAPPENING AGAIN.
FENCED IN, THE TROLLS WILL GO BACK TO INFIGHTING.
BUT SIRE--!
I HAVE SPOKEN, LAD.
YOU'RE FAR TOO EAGER TO GET YOUR PEOPLE KILLED.
YOU DO REALIZE YOU'LL BE KING ONE DAY?
WE WON'T GO TO WAR OVER ONE TRIBE OF RAIDERS.
THERE WILL BE NO ATTACKS ON THE TROLLS WITHOUT MY PERMISSION.
FANCY A PINT, MY PRINCE?
YOU BETTER DECIDE, CAPTAIN LOTHAR...
IT SEEMS I'M INCAPABLE OF MAKING THE RIGHT DECISION!

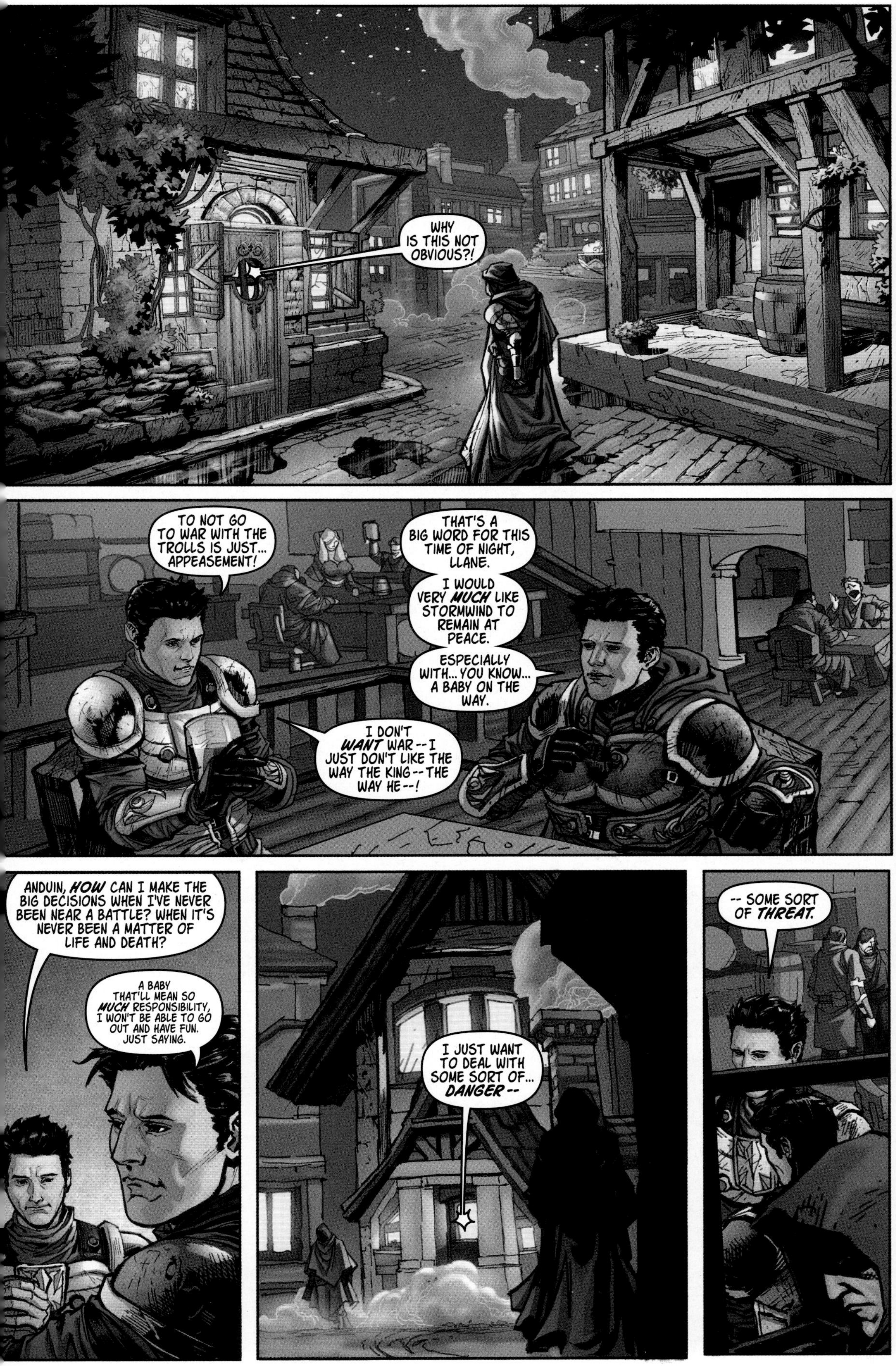
WHY IS THIS NOT OBVIOUS?!
TO NOT GO TO WAR WITH THE TROLLS IS JUST... APPEASEMENT!
THAT'S A BIG WORD FOR THIS TIME OF NIGHT, LLANE.
I WOULD VERY MUCH LIKE STORMWIND TO REMAIN AT PEACE.
ESPECIALLY WITH... YOU KNOW... A BABY ON THE WAY.
I DON'T WANT WAR -- I JUST DON'T LIKE THE WAY THE KING -- THE WAY HE --!
ANDUIN, HOW CAN I MAKE THE BIG DECISIONS WHEN I'VE NEVER BEEN NEAR A BATTLE? WHEN IT'S NEVER BEEN A MATTER OF LIFE AND DEATH?
A BABY THAT'LL MEAN SO MUCH RESPONSIBILITY, I WON'T BE ABLE TO GO OUT AND HAVE FUN. JUST SAYING.
I JUST WANT TO DEAL WITH SOME SORT OF... DANGER --
-- SOME SORT OF THREAT.

IS THAT THE PRINCE'S VOICE I HEAR? I THOUGHT THIS WAS A RESPECTABLE ESTABLISHMENT!

IT'S THE GUARDIAN!

WE GET *ALL* THE IMPORTANT PEOPLE.

AND YET OUR PRICES ARE SO REASONABLE.

MEDIVH?!

WHAT ARE YOU DOING BACK IN STORMWIND?

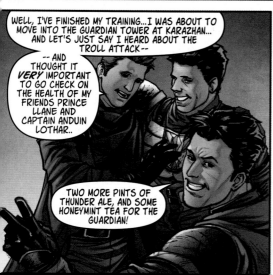

WELL, I'VE FINISHED MY TRAINING...I WAS ABOUT TO MOVE INTO THE GUARDIAN TOWER AT KARAZHAN... AND LET'S JUST SAY I HEARD ABOUT THE TROLL ATTACK--

-- AND THOUGHT IT *VERY* IMPORTANT TO GO CHECK ON THE HEALTH OF MY FRIENDS PRINCE LLANE AND CAPTAIN ANDUIN LOTHAR..

TWO MORE PINTS OF THUNDER ALE, AND SOME HONEYMINT TEA FOR THE GUARDIAN!

YOU'VE CHANGED SO MUCH. YOU LOOK...

...LIKE THE WEIGHT OF THE WORLD'S ON YOUR SHOULDERS.

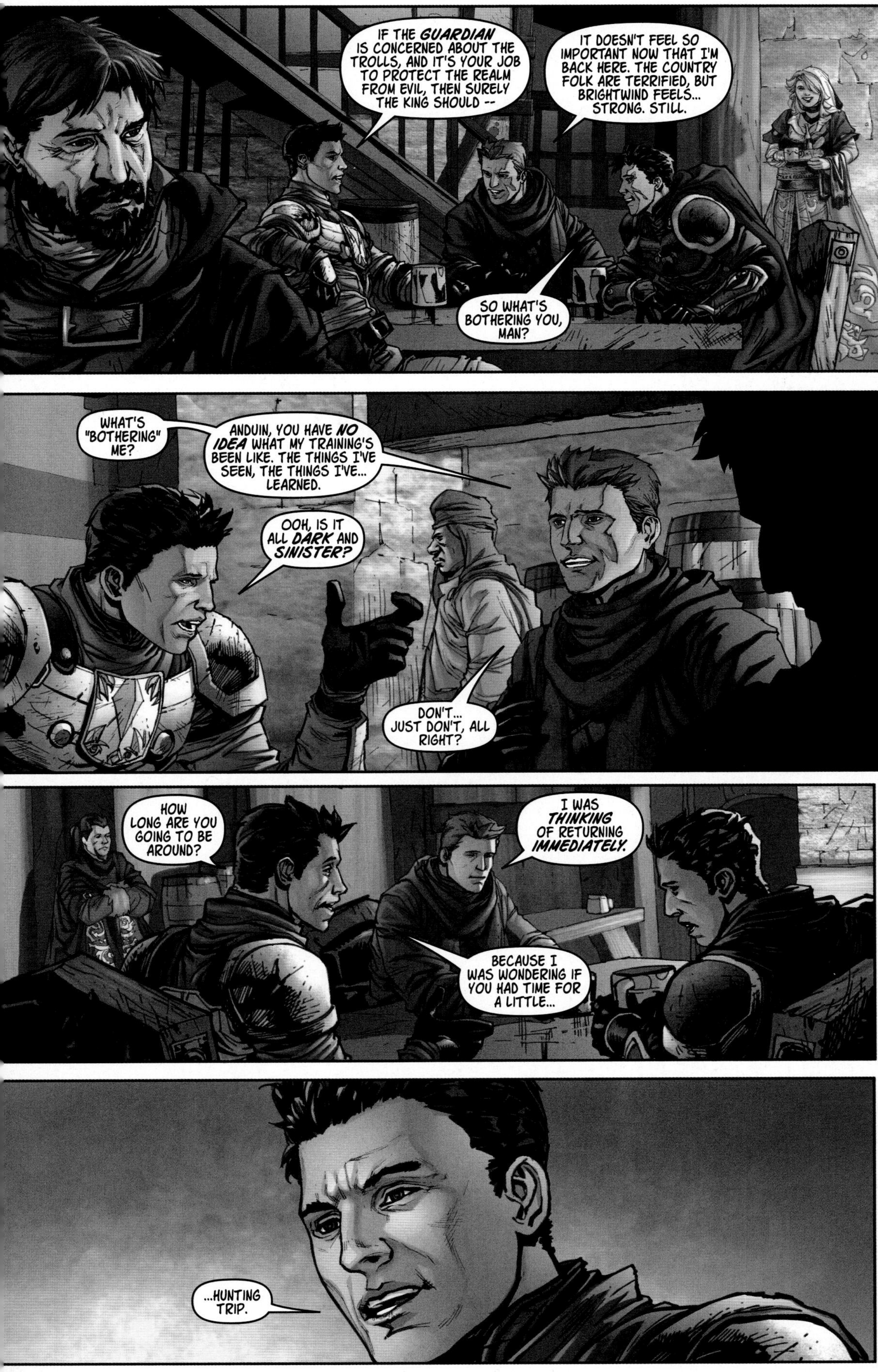

IF THE GUARDIAN IS CONCERNED ABOUT THE TROLLS, AND IT'S YOUR JOB TO PROTECT THE REALM FROM EVIL, THEN SURELY THE KING SHOULD --
IT DOESN'T FEEL SO IMPORTANT NOW THAT I'M BACK HERE. THE COUNTRY FOLK ARE TERRIFIED, BUT BRIGHTWIND FEELS... STRONG. STILL.
SO WHAT'S BOTHERING YOU, MAN?
WHAT'S "BOTHERING" ME?
ANDUIN, YOU HAVE NO IDEA WHAT MY TRAINING'S BEEN LIKE. THE THINGS I'VE SEEN, THE THINGS I'VE... LEARNED.
OOH, IS IT ALL DARK AND SINISTER?
DON'T... JUST DON'T, ALL RIGHT?
HOW LONG ARE YOU GOING TO BE AROUND?
I WAS THINKING OF RETURNING IMMEDIATELY.
BECAUSE I WAS WONDERING IF YOU HAD TIME FOR A LITTLE...
...HUNTING TRIP.

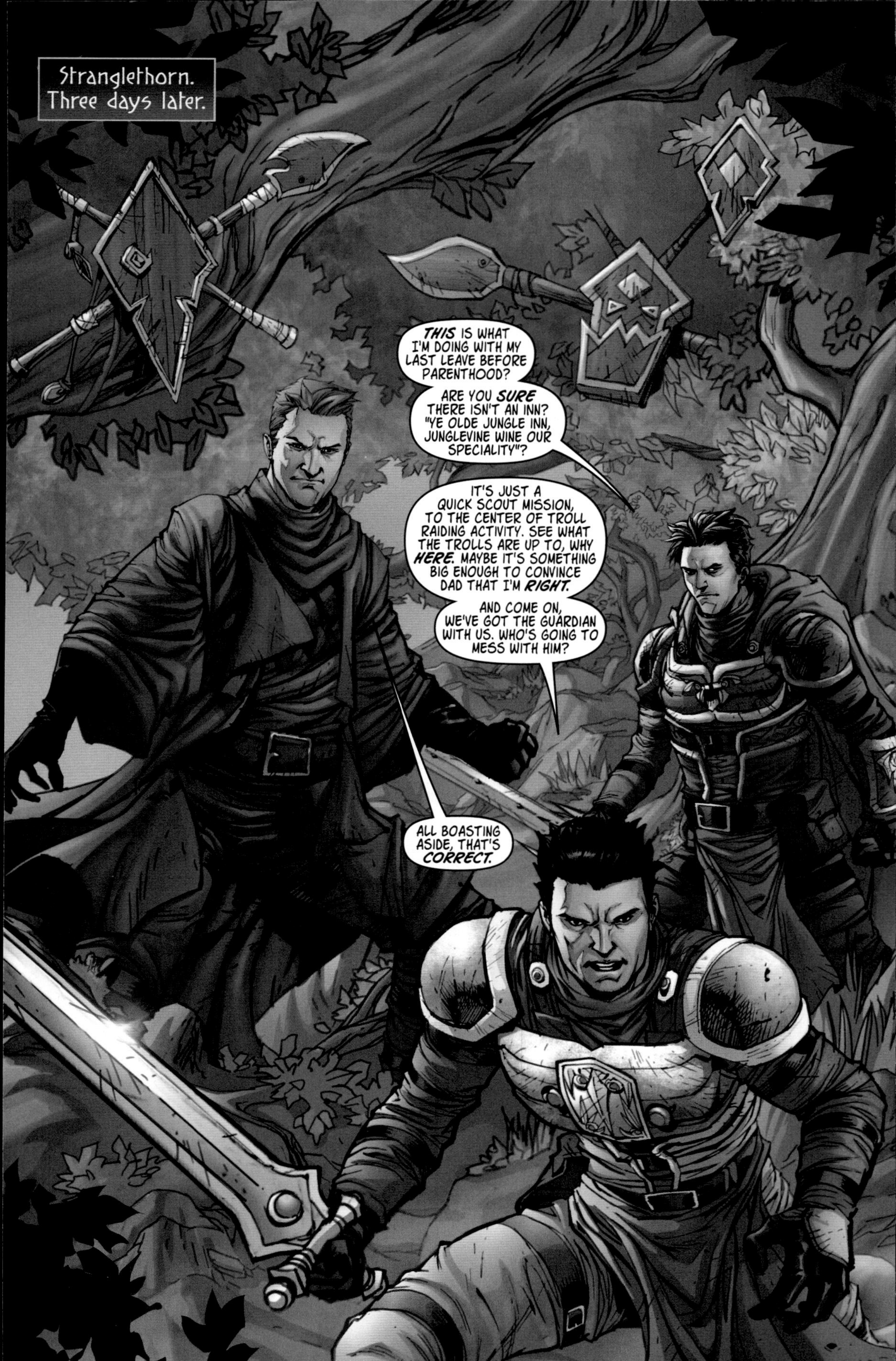
Stranglethorn. Three days later.
THIS IS WHAT I'M DOING WITH MY LAST LEAVE BEFORE PARENTHOOD?
ARE YOU SURE THERE ISN'T AN INN? "YE OLDE JUNGLE INN, JUNGLEVINE WINE OUR SPECIALITY"?
IT'S JUST A QUICK SCOUT MISSION, TO THE CENTER OF TROLL RAIDING ACTIVITY. SEE WHAT THE TROLLS ARE UP TO, WHY HERE. MAYBE IT'S SOMETHING BIG ENOUGH TO CONVINCE DAD THAT I'M RIGHT.
AND COME ON, WE'VE GOT THE GUARDIAN WITH US. WHO'S GOING TO MESS WITH HIM?
ALL BOASTING ASIDE, THAT'S CORRECT.

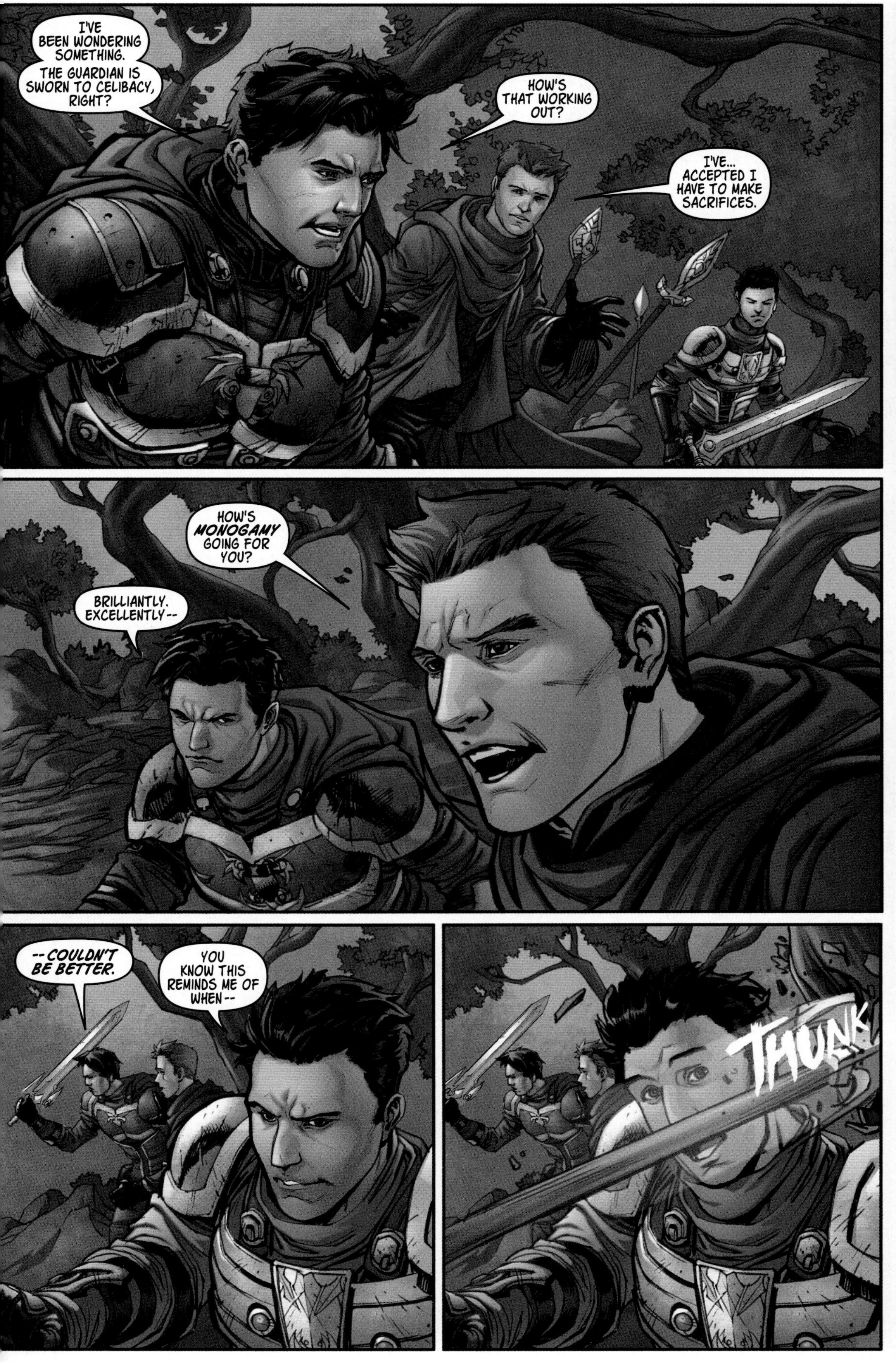
I'VE BEEN WONDERING SOMETHING.
THE GUARDIAN IS SWORN TO CELIBACY, RIGHT?
HOW'S THAT WORKING OUT?
I'VE... ACCEPTED I HAVE TO MAKE SACRIFICES.
HOW'S *MONOGAMY* GOING FOR YOU?
BRILLIANTLY. EXCELLENTLY--
--COULDN'T BE BETTER.
YOU KNOW THIS REMINDS ME OF WHEN--
THUNK

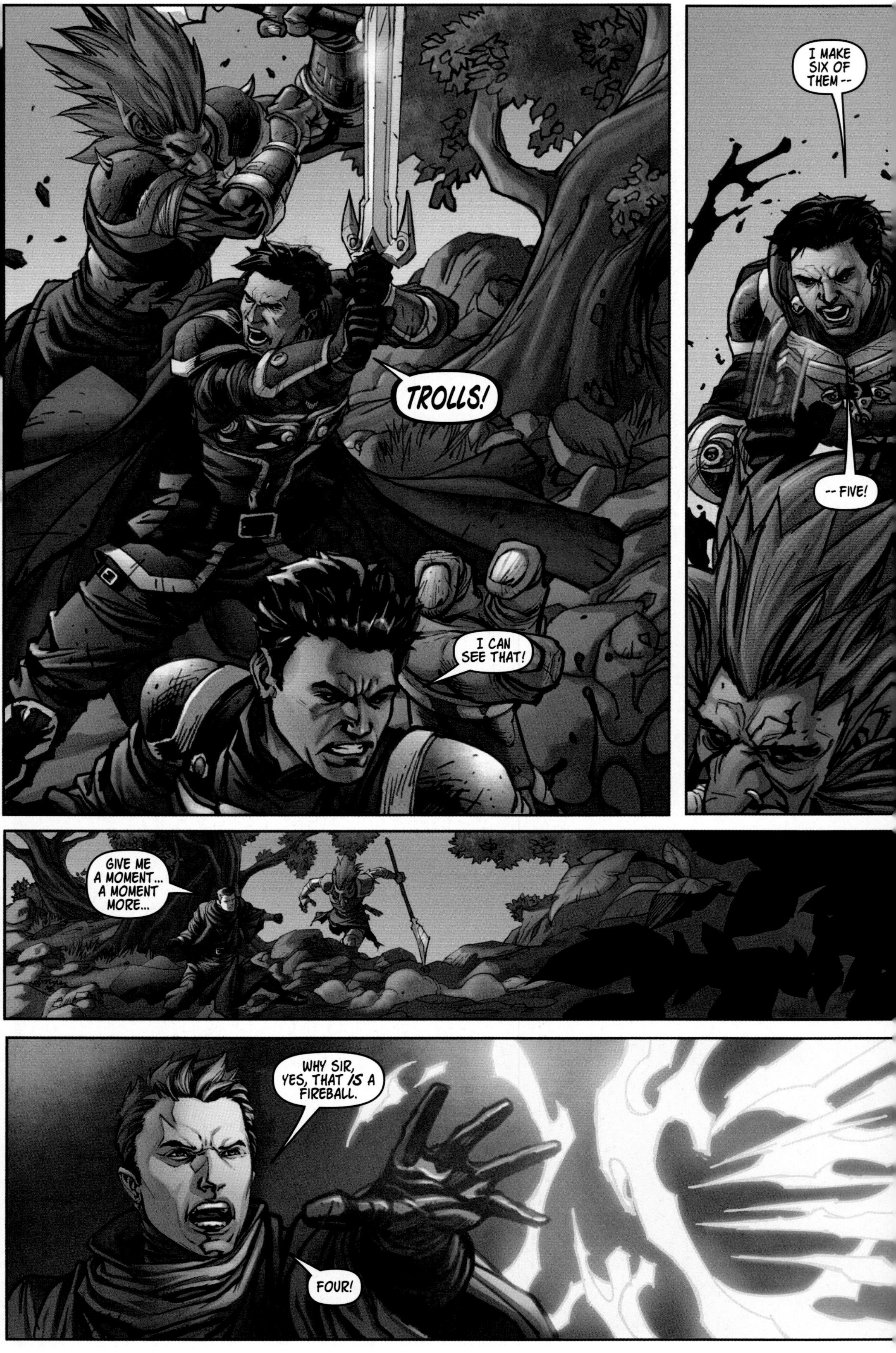
TROLLS!
I CAN SEE THAT!
I MAKE SIX OF THEM --
-- FIVE!
GIVE ME A MOMENT... A MOMENT MORE...
WHY SIR, YES, THAT IS A FIREBALL.
FOUR!

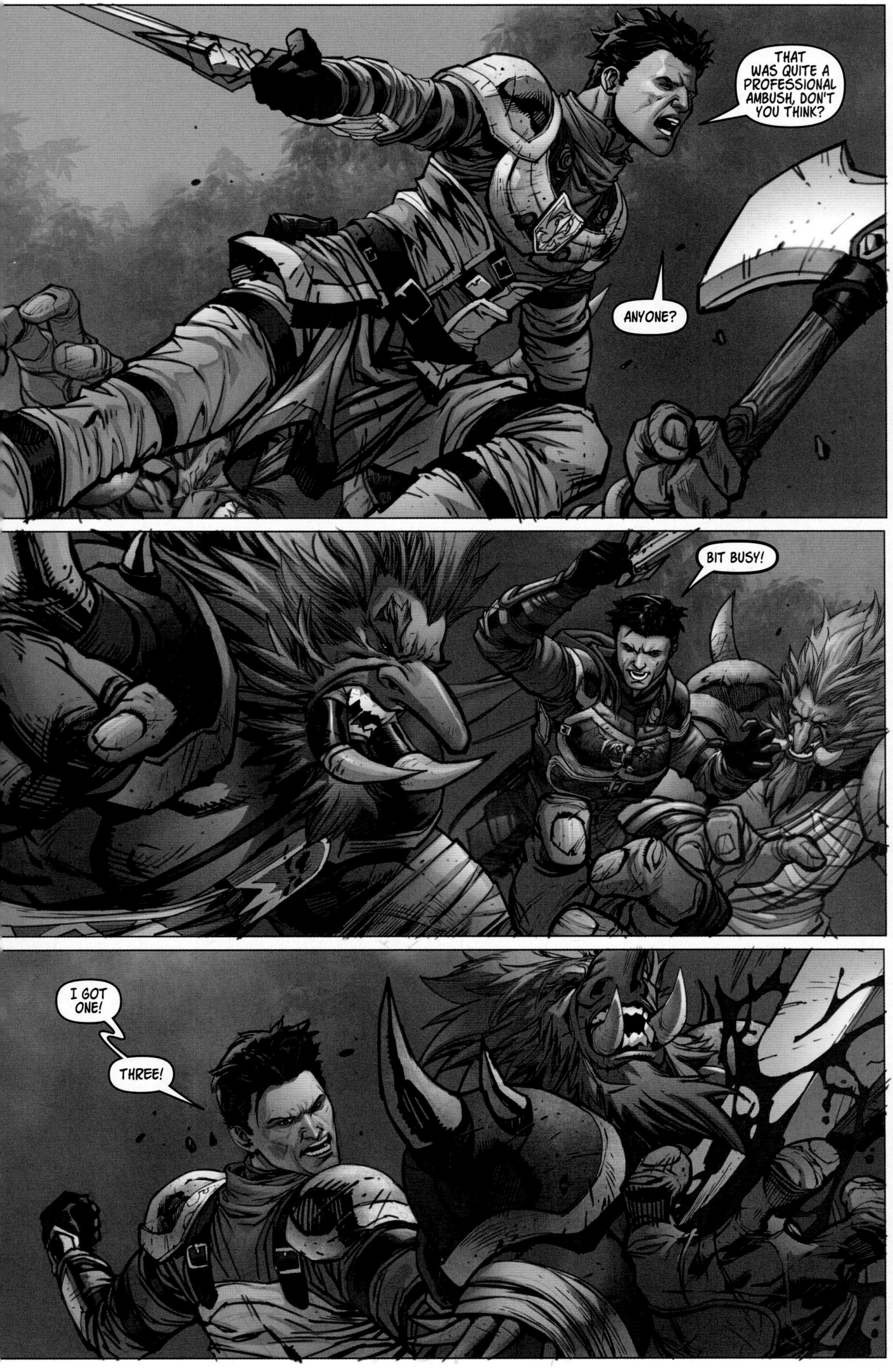
THAT WAS QUITE A PROFESSIONAL AMBUSH, DON'T YOU THINK?
ANYONE?
BIT BUSY!
I GOT ONE!
THREE!

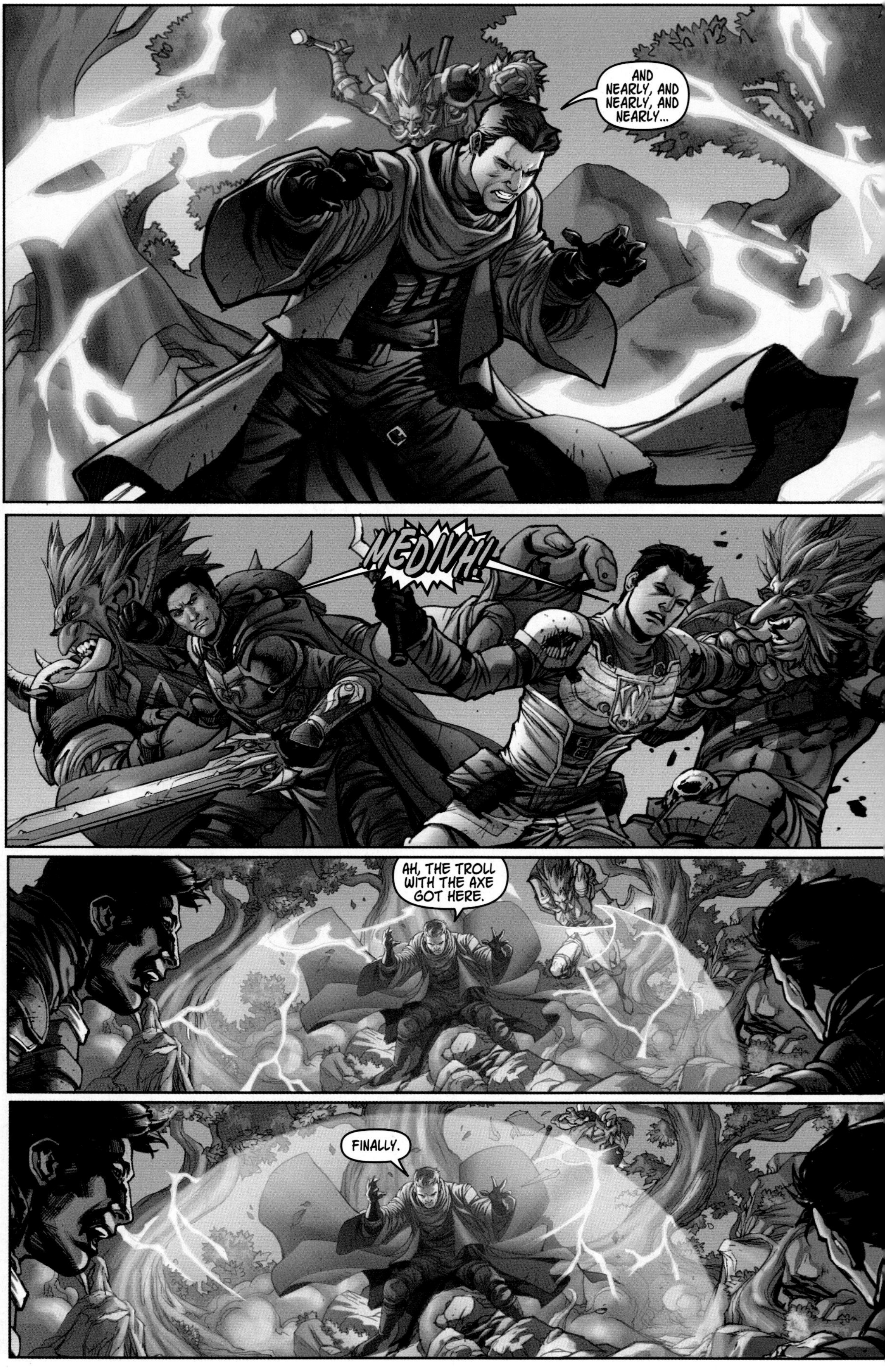
AND NEARLY, AND NEARLY, AND NEARLY...
MEDIVH!
AH, THE TROLL WITH THE AXE GOT HERE.
FINALLY.

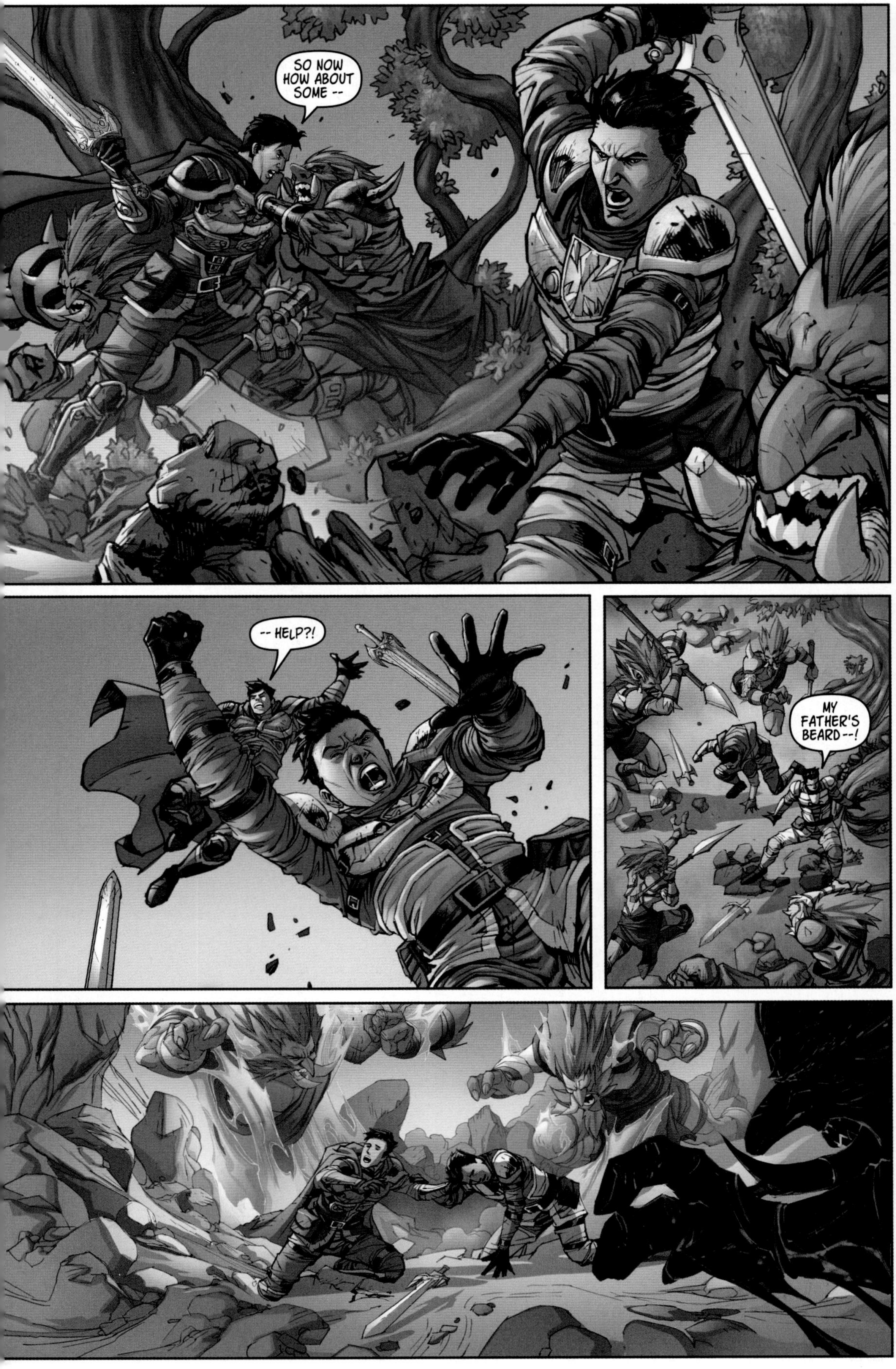
SO NOW HOW ABOUT SOME --
-- HELP?!
MY FATHER'S BEARD --!

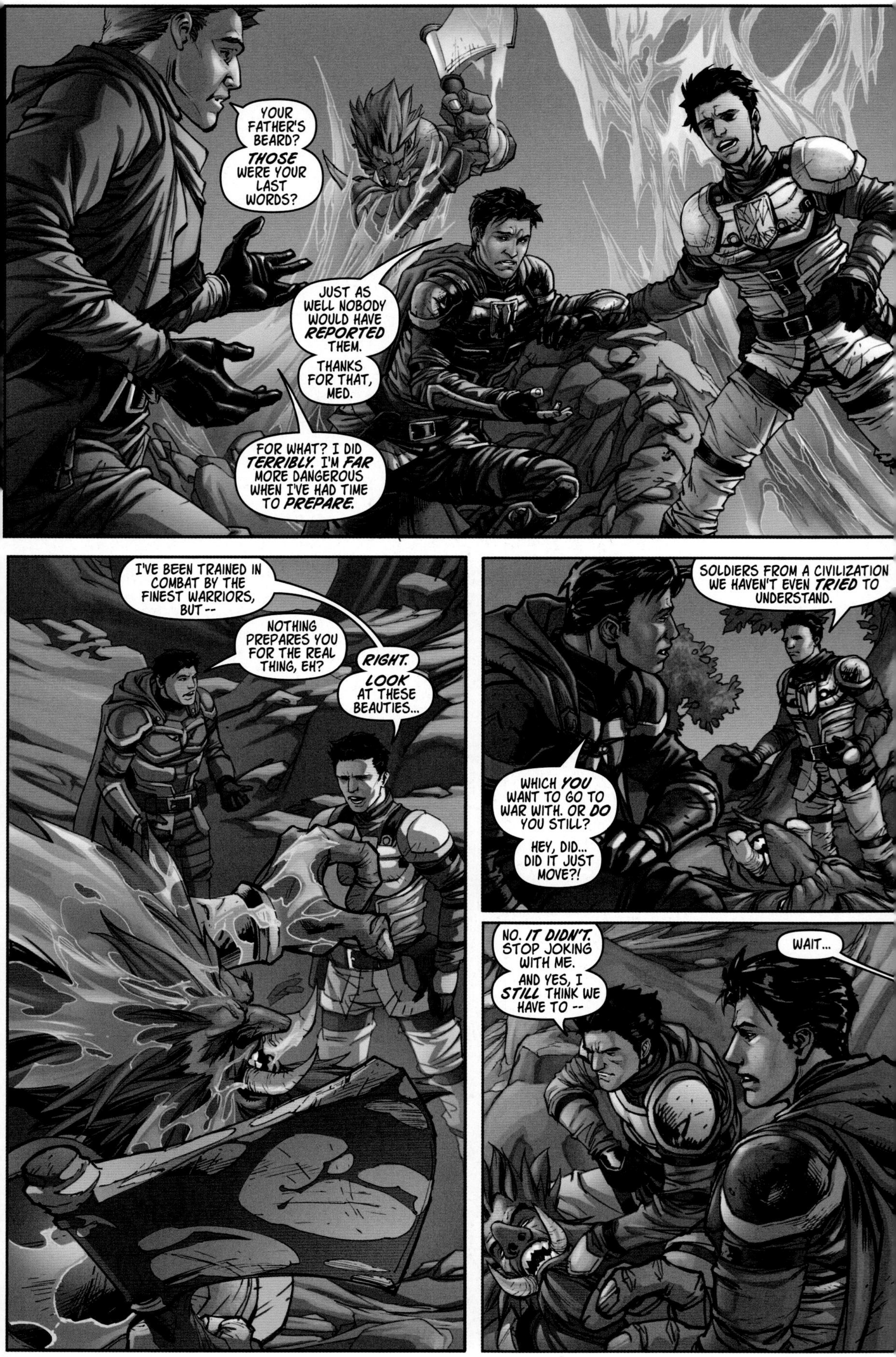
YOUR FATHER'S BEARD? *THOSE* WERE YOUR LAST WORDS?
JUST AS WELL NOBODY WOULD HAVE *REPORTED* THEM.
THANKS FOR THAT, MED.
FOR WHAT? I DID *TERRIBLY.* I'M *FAR* MORE DANGEROUS WHEN I'VE HAD TIME TO *PREPARE.*
I'VE BEEN TRAINED IN COMBAT BY THE FINEST WARRIORS, BUT --
NOTHING PREPARES YOU FOR THE REAL THING, EH?
RIGHT.
LOOK AT THESE BEAUTIES...
SOLDIERS FROM A CIVILIZATION WE HAVEN'T EVEN *TRIED* TO UNDERSTAND.
WHICH *YOU* WANT TO GO TO WAR WITH. OR *DO* YOU STILL?
HEY, DID... DID IT JUST MOVE?!
NO. *IT DIDN'T.* STOP JOKING WITH ME.
AND YES, I *STILL* THINK WE HAVE TO --
WAIT...

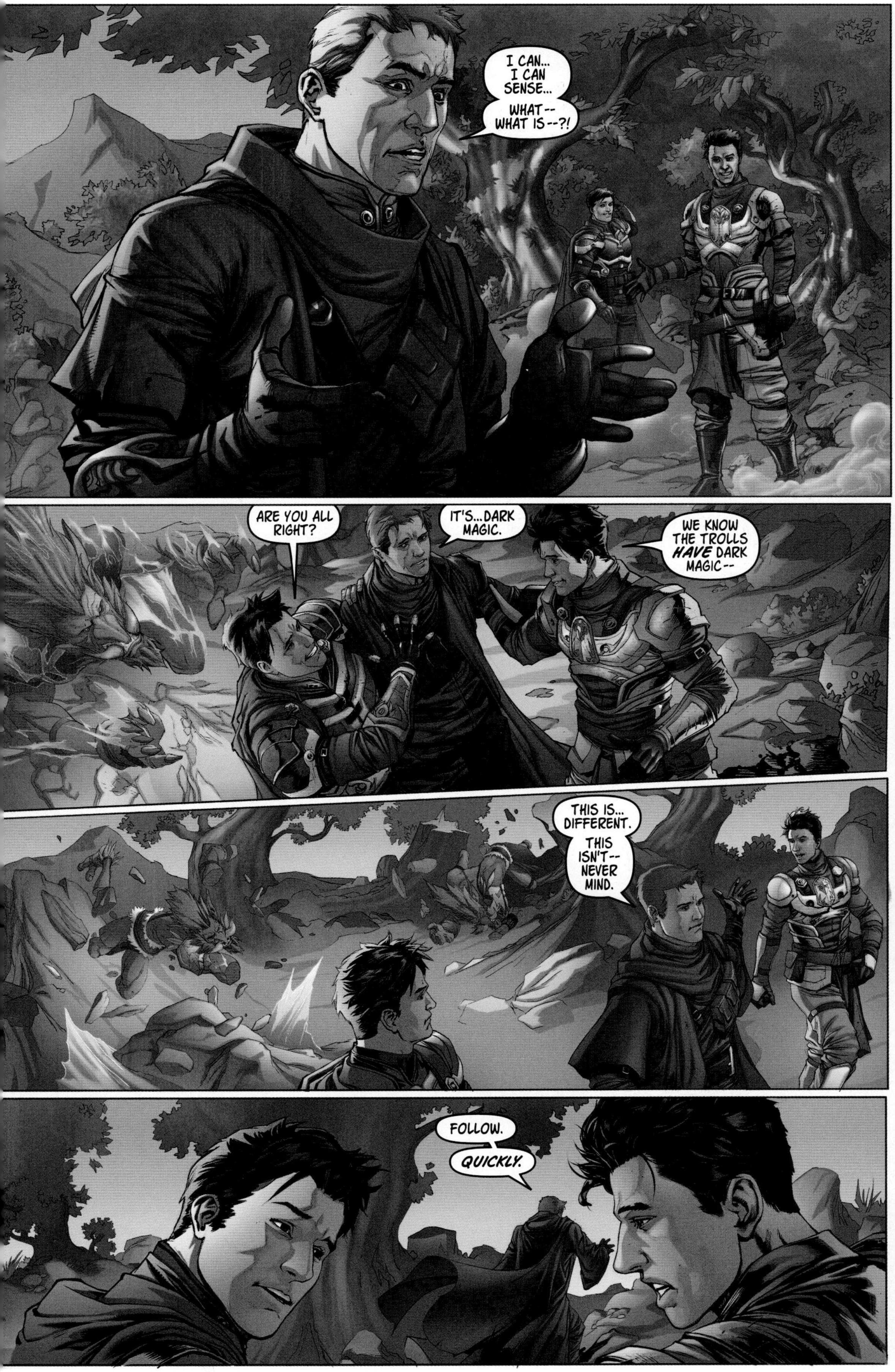
I CAN... I CAN SENSE...
WHAT-- WHAT IS--?!
ARE YOU ALL RIGHT?
IT'S...DARK MAGIC.
WE KNOW THE TROLLS *HAVE* DARK MAGIC--
THIS IS... DIFFERENT.
THIS ISN'T-- NEVER MIND.
FOLLOW.
QUICKLY.

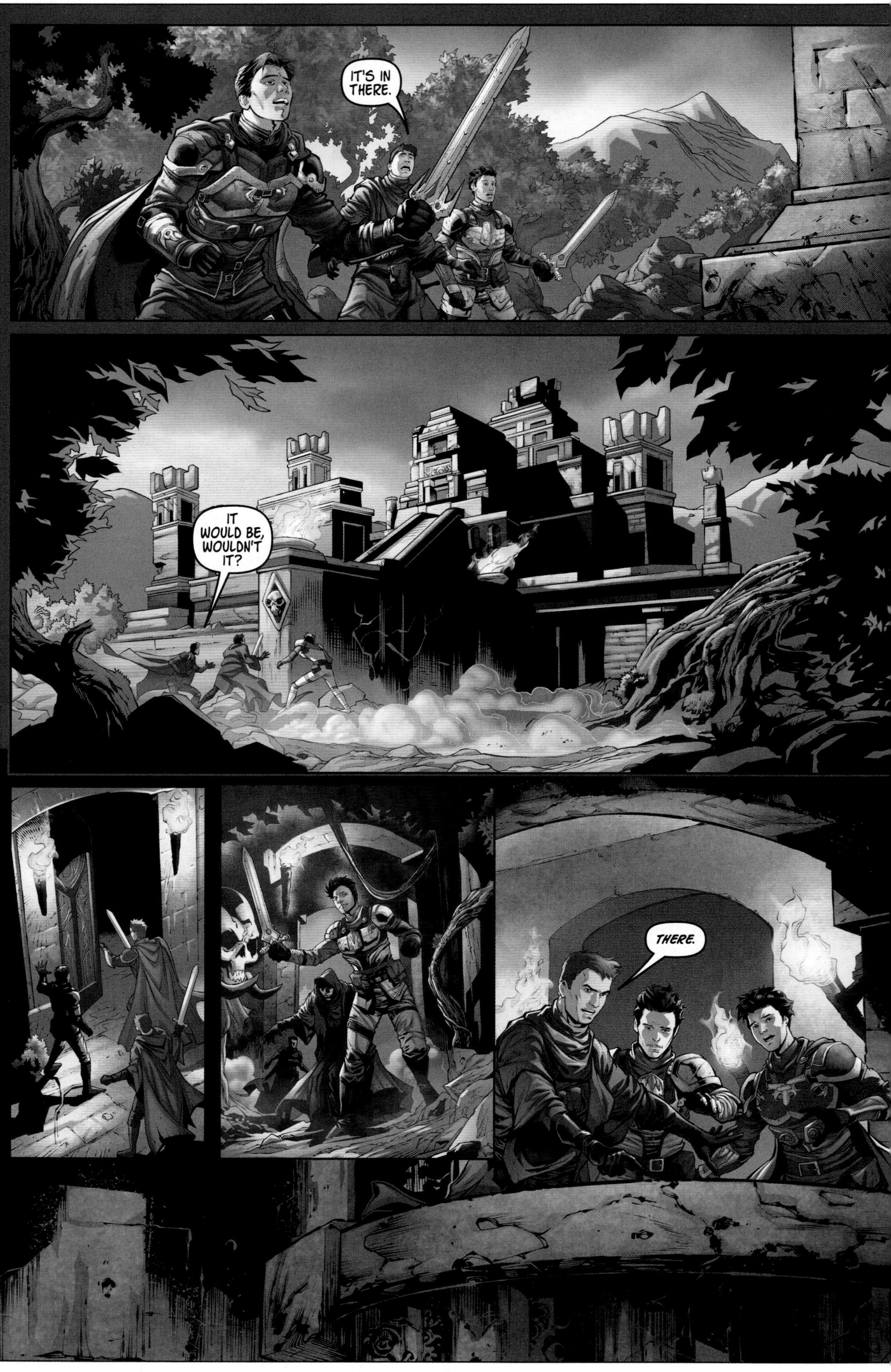
IT'S IN THERE.
IT WOULD BE, WOULDN'T IT?
THERE.

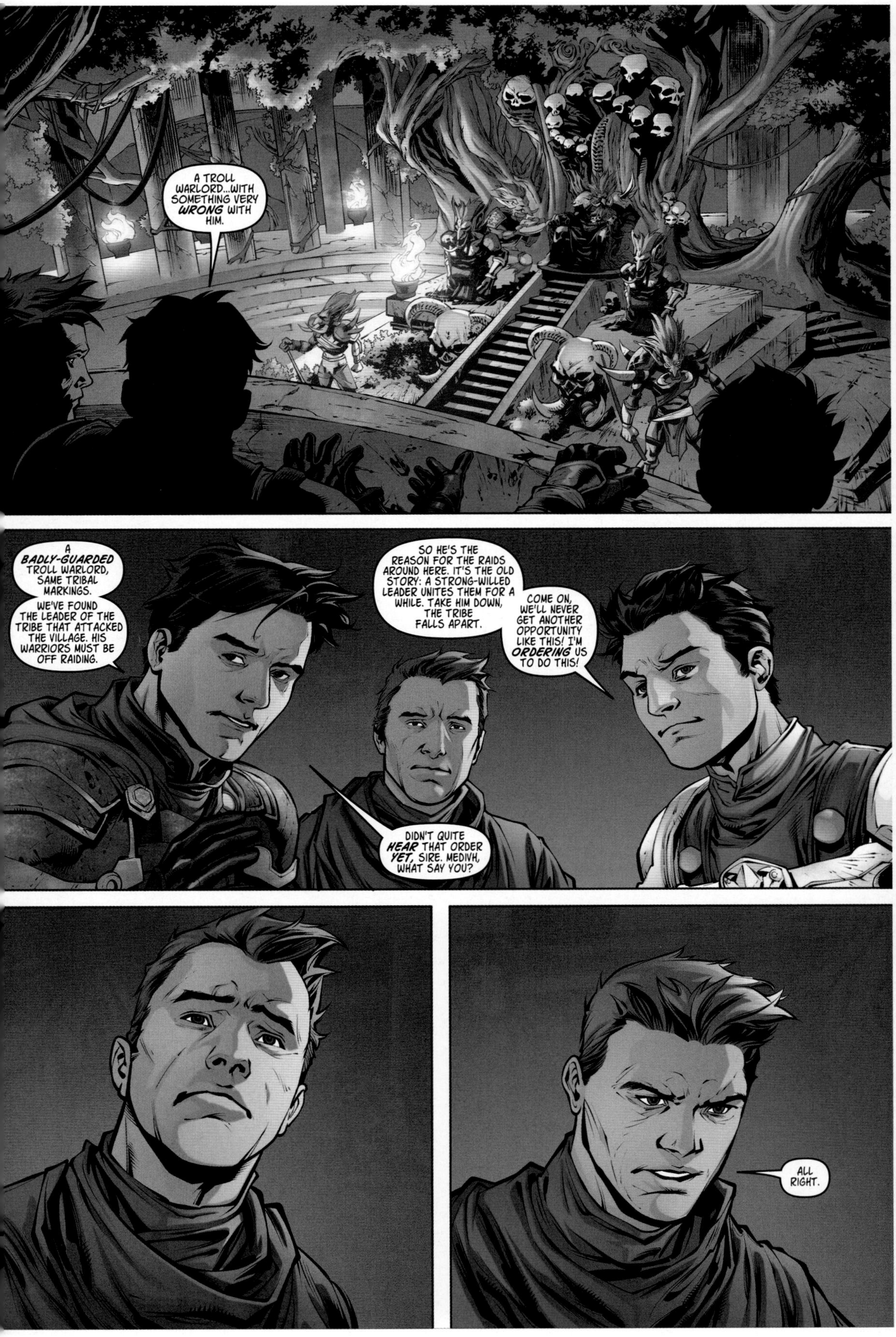

A TROLL WARLORD...WITH SOMETHING VERY WRONG WITH HIM.
A BADLY-GUARDED TROLL WARLORD, SAME TRIBAL MARKINGS.
WE'VE FOUND THE LEADER OF THE TRIBE THAT ATTACKED THE VILLAGE. HIS WARRIORS MUST BE OFF RAIDING.
SO HE'S THE REASON FOR THE RAIDS AROUND HERE. IT'S THE OLD STORY: A STRONG-WILLED LEADER UNITES THEM FOR A WHILE. TAKE HIM DOWN, THE TRIBE FALLS APART.
COME ON, WE'LL NEVER GET ANOTHER OPPORTUNITY LIKE THIS! I'M ORDERING US TO DO THIS!
DIDN'T QUITE HEAR THAT ORDER YET, SIRE. MEDIVH, WHAT SAY YOU?
ALL RIGHT.

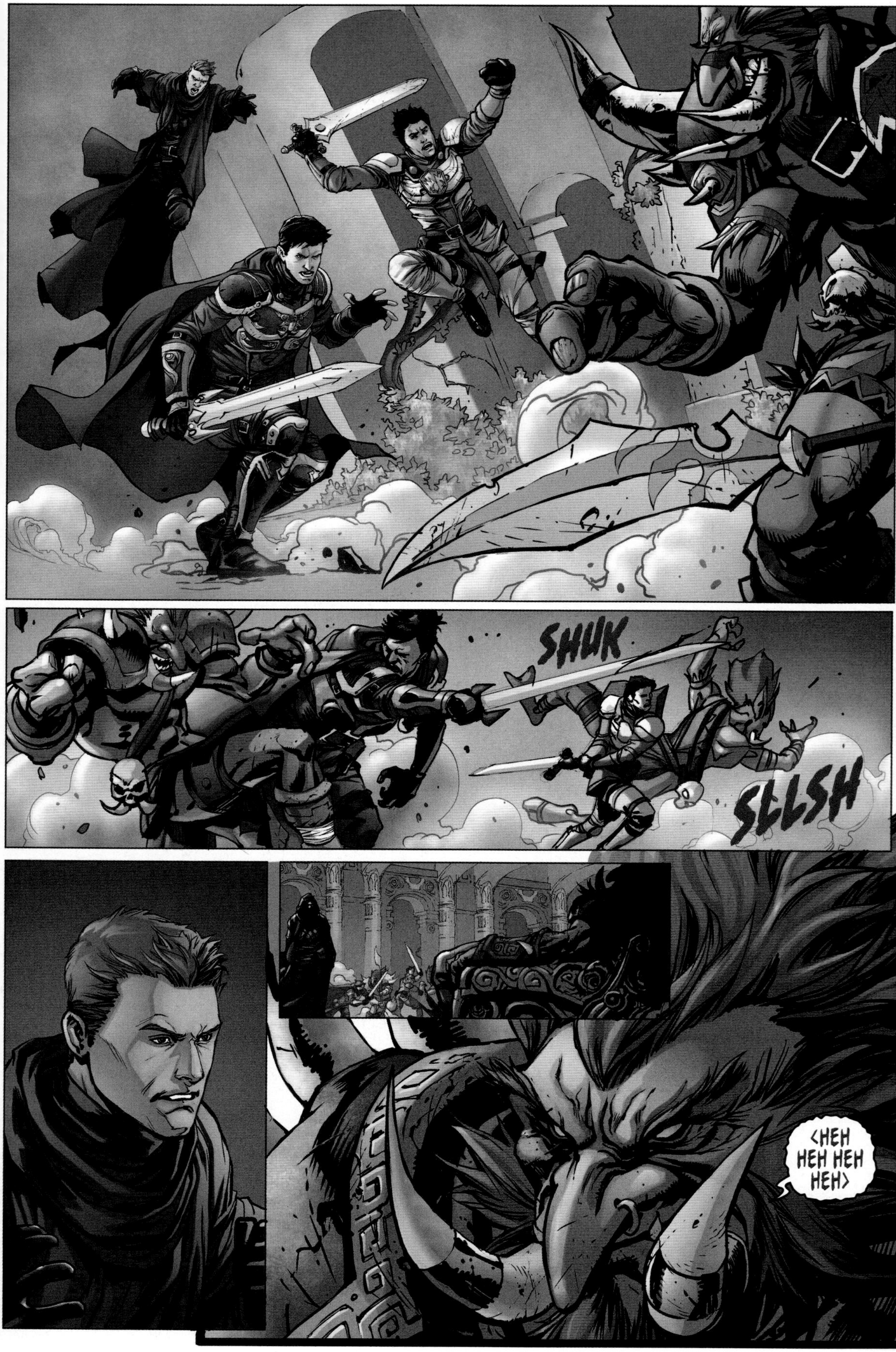
SHUK
SLLSH
<HEH HEH HEH HEH>

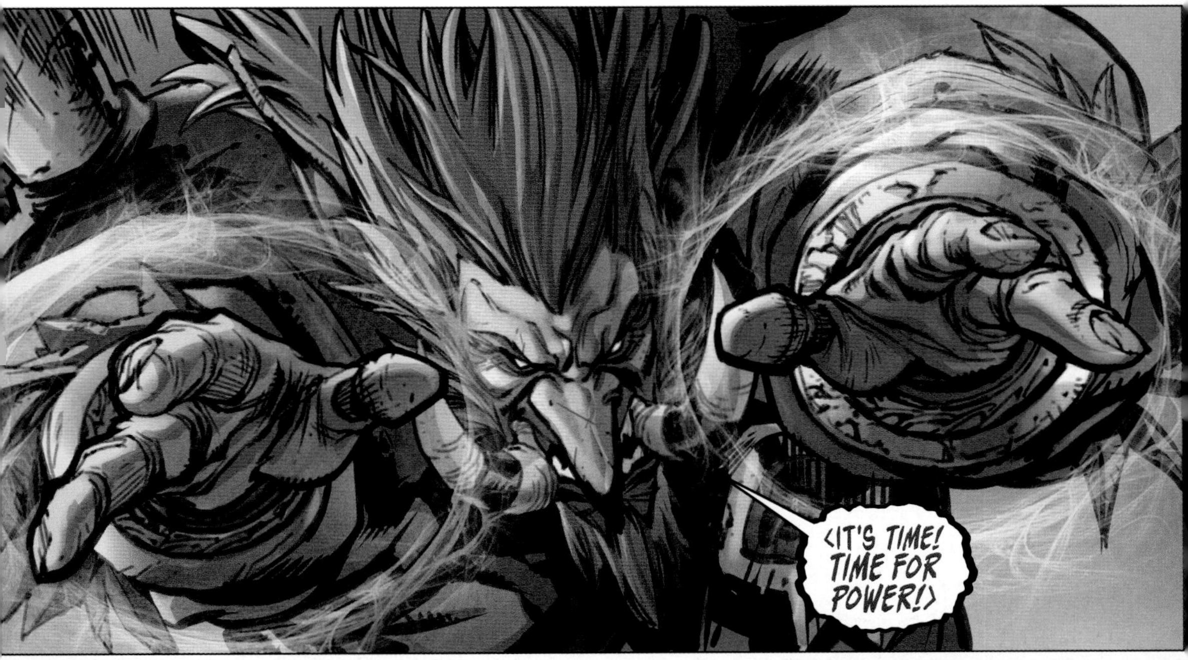
<IT'S TIME! TIME FOR POWER!>

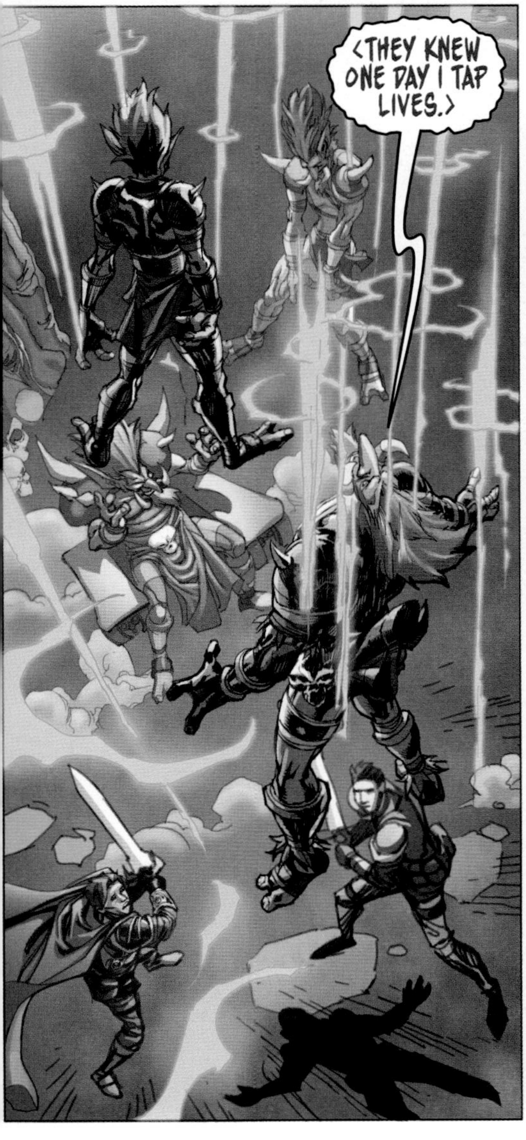
<THEY KNEW ONE DAY I TAP LIVES.>

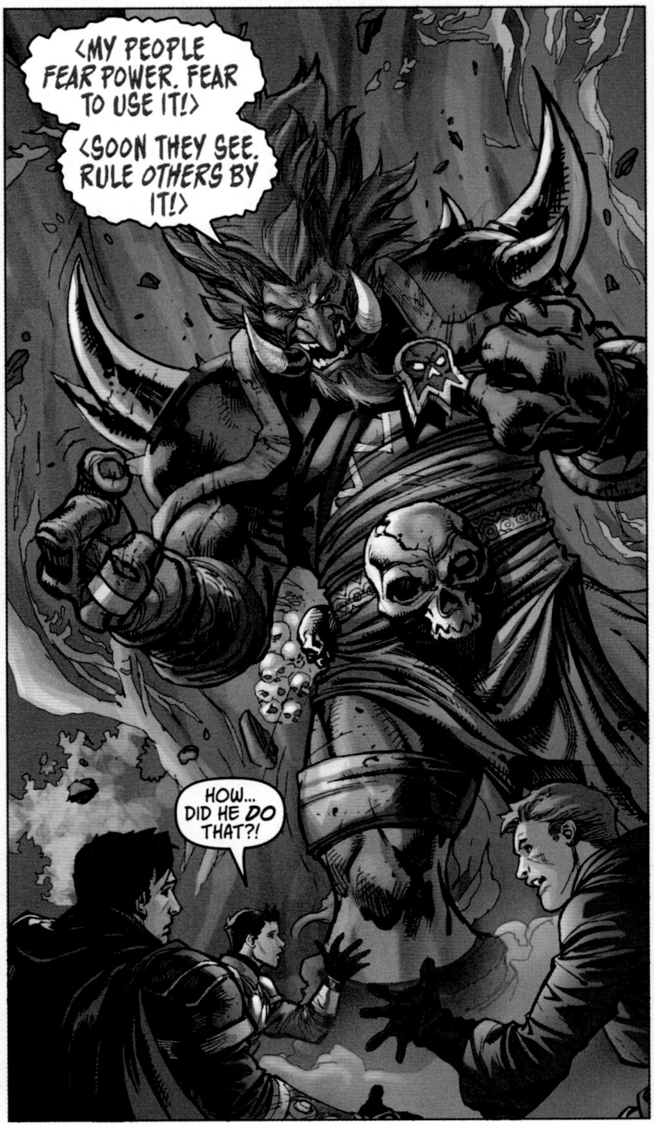
<MY PEOPLE FEAR POWER. FEAR TO USE IT!>
<SOON THEY SEE. RULE OTHERS BY IT!>
HOW... DID HE *DO* THAT?!

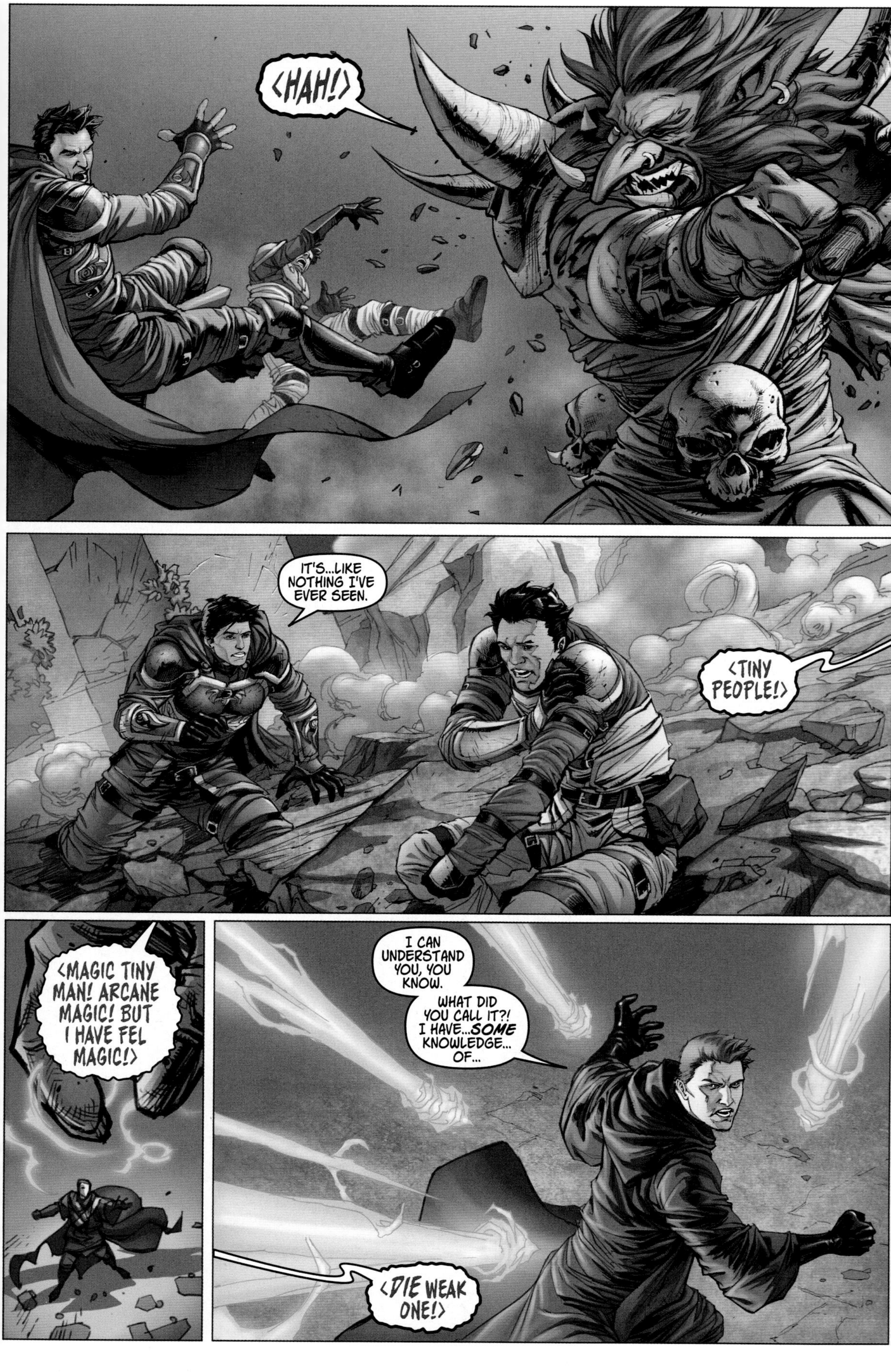
<HAH!>
IT'S...LIKE NOTHING I'VE EVER SEEN.
<TINY PEOPLE!>
<MAGIC TINY MAN! ARCANE MAGIC! BUT I HAVE FEL MAGIC!>
I CAN UNDERSTAND YOU, YOU KNOW.
WHAT DID YOU CALL IT?! I HAVE...SOME KNOWLEDGE... OF...
<DIE WEAK ONE!>

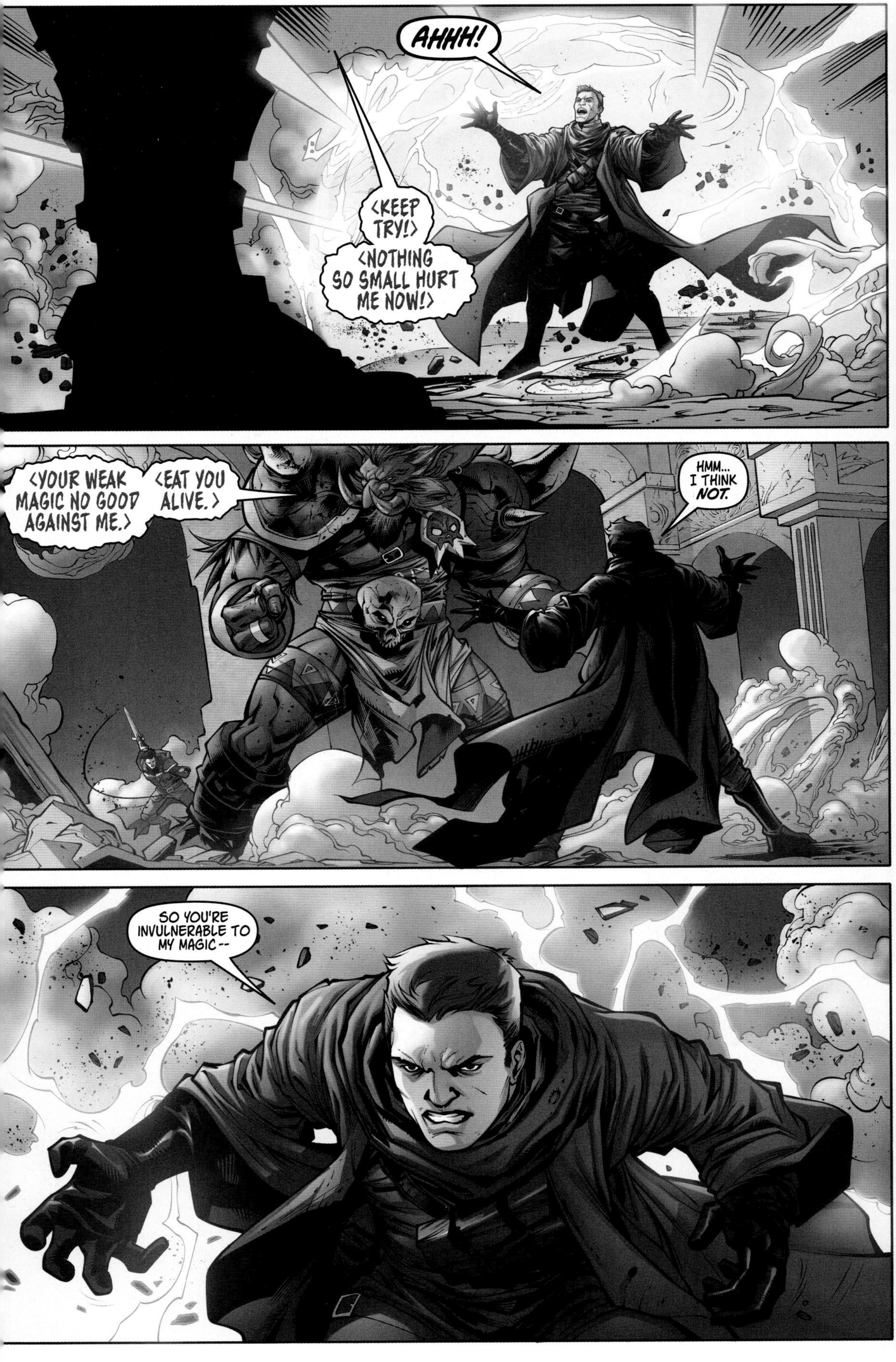
AHHH!
<KEEP TRY!>
<NOTHING SO SMALL HURT ME NOW!>
<YOUR WEAK MAGIC NO GOOD AGAINST ME.>
<EAT YOU ALIVE.>
HMM... I THINK *NOT.*
SO YOU'RE INVULNERABLE TO MY MAGIC --

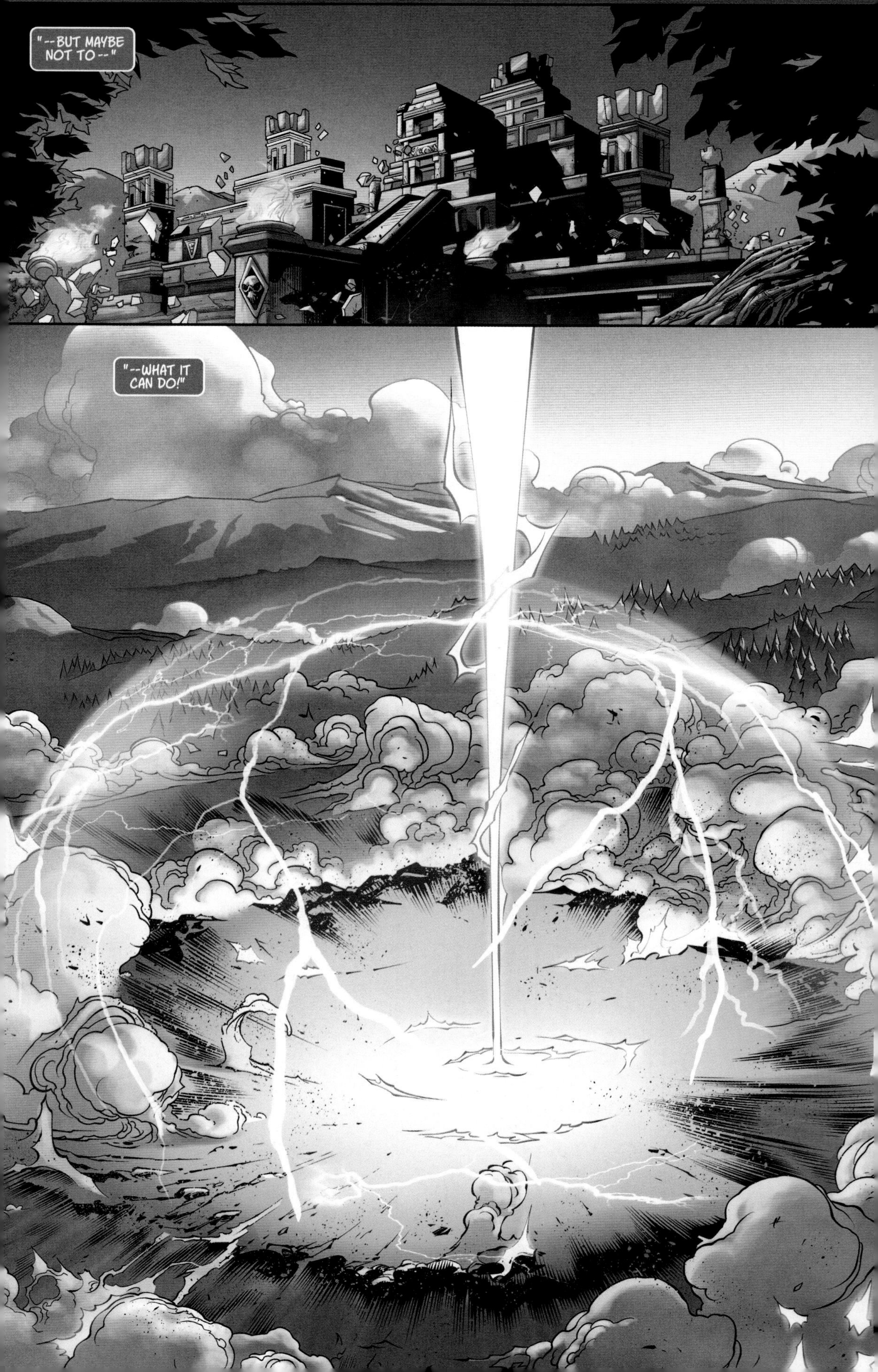
"--BUT MAYBE NOT TO--"
"--WHAT IT CAN DO!"

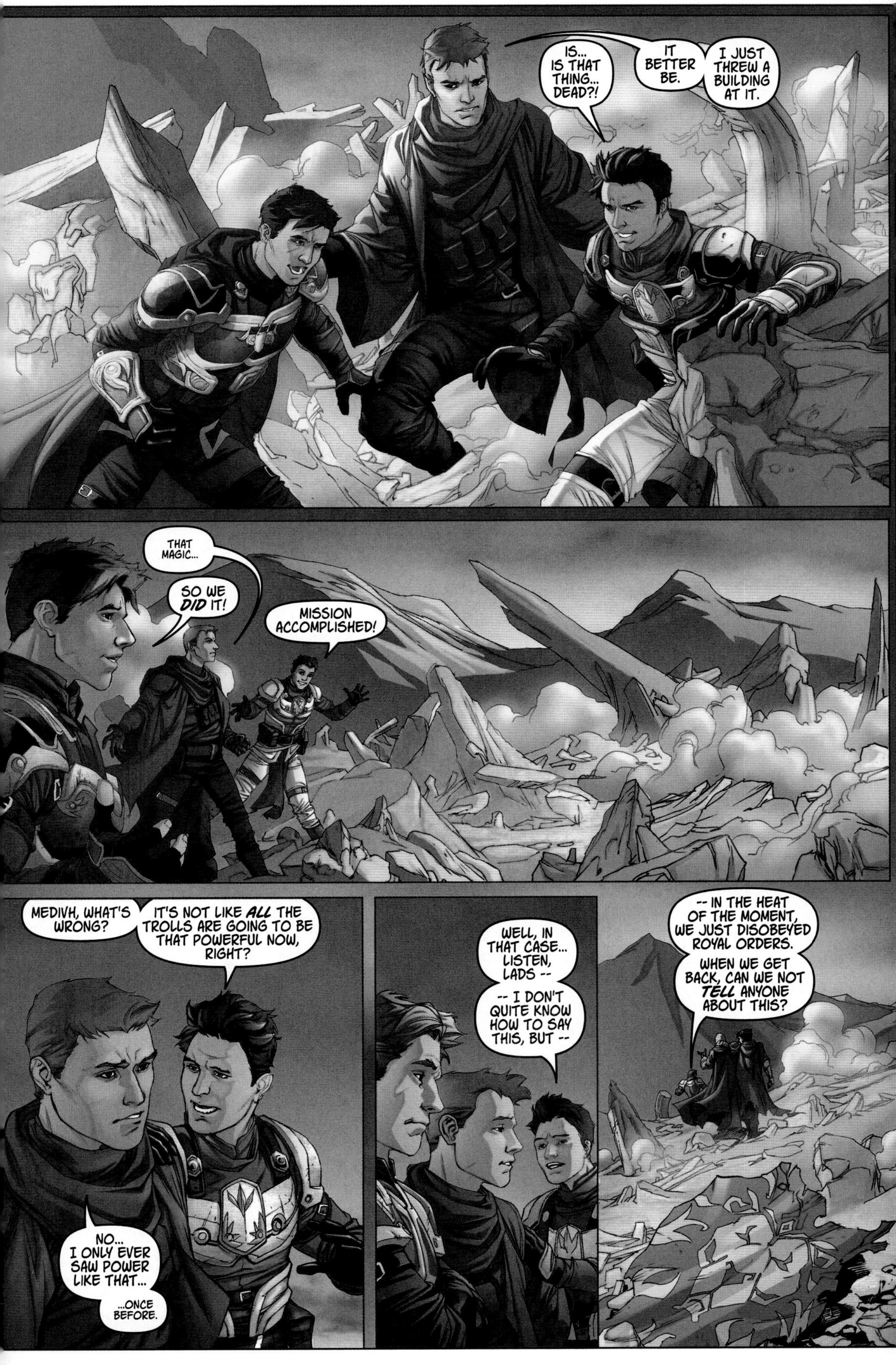
IS... IS THAT THING... DEAD?!
IT BETTER BE.
I JUST THREW A BUILDING AT IT.
THAT MAGIC...
SO WE DID IT!
MISSION ACCOMPLISHED!
MEDIVH, WHAT'S WRONG?
IT'S NOT LIKE ALL THE TROLLS ARE GOING TO BE THAT POWERFUL NOW, RIGHT?
NO... I ONLY EVER SAW POWER LIKE THAT...
...ONCE BEFORE.
WELL, IN THAT CASE... LISTEN, LADS --
-- I DON'T QUITE KNOW HOW TO SAY THIS, BUT --
-- IN THE HEAT OF THE MOMENT, WE JUST DISOBEYED ROYAL ORDERS.
WHEN WE GET BACK, CAN WE NOT TELL ANYONE ABOUT THIS?

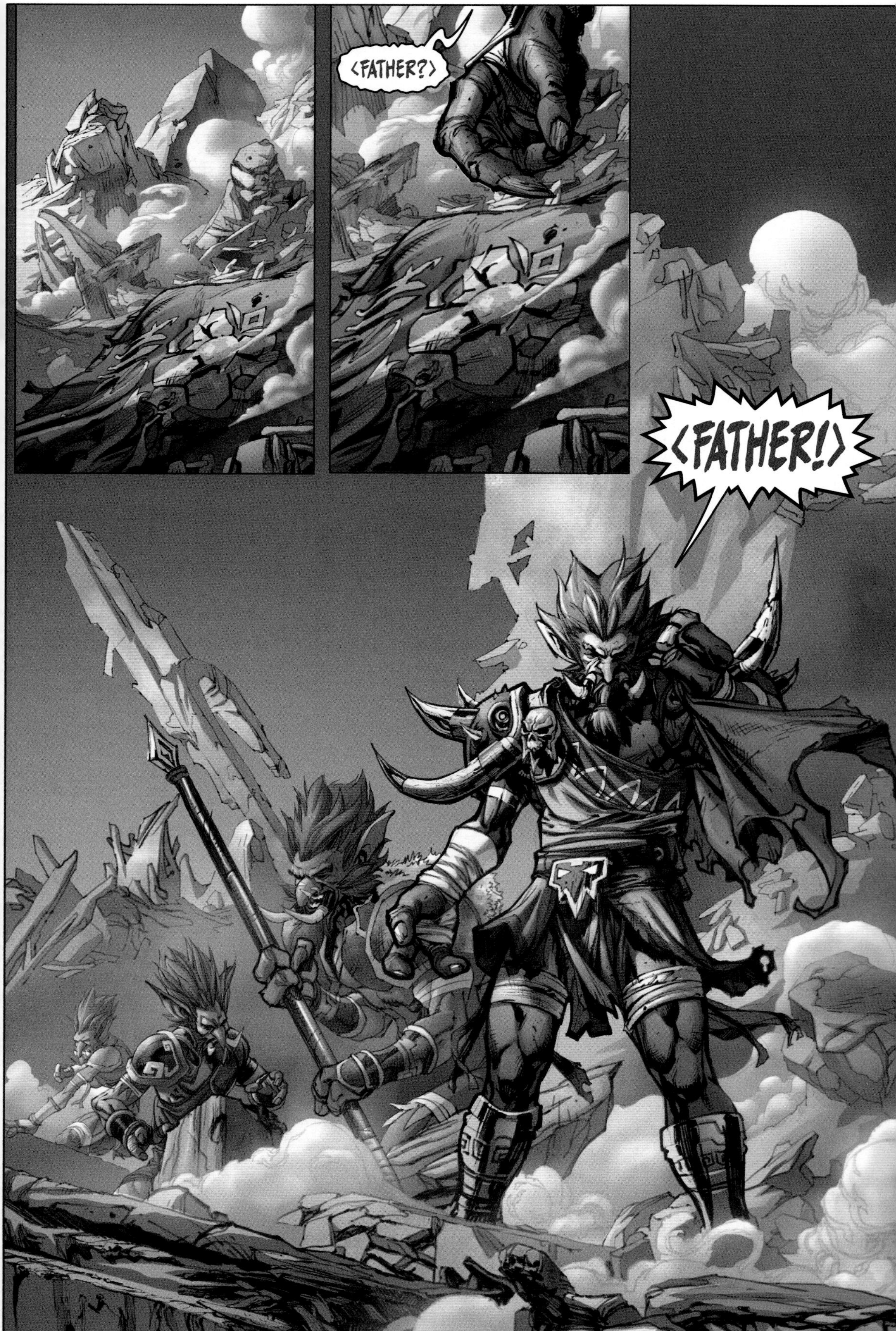
<FATHER?>
<FATHER!>

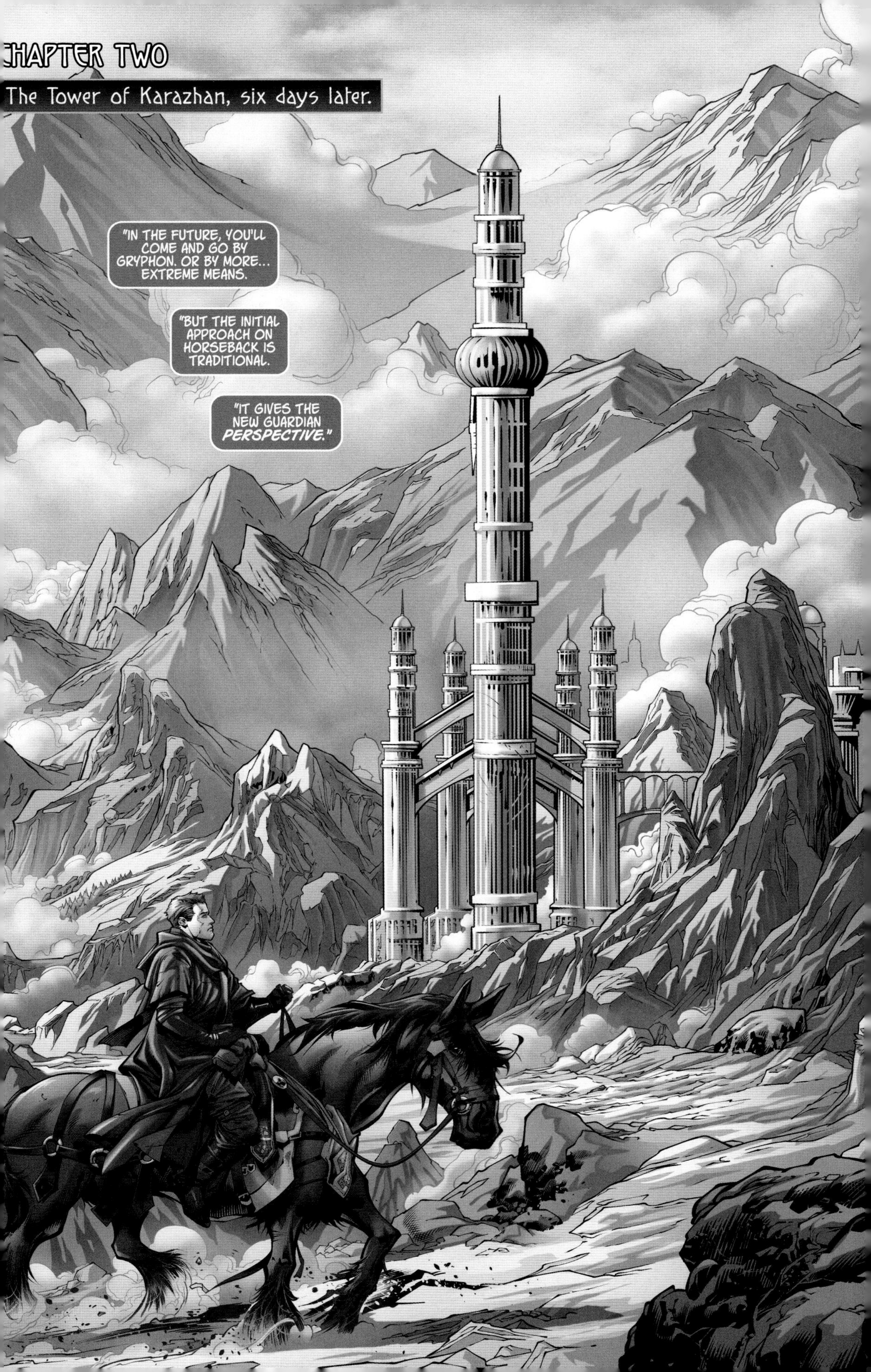
CHAPTER TWO
The Tower of Karazhan, six days later.
"IN THE FUTURE, YOU'LL COME AND GO BY GRYPHON. OR BY MORE... EXTREME MEANS.
"BUT THE INITIAL APPROACH ON HORSEBACK IS TRADITIONAL.
"IT GIVES THE NEW GUARDIAN PERSPECTIVE."

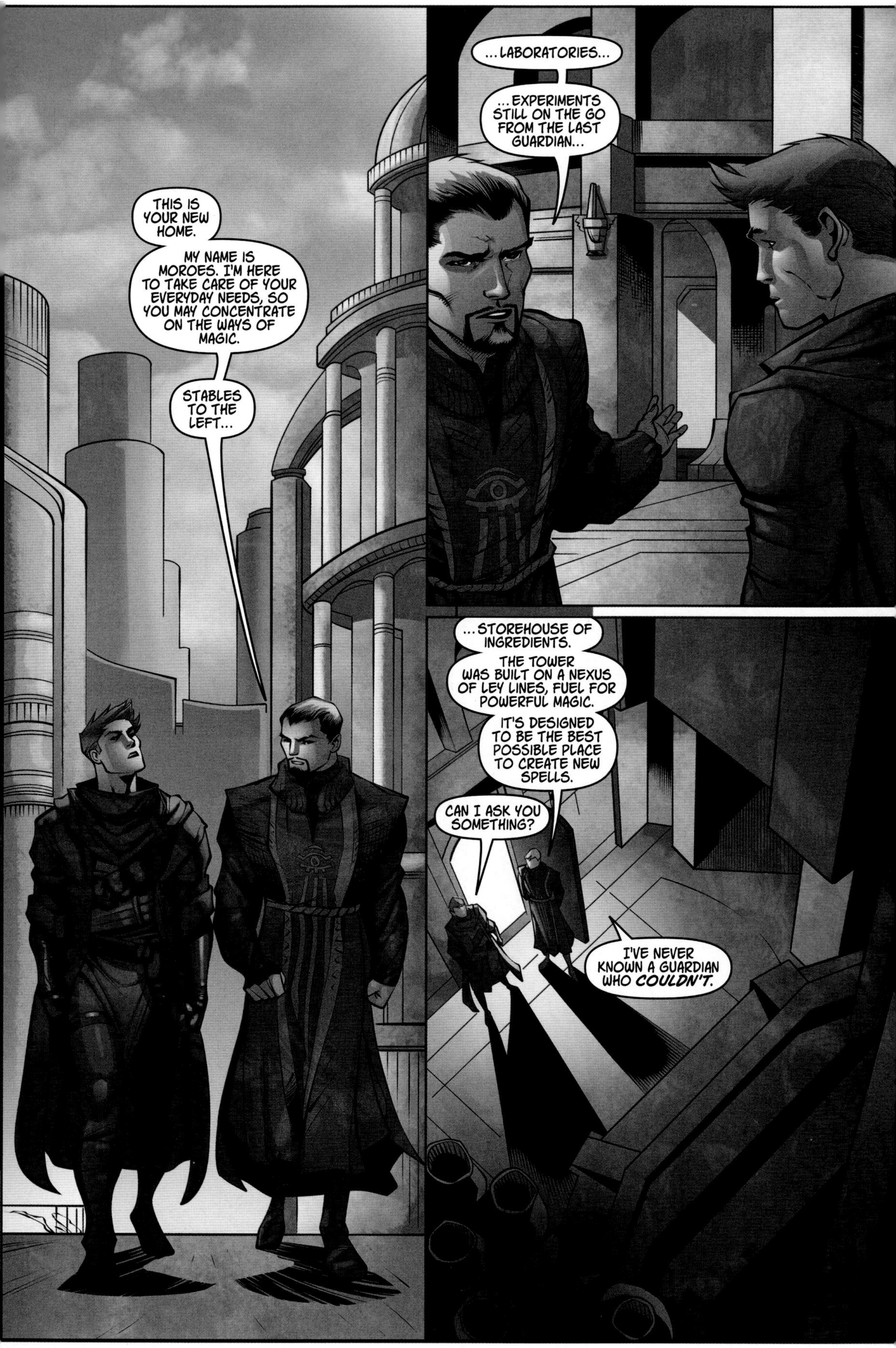
THIS IS YOUR NEW HOME.
MY NAME IS MOROES. I'M HERE TO TAKE CARE OF YOUR EVERYDAY NEEDS, SO YOU MAY CONCENTRATE ON THE WAYS OF MAGIC.
STABLES TO THE LEFT...
...LABORATORIES...
...EXPERIMENTS STILL ON THE GO FROM THE LAST GUARDIAN...
...STOREHOUSE OF INGREDIENTS.
THE TOWER WAS BUILT ON A NEXUS OF LEY LINES, FUEL FOR POWERFUL MAGIC.
IT'S DESIGNED TO BE THE BEST POSSIBLE PLACE TO CREATE NEW SPELLS.
CAN I ASK YOU SOMETHING?
I'VE NEVER KNOWN A GUARDIAN WHO *COULDN'T*.

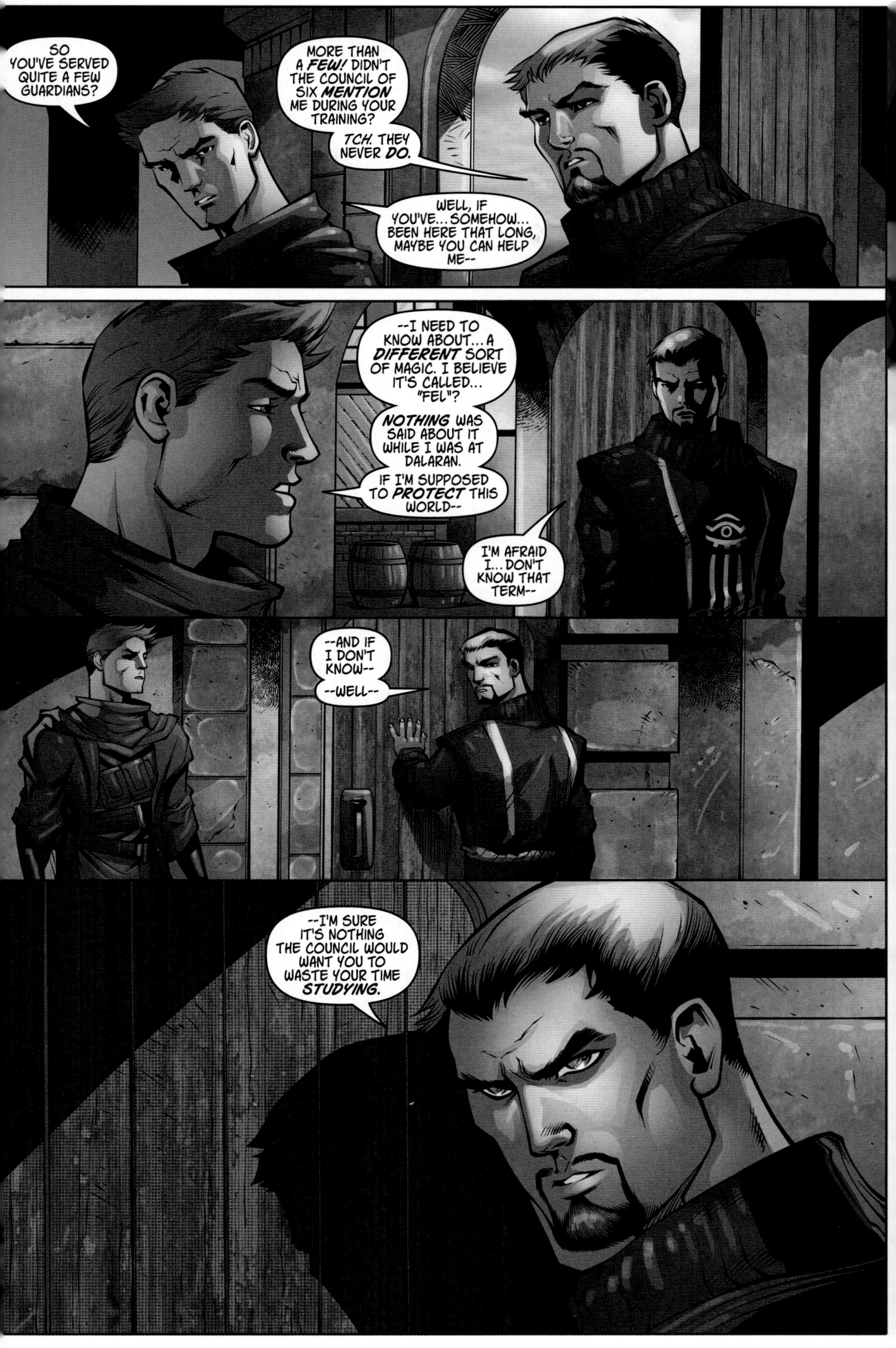
SO YOU'VE SERVED QUITE A FEW GUARDIANS?
MORE THAN A FEW! DIDN'T THE COUNCIL OF SIX MENTION ME DURING YOUR TRAINING?
TCH. THEY NEVER DO.
WELL, IF YOU'VE... SOMEHOW... BEEN HERE THAT LONG, MAYBE YOU CAN HELP ME--
--I NEED TO KNOW ABOUT... A DIFFERENT SORT OF MAGIC. I BELIEVE IT'S CALLED... "FEL"?
NOTHING WAS SAID ABOUT IT WHILE I WAS AT DALARAN.
IF I'M SUPPOSED TO PROTECT THIS WORLD--
I'M AFRAID I... DON'T KNOW THAT TERM--
--AND IF I DON'T KNOW--
--WELL--
--I'M SURE IT'S NOTHING THE COUNCIL WOULD WANT YOU TO WASTE YOUR TIME STUDYING.

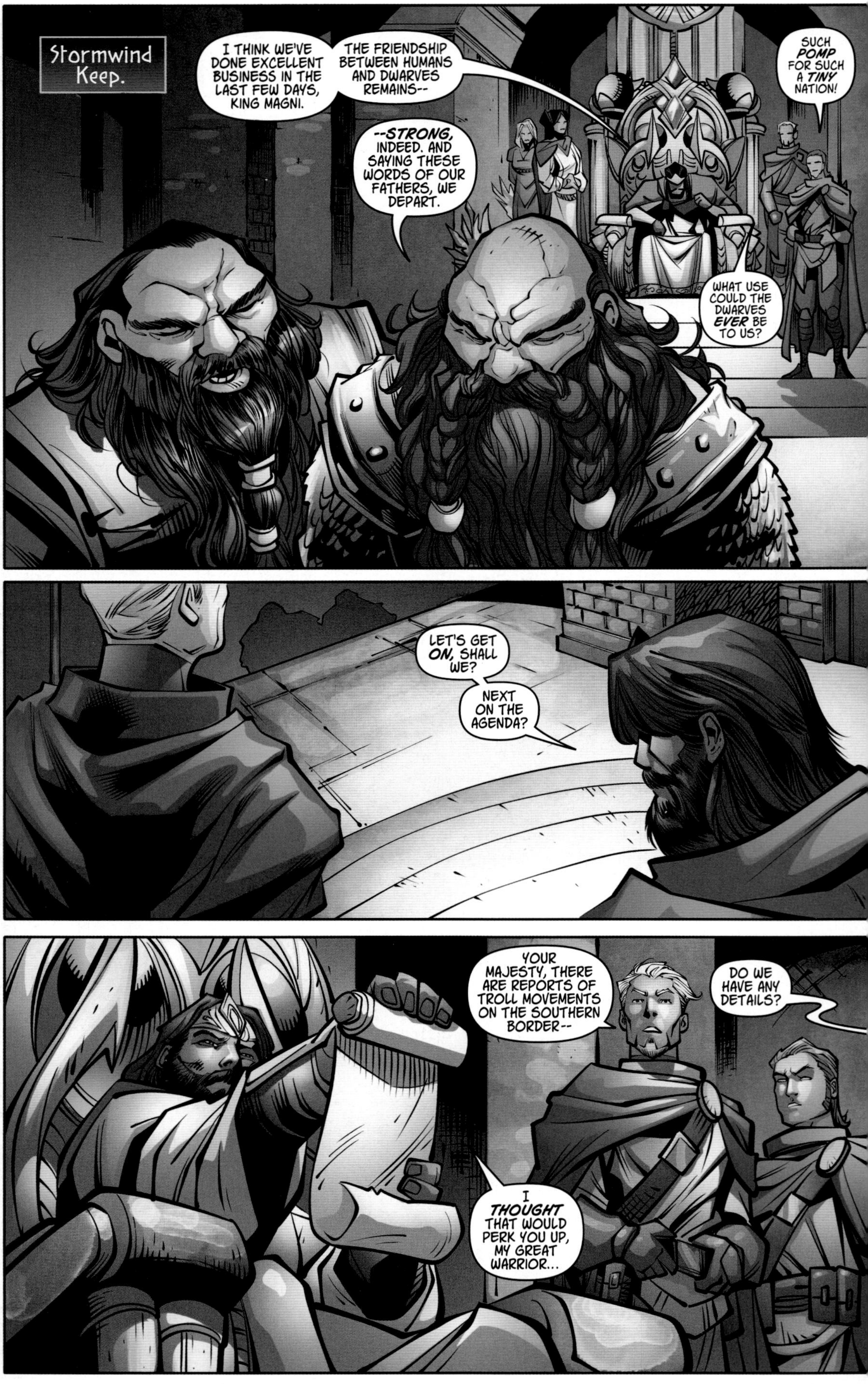
Stormwind Keep.
I THINK WE'VE DONE EXCELLENT BUSINESS IN THE LAST FEW DAYS, KING MAGNI.
THE FRIENDSHIP BETWEEN HUMANS AND DWARVES REMAINS--
--STRONG, INDEED. AND SAYING THESE WORDS OF OUR FATHERS, WE DEPART.
SUCH POMP FOR SUCH A TINY NATION!
WHAT USE COULD THE DWARVES EVER BE TO US?
LET'S GET ON, SHALL WE?
NEXT ON THE AGENDA?
YOUR MAJESTY, THERE ARE REPORTS OF TROLL MOVEMENTS ON THE SOUTHERN BORDER--
DO WE HAVE ANY DETAILS?
I THOUGHT THAT WOULD PERK YOU UP, MY GREAT WARRIOR...

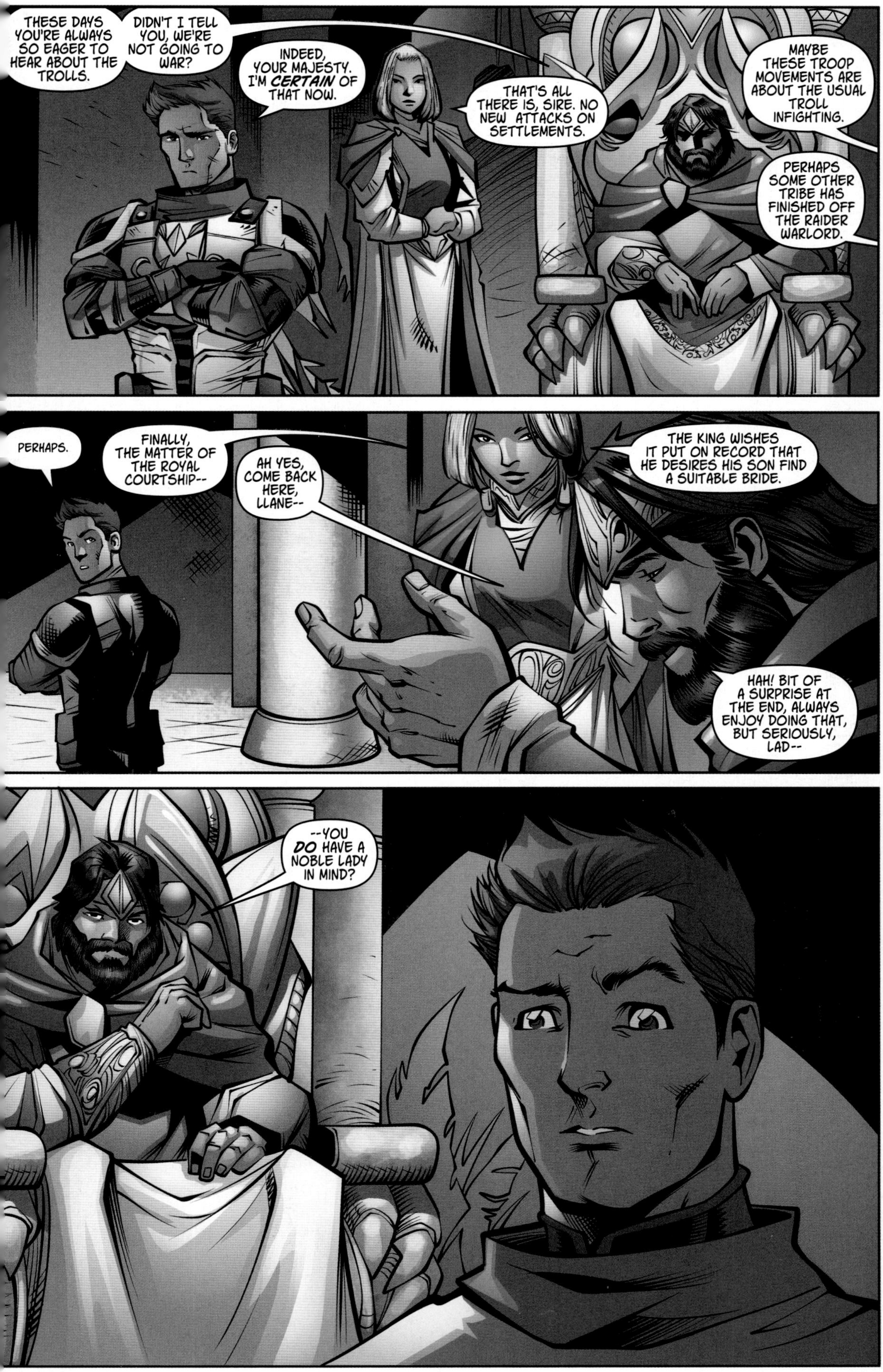
THESE DAYS YOU'RE ALWAYS SO EAGER TO HEAR ABOUT THE TROLLS.
DIDN'T I TELL YOU, WE'RE NOT GOING TO WAR?
INDEED, YOUR MAJESTY. I'M *CERTAIN* OF THAT NOW.
THAT'S ALL THERE IS, SIRE. NO NEW ATTACKS ON SETTLEMENTS.
MAYBE THESE TROOP MOVEMENTS ARE ABOUT THE USUAL TROLL INFIGHTING.
PERHAPS SOME OTHER TRIBE HAS FINISHED OFF THE RAIDER WARLORD.
PERHAPS.
FINALLY, THE MATTER OF THE ROYAL COURTSHIP--
AH YES, COME BACK HERE, LLANE--
THE KING WISHES IT PUT ON RECORD THAT HE DESIRES HIS SON FIND A SUITABLE BRIDE.
HAH! BIT OF A SURPRISE AT THE END, ALWAYS ENJOY DOING THAT, BUT SERIOUSLY, LAD--
--YOU *DO* HAVE A NOBLE LADY IN MIND?

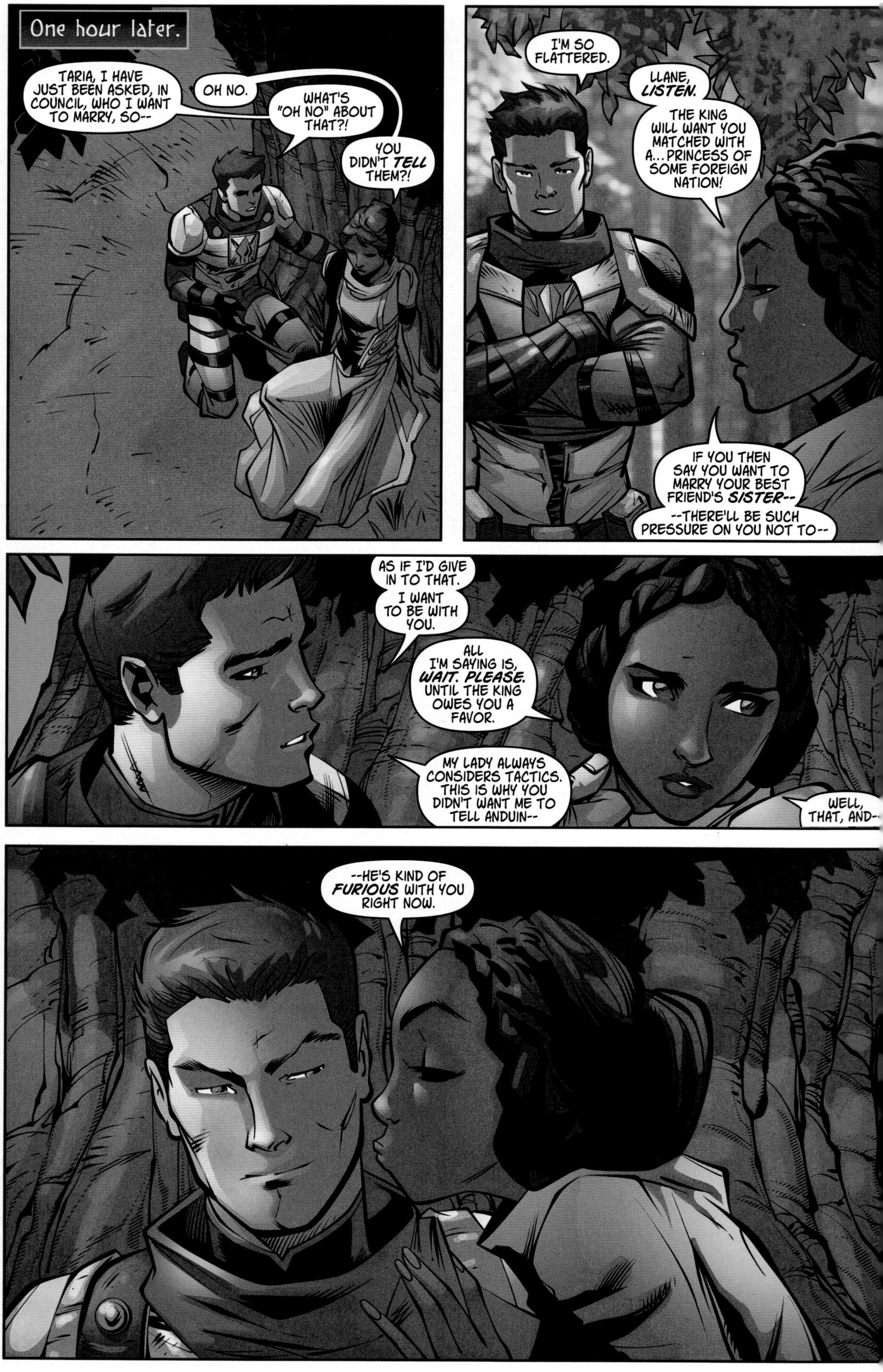
One hour later.
TARIA, I HAVE JUST BEEN ASKED, IN COUNCIL, WHO I WANT TO MARRY, SO--
OH NO.
WHAT'S "OH NO" ABOUT THAT?!
YOU DIDN'T TELL THEM?!
I'M SO FLATTERED.
LLANE, LISTEN.
THE KING WILL WANT YOU MATCHED WITH A... PRINCESS OF SOME FOREIGN NATION!
IF YOU THEN SAY YOU WANT TO MARRY YOUR BEST FRIEND'S SISTER--
--THERE'LL BE SUCH PRESSURE ON YOU NOT TO--
AS IF I'D GIVE IN TO THAT.
I WANT TO BE WITH YOU.
ALL I'M SAYING IS, WAIT. PLEASE. UNTIL THE KING OWES YOU A FAVOR.
MY LADY ALWAYS CONSIDERS TACTICS. THIS IS WHY YOU DIDN'T WANT ME TO TELL ANDUIN--
WELL, THAT, AND--
--HE'S KIND OF FURIOUS WITH YOU RIGHT NOW.

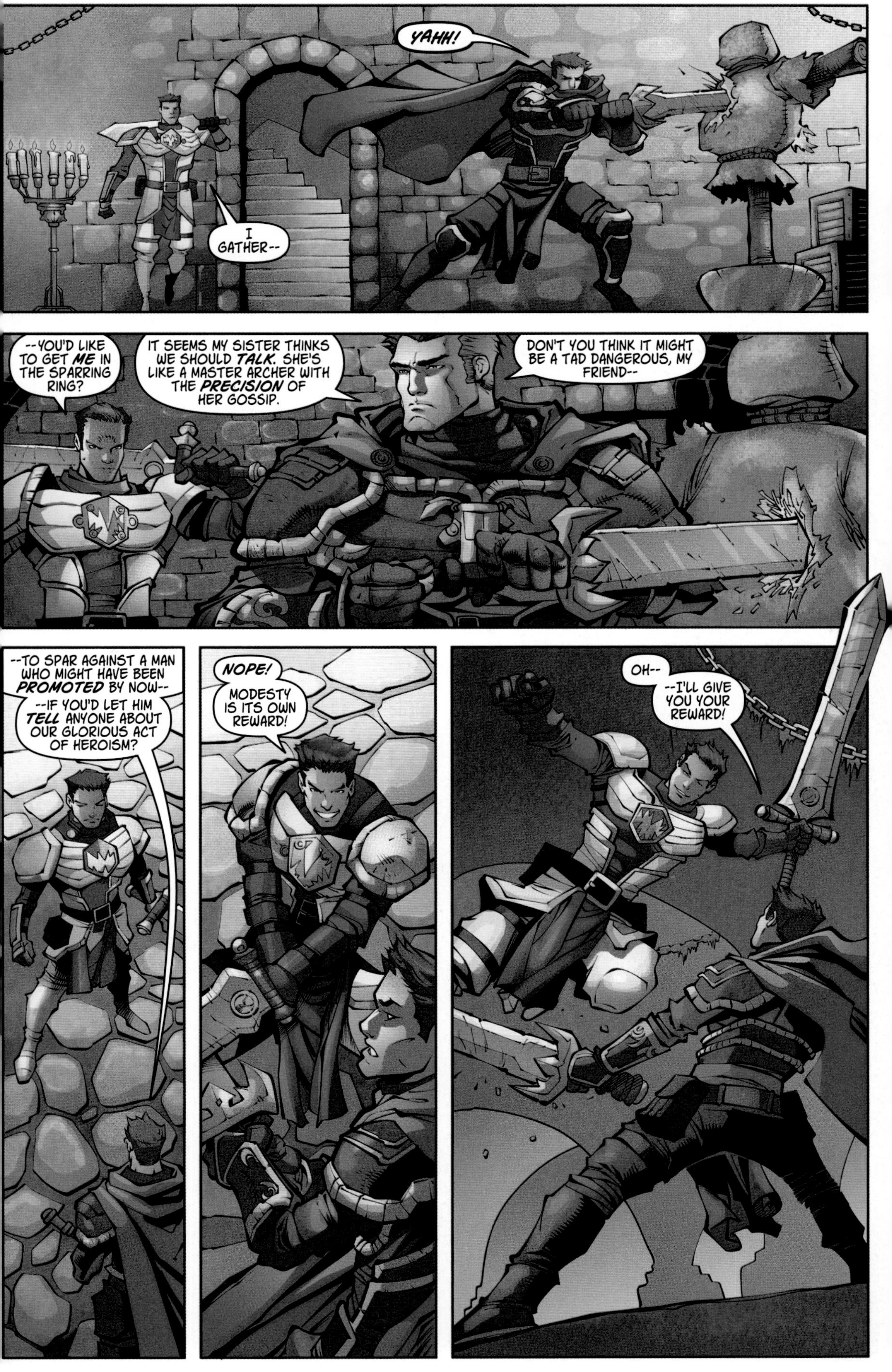
YAHH!
I GATHER--
--YOU'D LIKE TO GET ME IN THE SPARRING RING?
IT SEEMS MY SISTER THINKS WE SHOULD TALK. SHE'S LIKE A MASTER ARCHER WITH THE PRECISION OF HER GOSSIP.
DON'T YOU THINK IT MIGHT BE A TAD DANGEROUS, MY FRIEND--
--TO SPAR AGAINST A MAN WHO MIGHT HAVE BEEN PROMOTED BY NOW--
--IF YOU'D LET HIM TELL ANYONE ABOUT OUR GLORIOUS ACT OF HEROISM?
NOPE!
MODESTY IS ITS OWN REWARD!
OH--
--I'LL GIVE YOU YOUR REWARD!

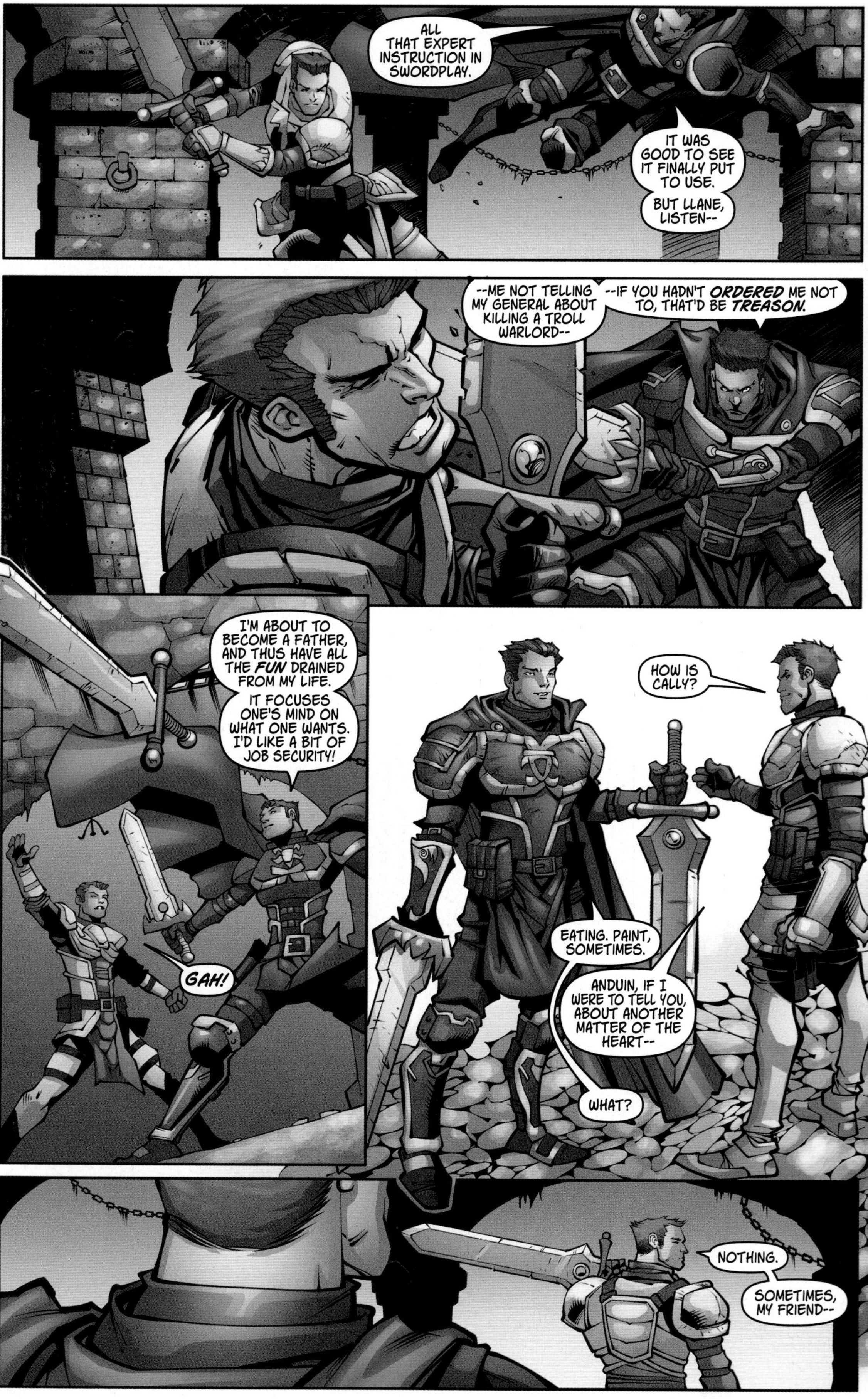
ALL THAT EXPERT INSTRUCTION IN SWORDPLAY.
IT WAS GOOD TO SEE IT FINALLY PUT TO USE.
BUT LLANE, LISTEN--
--ME NOT TELLING MY GENERAL ABOUT KILLING A TROLL WARLORD--
--IF YOU HADN'T ORDERED ME NOT TO, THAT'D BE TREASON.
I'M ABOUT TO BECOME A FATHER, AND THUS HAVE ALL THE FUN DRAINED FROM MY LIFE.
IT FOCUSES ONE'S MIND ON WHAT ONE WANTS. I'D LIKE A BIT OF JOB SECURITY!
GAH!
HOW IS CALLY?
EATING. PAINT, SOMETIMES.
ANDUIN, IF I WERE TO TELL YOU, ABOUT ANOTHER MATTER OF THE HEART--
WHAT?
NOTHING.
SOMETIMES, MY FRIEND--

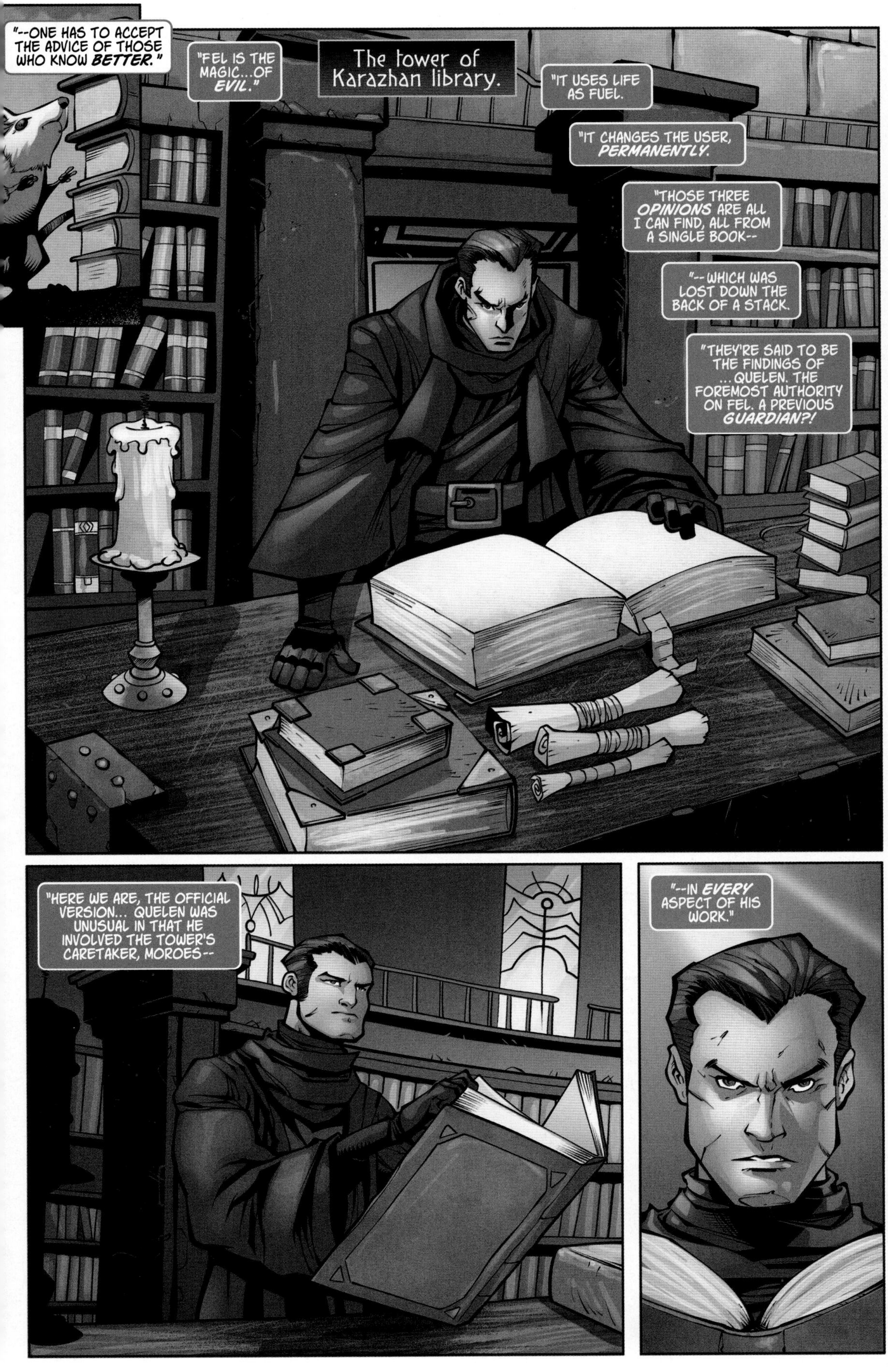
"--ONE HAS TO ACCEPT THE ADVICE OF THOSE WHO KNOW *BETTER.*"
"FEL IS THE MAGIC...OF *EVIL.*"
The tower of Karazhan library.
"IT USES LIFE AS FUEL.
"IT CHANGES THE USER, *PERMANENTLY.*
"THOSE THREE *OPINIONS* ARE ALL I CAN FIND, ALL FROM A SINGLE BOOK--
"--WHICH WAS LOST DOWN THE BACK OF A STACK.
"THEY'RE SAID TO BE THE FINDINGS OF ...QUELEN. THE FOREMOST AUTHORITY ON FEL. A PREVIOUS *GUARDIAN?!*
"HERE WE ARE, THE OFFICIAL VERSION... QUELEN WAS UNUSUAL IN THAT HE INVOLVED THE TOWER'S CARETAKER, MOROES--
"--IN *EVERY* ASPECT OF HIS WORK."

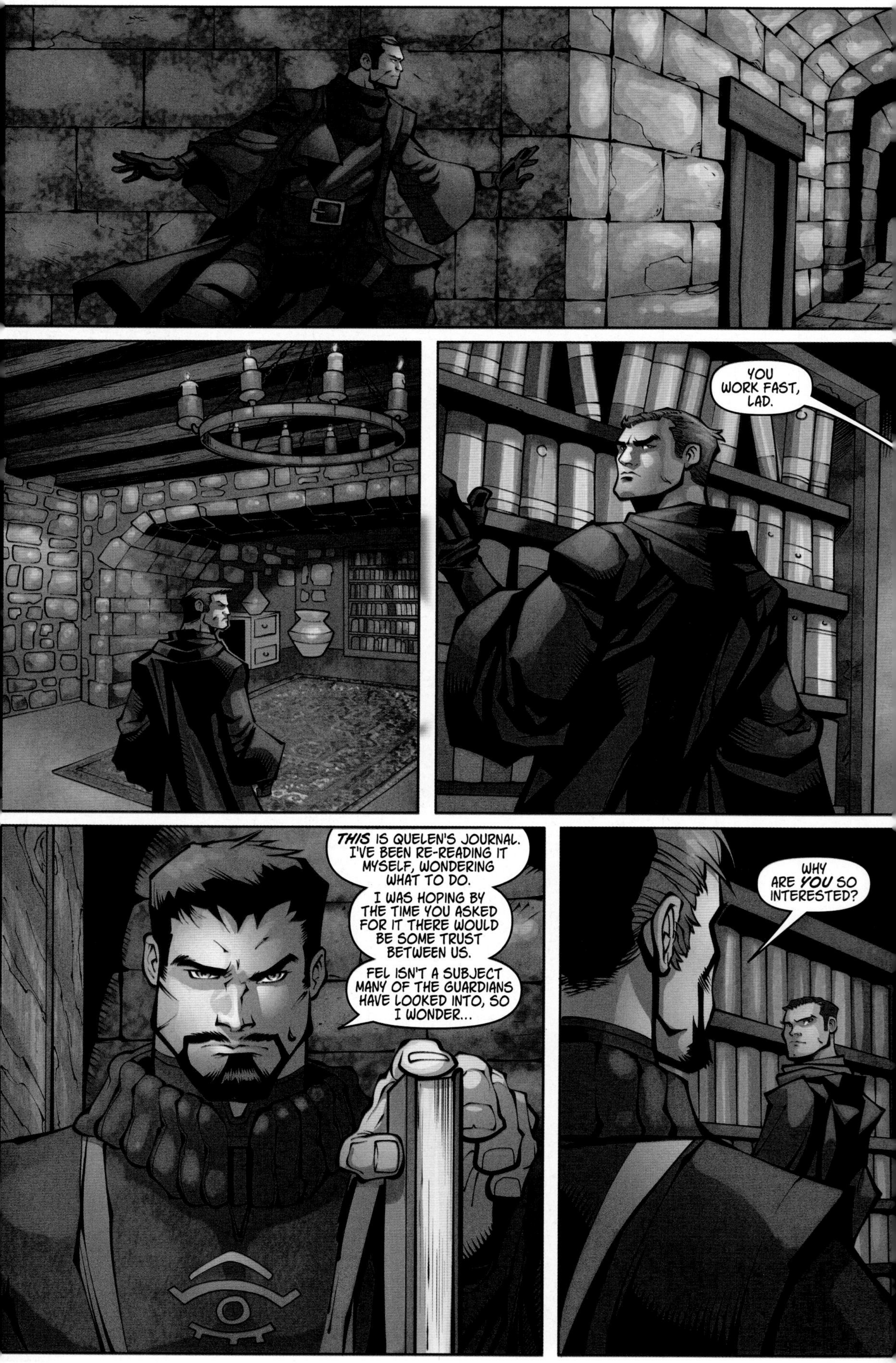
YOU WORK FAST, LAD.
THIS IS QUELEN'S JOURNAL. I'VE BEEN RE-READING IT MYSELF, WONDERING WHAT TO DO.
I WAS HOPING BY THE TIME YOU ASKED FOR IT THERE WOULD BE SOME TRUST BETWEEN US.
FEL ISN'T A SUBJECT MANY OF THE GUARDIANS HAVE LOOKED INTO, SO I WONDER...
WHY ARE YOU SO INTERESTED?

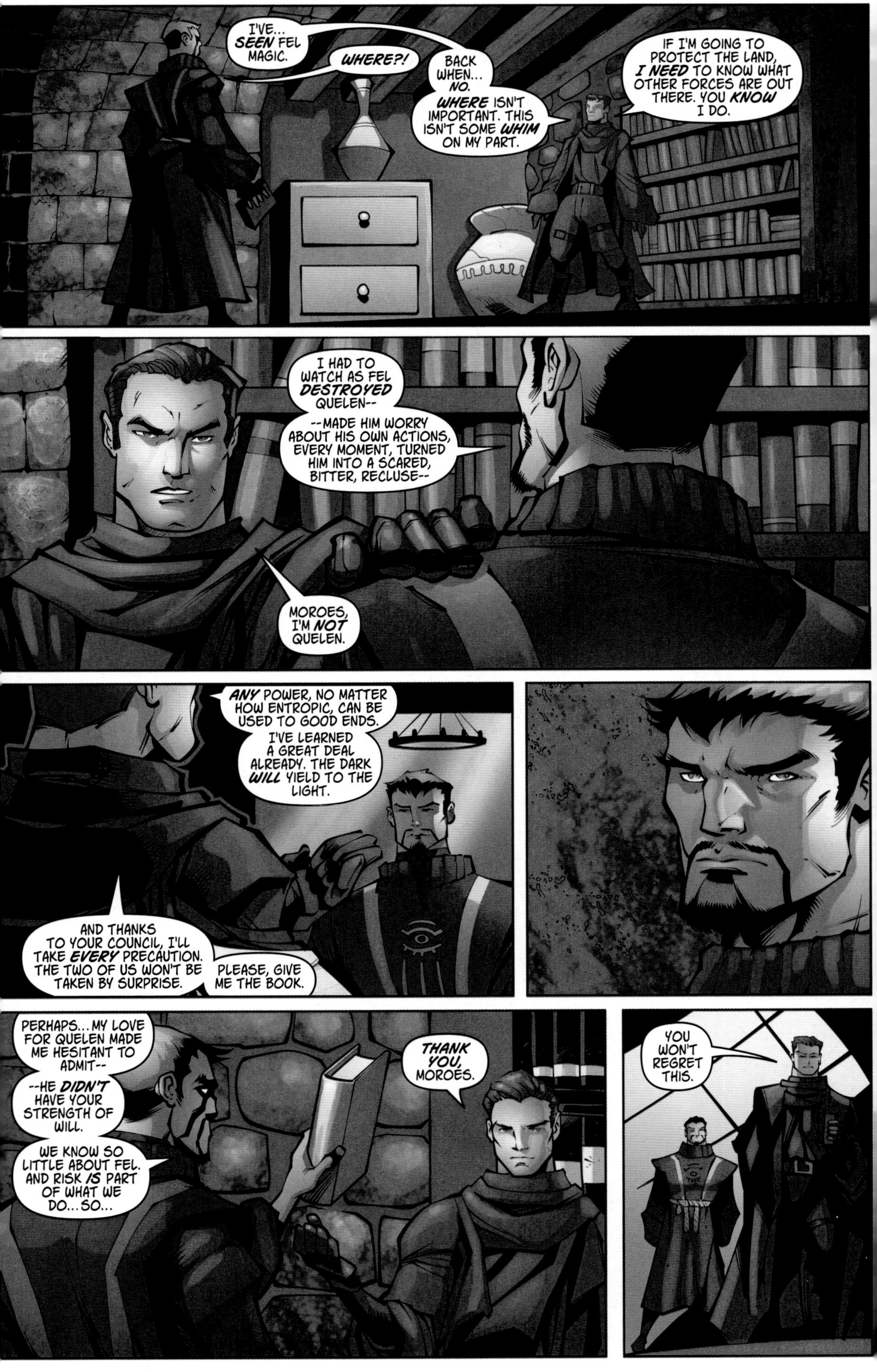
I'VE... SEEN FEL MAGIC.
WHERE?!
BACK WHEN... NO. WHERE ISN'T IMPORTANT. THIS ISN'T SOME WHIM ON MY PART.
IF I'M GOING TO PROTECT THE LAND, I NEED TO KNOW WHAT OTHER FORCES ARE OUT THERE. YOU KNOW I DO.
I HAD TO WATCH AS FEL DESTROYED QUELEN--
--MADE HIM WORRY ABOUT HIS OWN ACTIONS, EVERY MOMENT, TURNED HIM INTO A SCARED, BITTER, RECLUSE--
MOROES, I'M NOT QUELEN.
ANY POWER, NO MATTER HOW ENTROPIC, CAN BE USED TO GOOD ENDS.
I'VE LEARNED A GREAT DEAL ALREADY. THE DARK WILL YIELD TO THE LIGHT.
AND THANKS TO YOUR COUNCIL, I'LL TAKE EVERY PRECAUTION. THE TWO OF US WON'T BE TAKEN BY SURPRISE.
PLEASE, GIVE ME THE BOOK.
PERHAPS... MY LOVE FOR QUELEN MADE ME HESITANT TO ADMIT--
--HE DIDN'T HAVE YOUR STRENGTH OF WILL.
WE KNOW SO LITTLE ABOUT FEL. AND RISK IS PART OF WHAT WE DO... SO...
THANK YOU, MOROES.
YOU WON'T REGRET THIS.

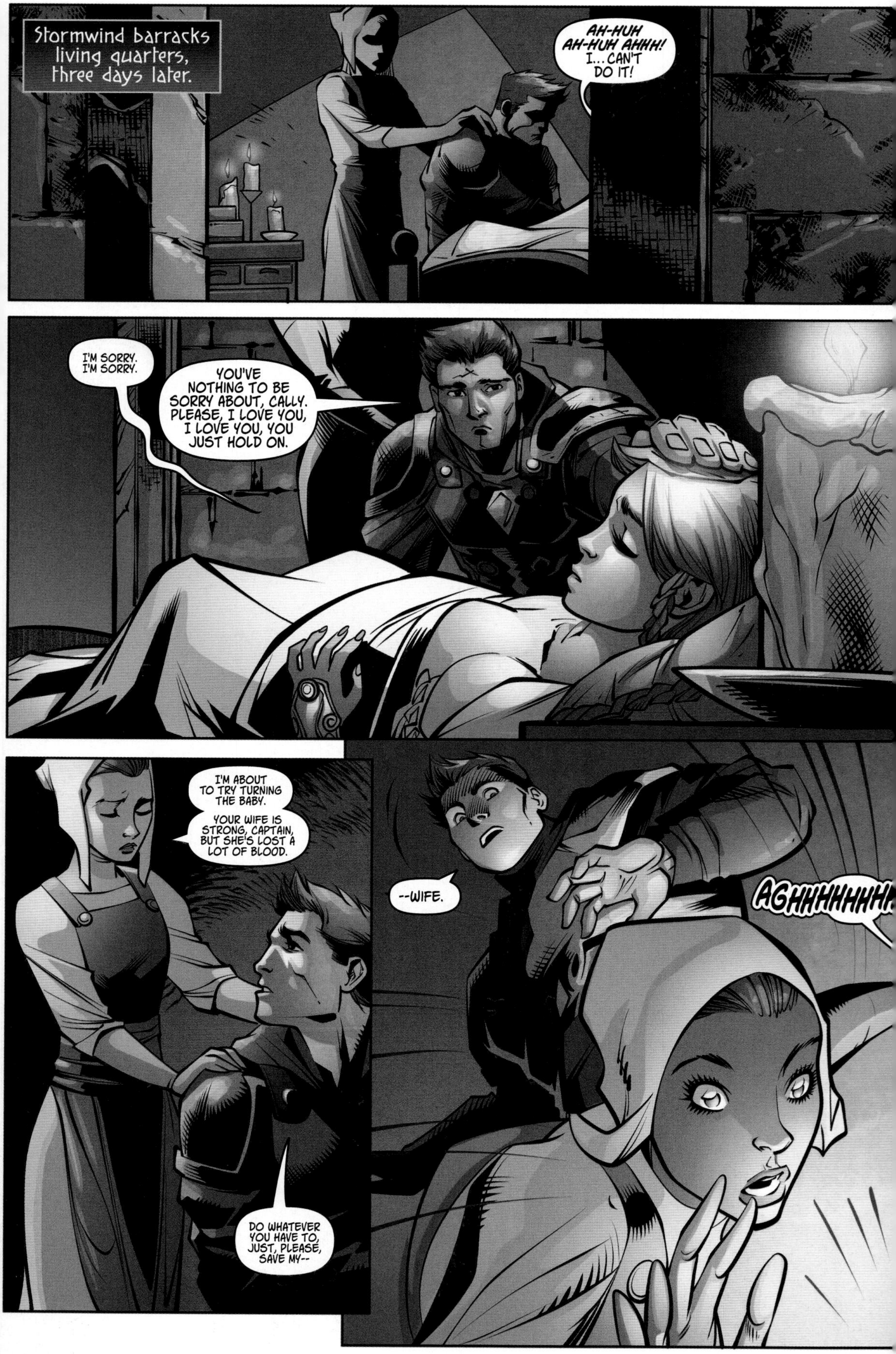
Stormwind barracks living quarters, three days later.
AH-HUH AH-HUH AHHH! I... CAN'T DO IT!
I'M SORRY. I'M SORRY.
YOU'VE NOTHING TO BE SORRY ABOUT, CALLY. PLEASE, I LOVE YOU, I LOVE YOU, YOU JUST HOLD ON.
I'M ABOUT TO TRY TURNING THE BABY.
YOUR WIFE IS STRONG, CAPTAIN, BUT SHE'S LOST A LOT OF BLOOD.
DO WHATEVER YOU HAVE TO, JUST, PLEASE, SAVE MY--
--WIFE.
AGHHHHHHH

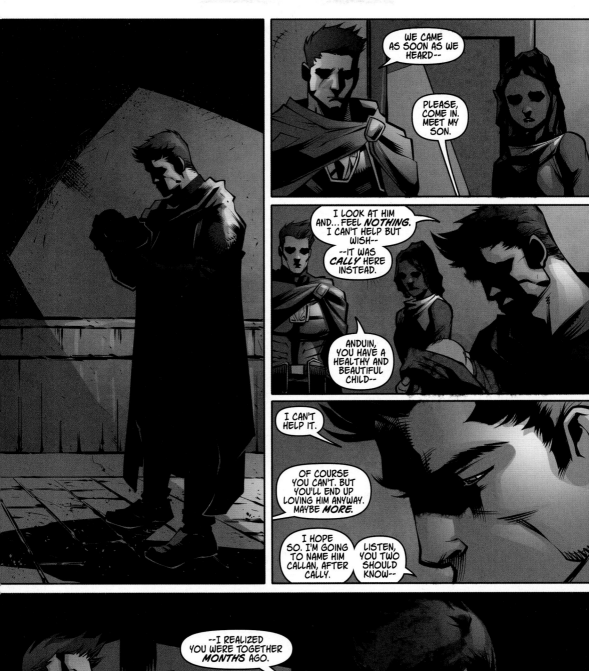

WE CAME AS SOON AS WE HEARD--

PLEASE, COME IN. MEET MY SON.

I LOOK AT HIM AND...FEEL *NOTHING*. I CAN'T HELP BUT WISH--

--IT WAS *CALLY* HERE INSTEAD.

ANDUIN, YOU HAVE A HEALTHY AND BEAUTIFUL CHILD--

I CAN'T HELP IT.

OF COURSE YOU CAN'T. BUT YOU'LL END UP LOVING HIM ANYWAY. MAYBE *MORE*.

I HOPE SO. I'M GOING TO NAME HIM CALLAN, AFTER CALLY.

LISTEN, YOU TWO SHOULD KNOW--

--I REALIZED YOU WERE TOGETHER *MONTHS* AGO.

I DIDN'T TELL HIM.

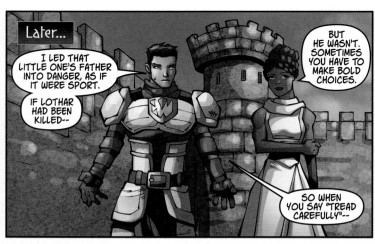

Later...

I LED THAT LITTLE ONE'S FATHER INTO DANGER, AS IF IT WERE SPORT.

IF LOTHAR HAD BEEN KILLED--

BUT HE WASN'T. SOMETIMES YOU HAVE TO MAKE BOLD CHOICES.

SO WHEN YOU SAY "TREAD CAREFULLY"--

I SAY TAKE CARE WHEN YOU HAVE TO, AND BE BOLD WHEN YOU HAVE TO.

A GREAT LEADER IS ONE WHO'S PREPARED TO TAKE COMPLETE RESPONSIBILITY FOR KNOWING THE DIFFERENCE.

YES, YES, I SEE. IN WHICH CASE--

AH, LAD--

--VISITING LOTHAR, EH? TERRIBLE BUSINESS. WHO'S *THIS*?

I NEED A MOMENT TO DISCOVER THAT, SIRE--

--BECAUSE IF SHE'LL DO ME THE HONOR OF BECOMING MY WIFE--

--THEN THIS YOUNG LADY IS MY *FIANCÉE.*

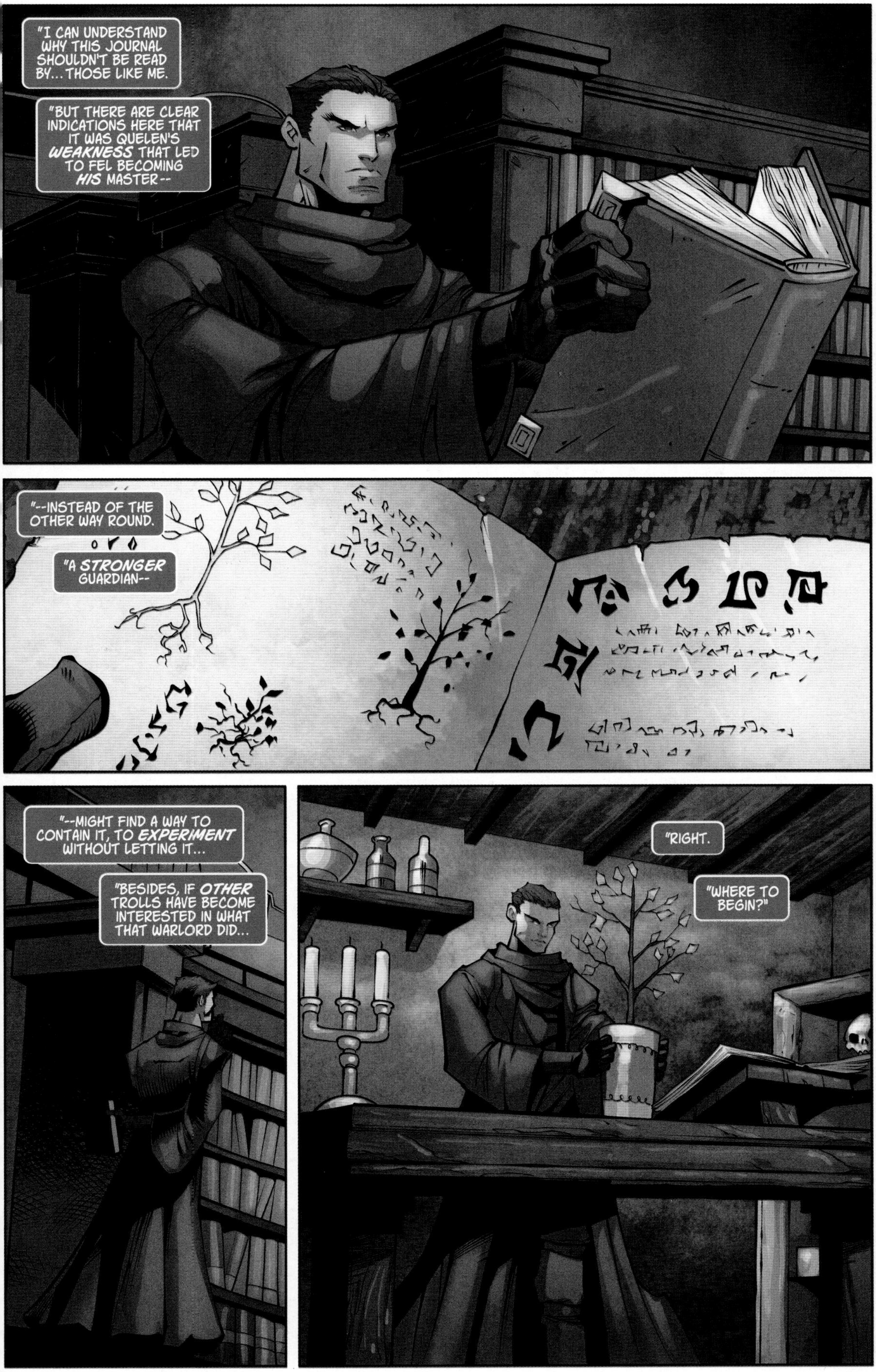
"I CAN UNDERSTAND WHY THIS JOURNAL SHOULDN'T BE READ BY... THOSE LIKE ME.
"BUT THERE ARE CLEAR INDICATIONS HERE THAT IT WAS QUELEN'S *WEAKNESS* THAT LED TO FEL BECOMING *HIS* MASTER--
"--INSTEAD OF THE OTHER WAY ROUND.
"A *STRONGER* GUARDIAN--
"--MIGHT FIND A WAY TO CONTAIN IT, TO *EXPERIMENT* WITHOUT LETTING IT...
"BESIDES, IF *OTHER* TROLLS HAVE BECOME INTERESTED IN WHAT THAT WARLORD DID...
"RIGHT.
"WHERE TO BEGIN?"

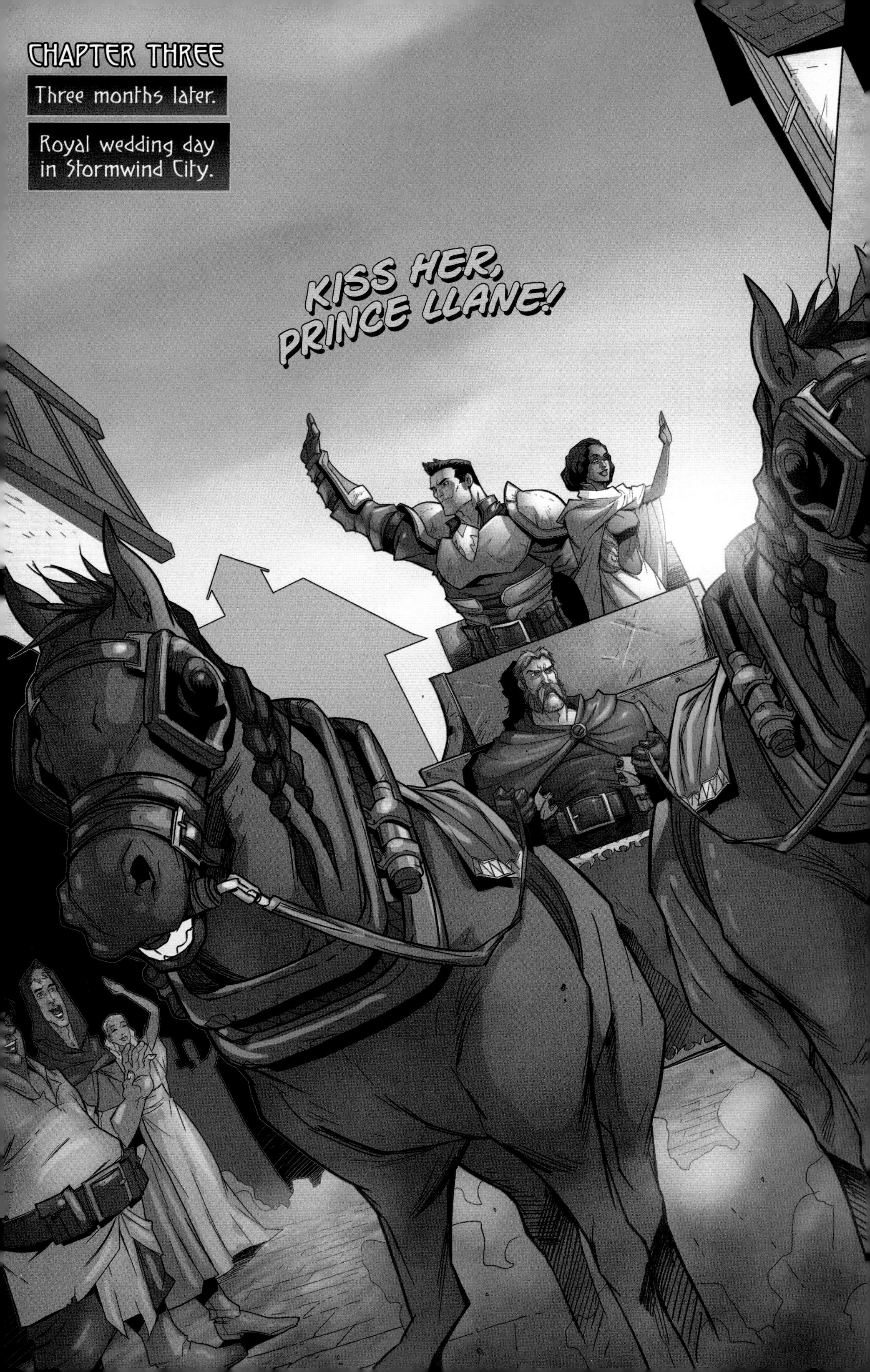
CHAPTER THREE
Three months later.
Royal wedding day in Stormwind City.
KISS HER, PRINCE LLANE!

HOORAY!

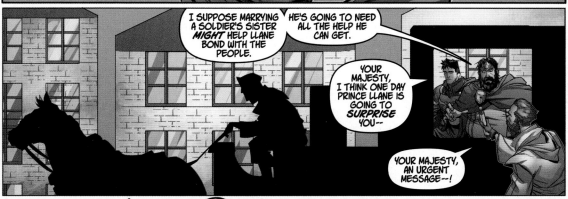

I SUPPOSE MARRYING A SOLDIER'S SISTER *MIGHT* HELP LLANE BOND WITH THE PEOPLE.

HE'S GOING TO NEED ALL THE HELP HE CAN GET.

YOUR MAJESTY, I THINK ONE DAY PRINCE LLANE IS GOING TO *SURPRISE* YOU--

YOUR MAJESTY, AN URGENT MESSAGE--!

EMERGENCY COUNCIL MEETING!

ALL IN THE INNER CIRCLE WILL ATTEND ME, IMMEDIATELY!

YOU TOO, BOY!

SO... CHANCES OF A HONEYMOON?

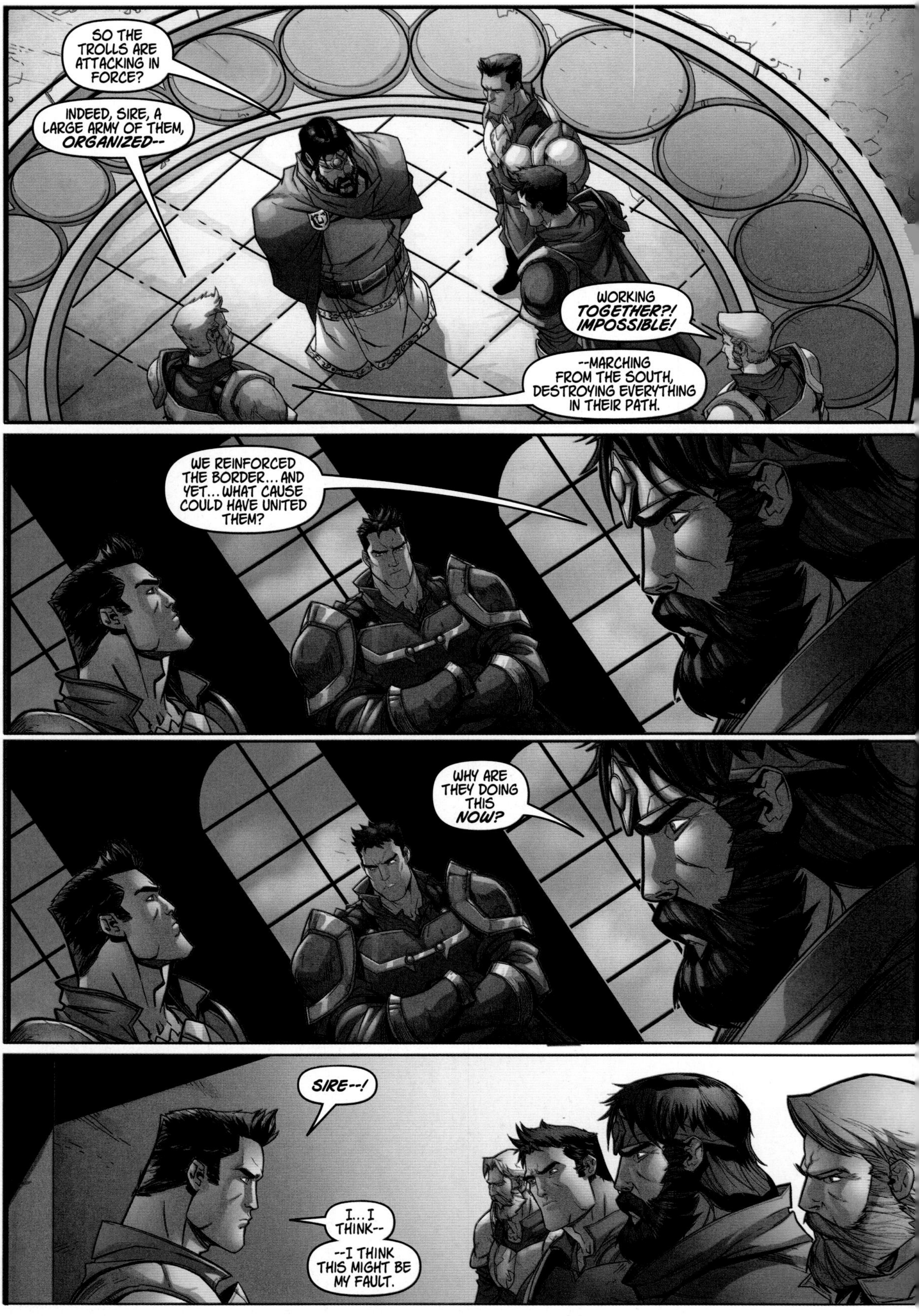
SO THE TROLLS ARE ATTACKING IN FORCE?
INDEED, SIRE, A LARGE ARMY OF THEM, ORGANIZED--
WORKING TOGETHER?! IMPOSSIBLE!
--MARCHING FROM THE SOUTH, DESTROYING EVERYTHING IN THEIR PATH.
WE REINFORCED THE BORDER... AND YET... WHAT CAUSE COULD HAVE UNITED THEM?
WHY ARE THEY DOING THIS NOW?
SIRE--!
I... I THINK--
--I THINK THIS MIGHT BE MY FAULT.

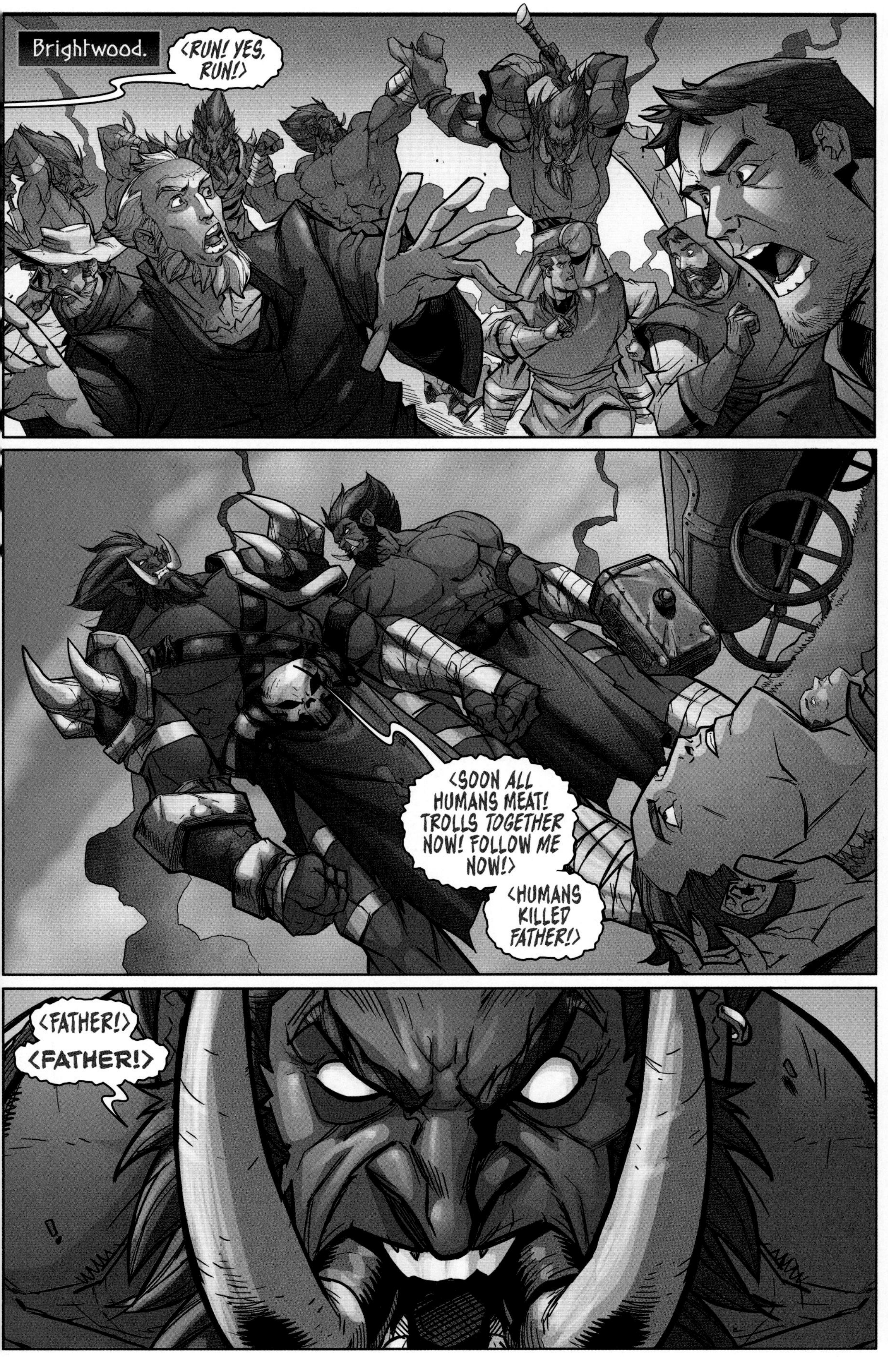
Brightwood.
<RUN! YES, RUN!>
<SOON ALL HUMANS MEAT! TROLLS TOGETHER NOW! FOLLOW ME NOW!>
<HUMANS KILLED FATHER!>
<FATHER!>
<FATHER!>

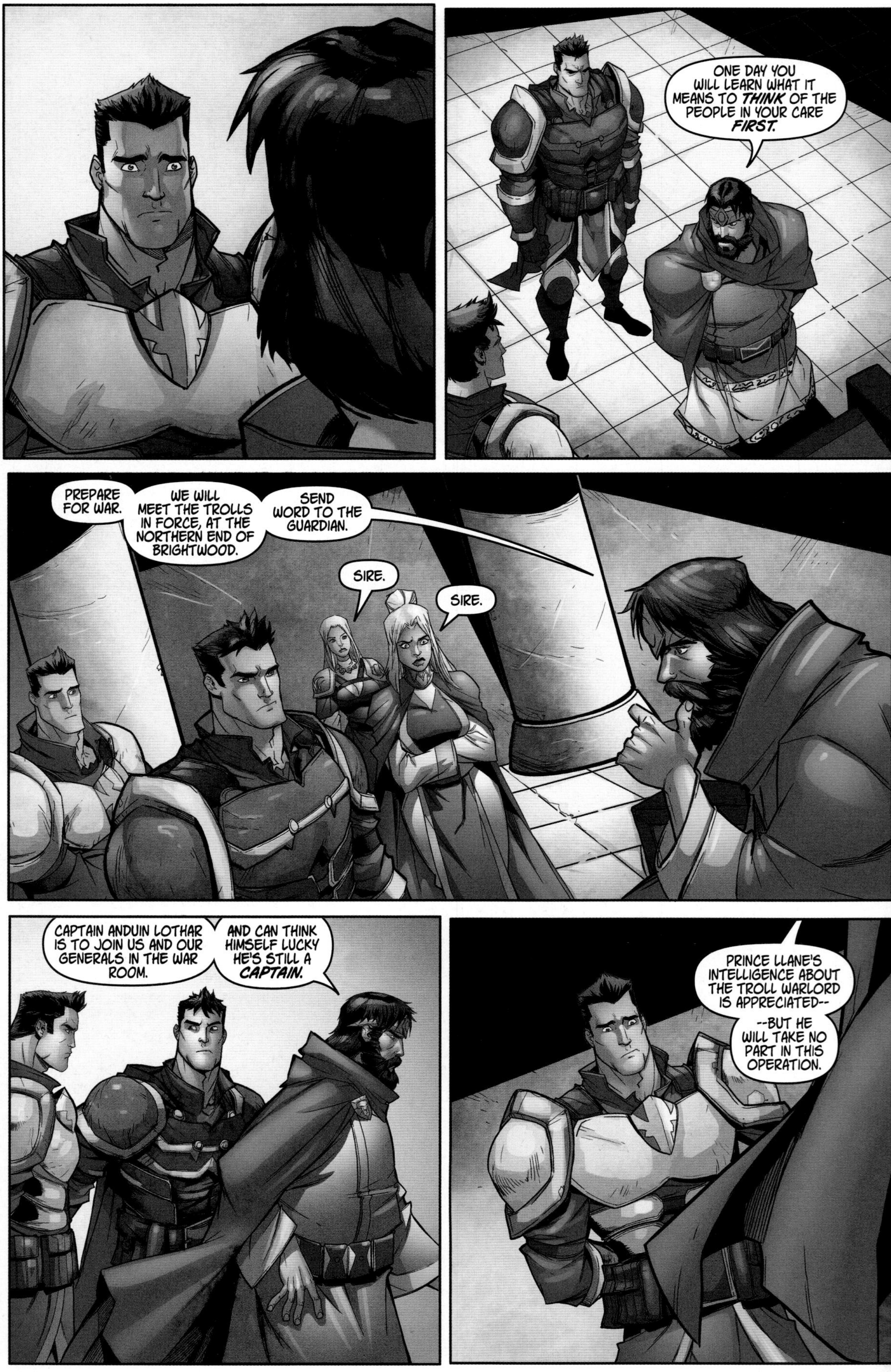
ONE DAY YOU WILL LEARN WHAT IT MEANS TO THINK OF THE PEOPLE IN YOUR CARE FIRST.
PREPARE FOR WAR.
WE WILL MEET THE TROLLS IN FORCE, AT THE NORTHERN END OF BRIGHTWOOD.
SEND WORD TO THE GUARDIAN.
SIRE.
SIRE.
CAPTAIN ANDUIN LOTHAR IS TO JOIN US AND OUR GENERALS IN THE WAR ROOM.
AND CAN THINK HIMSELF LUCKY HE'S STILL A CAPTAIN.
PRINCE LLANE'S INTELLIGENCE ABOUT THE TROLL WARLORD IS APPRECIATED--
--BUT HE WILL TAKE NO PART IN THIS OPERATION.

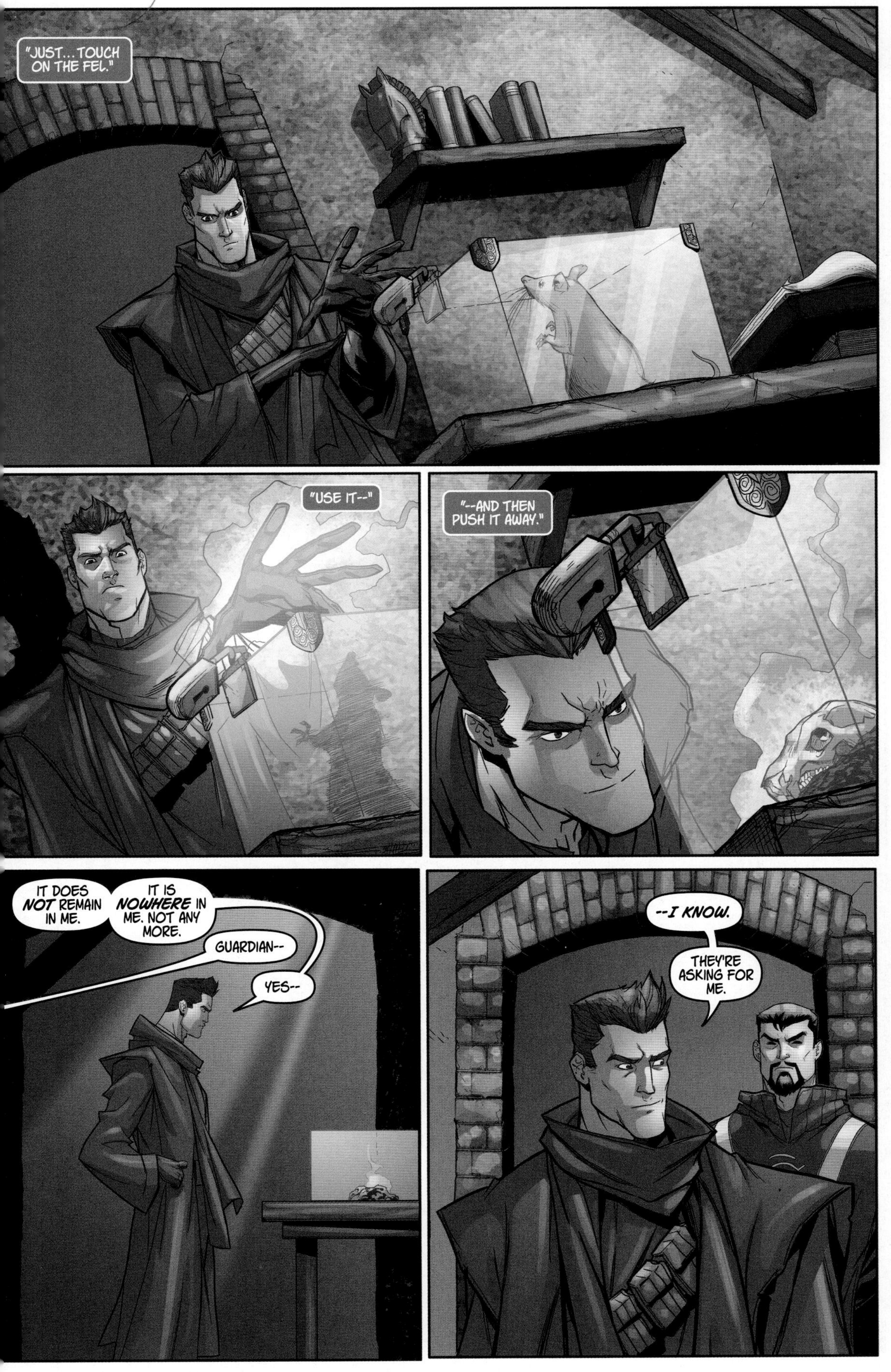
"JUST... TOUCH ON THE FEL."
"USE IT--"
"--AND THEN PUSH IT AWAY."
IT DOES NOT REMAIN IN ME.
IT IS NOWHERE IN ME. NOT ANY MORE.
GUARDIAN--
YES--
--I KNOW.
THEY'RE ASKING FOR ME.

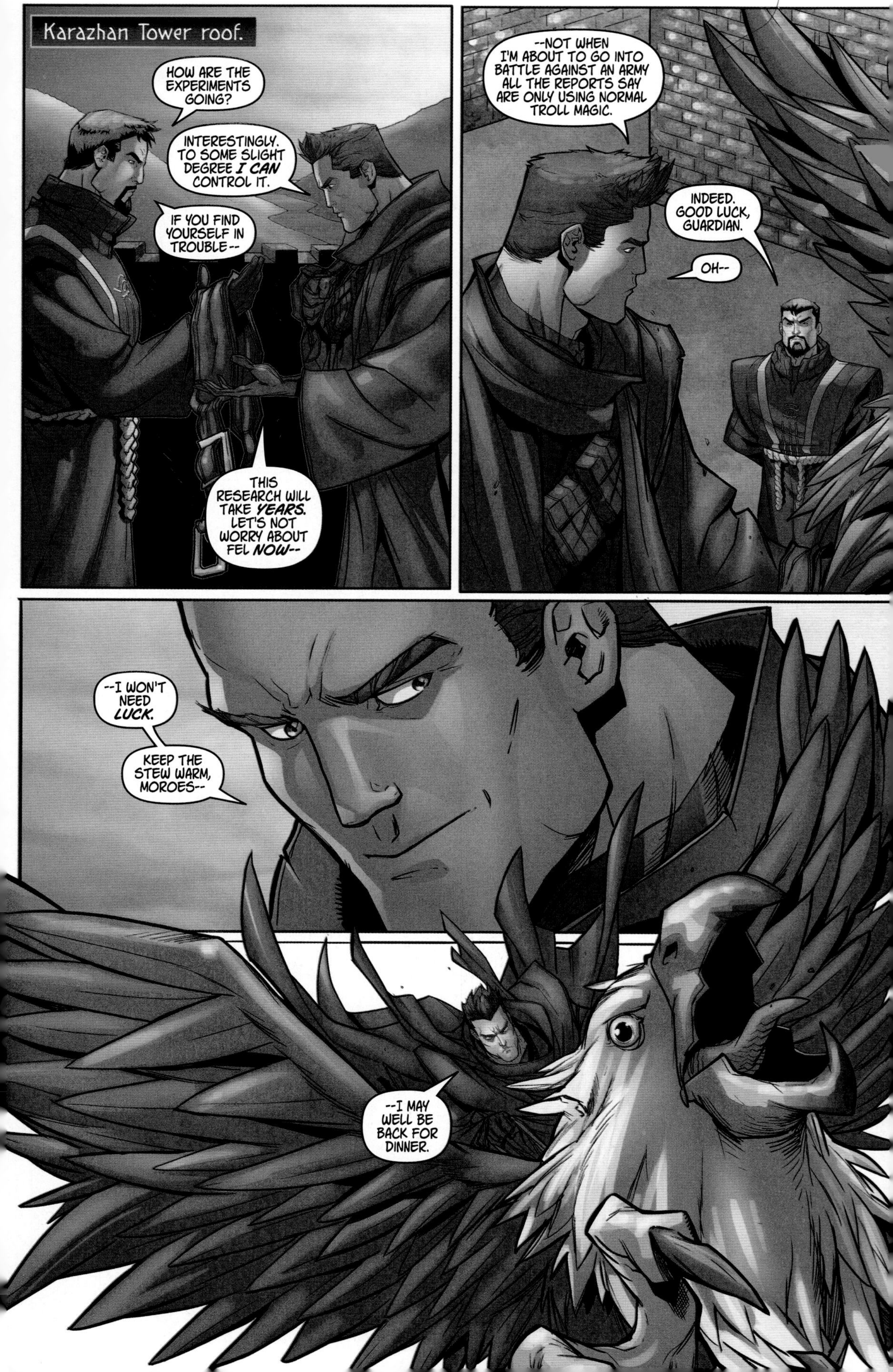
Karazhan Tower roof.
HOW ARE THE EXPERIMENTS GOING?
INTERESTINGLY. TO SOME SLIGHT DEGREE I CAN CONTROL IT.
IF YOU FIND YOURSELF IN TROUBLE--
THIS RESEARCH WILL TAKE YEARS. LET'S NOT WORRY ABOUT FEL NOW--
--NOT WHEN I'M ABOUT TO GO INTO BATTLE AGAINST AN ARMY ALL THE REPORTS SAY ARE ONLY USING NORMAL TROLL MAGIC.
INDEED. GOOD LUCK, GUARDIAN.
OH--
--I WON'T NEED LUCK.
KEEP THE STEW WARM, MOROES--
--I MAY WELL BE BACK FOR DINNER.

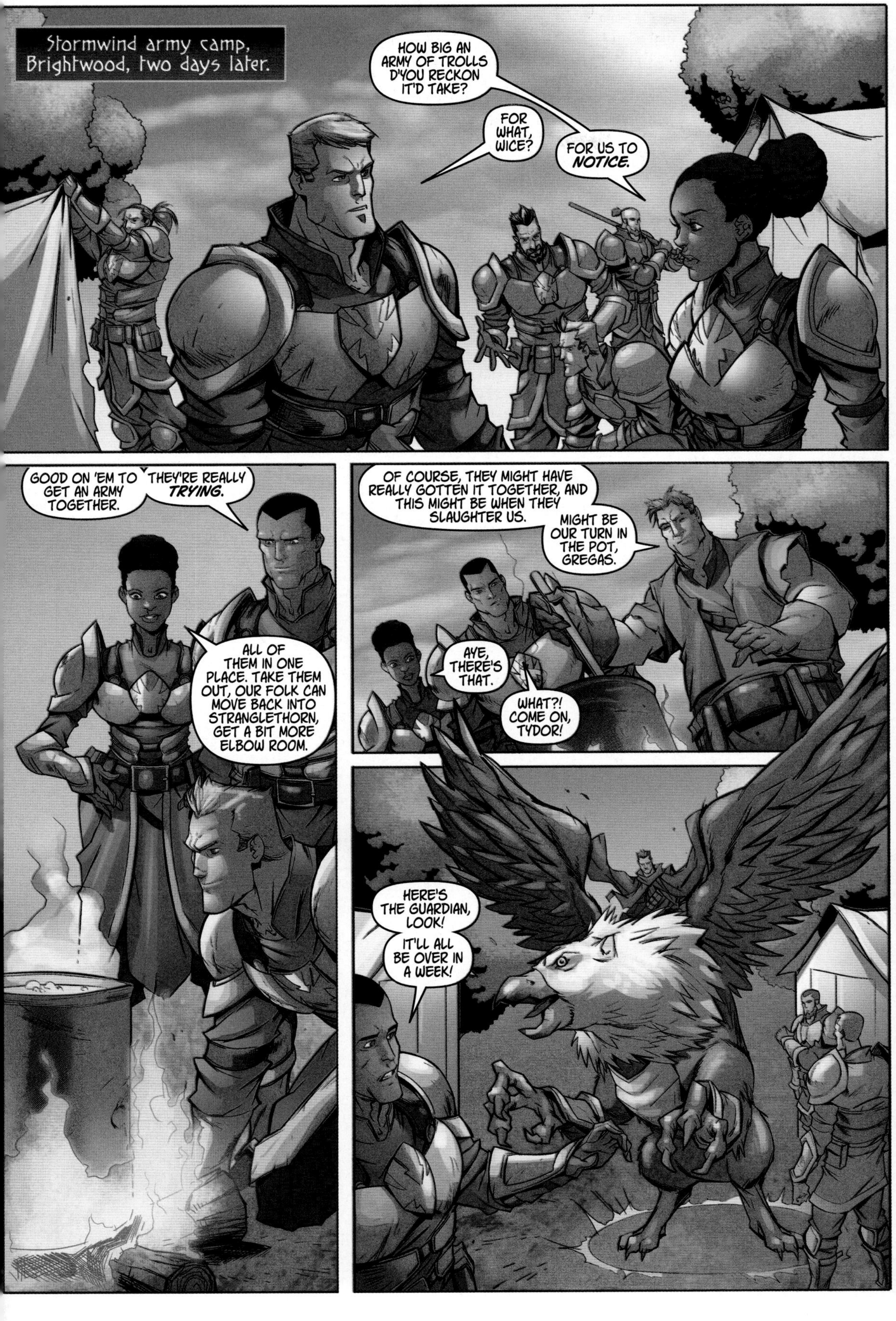

Stormwind army camp, Brightwood, two days later.
HOW BIG AN ARMY OF TROLLS D'YOU RECKON IT'D TAKE?
FOR WHAT, WICE?
FOR US TO *NOTICE*.
GOOD ON 'EM TO GET AN ARMY TOGETHER.
THEY'RE REALLY *TRYING*.
ALL OF THEM IN ONE PLACE. TAKE THEM OUT, OUR FOLK CAN MOVE BACK INTO STRANGLETHORN, GET A BIT MORE ELBOW ROOM.
OF COURSE, THEY MIGHT HAVE REALLY GOTTEN IT TOGETHER, AND THIS MIGHT BE WHEN THEY SLAUGHTER US.
MIGHT BE OUR TURN IN THE POT, GREGAS.
AYE, THERE'S THAT.
WHAT?! COME ON, TYDOR!
HERE'S THE GUARDIAN, LOOK!
IT'LL ALL BE OVER IN A WEEK!

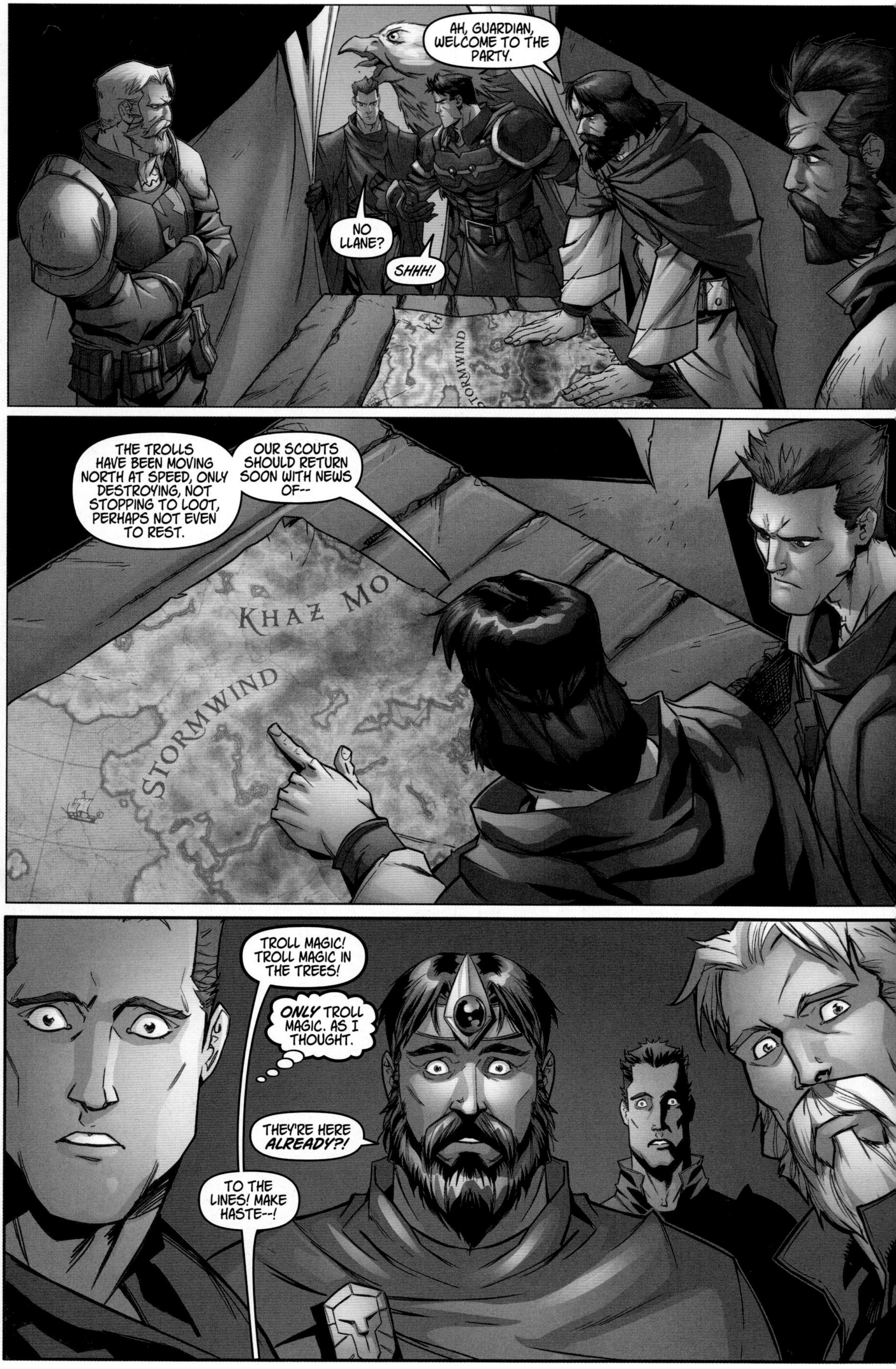
AH, GUARDIAN, WELCOME TO THE PARTY.
NO LLANE?
SHHH!
STORMWIND
THE TROLLS HAVE BEEN MOVING NORTH AT SPEED, ONLY DESTROYING, NOT STOPPING TO LOOT, PERHAPS NOT EVEN TO REST.
OUR SCOUTS SHOULD RETURN SOON WITH NEWS OF--
KHAZ MO
STORMWIND
TROLL MAGIC! TROLL MAGIC IN THE TREES!
ONLY TROLL MAGIC. AS I THOUGHT.
THEY'RE HERE ALREADY?!
TO THE LINES! MAKE HASTE--!

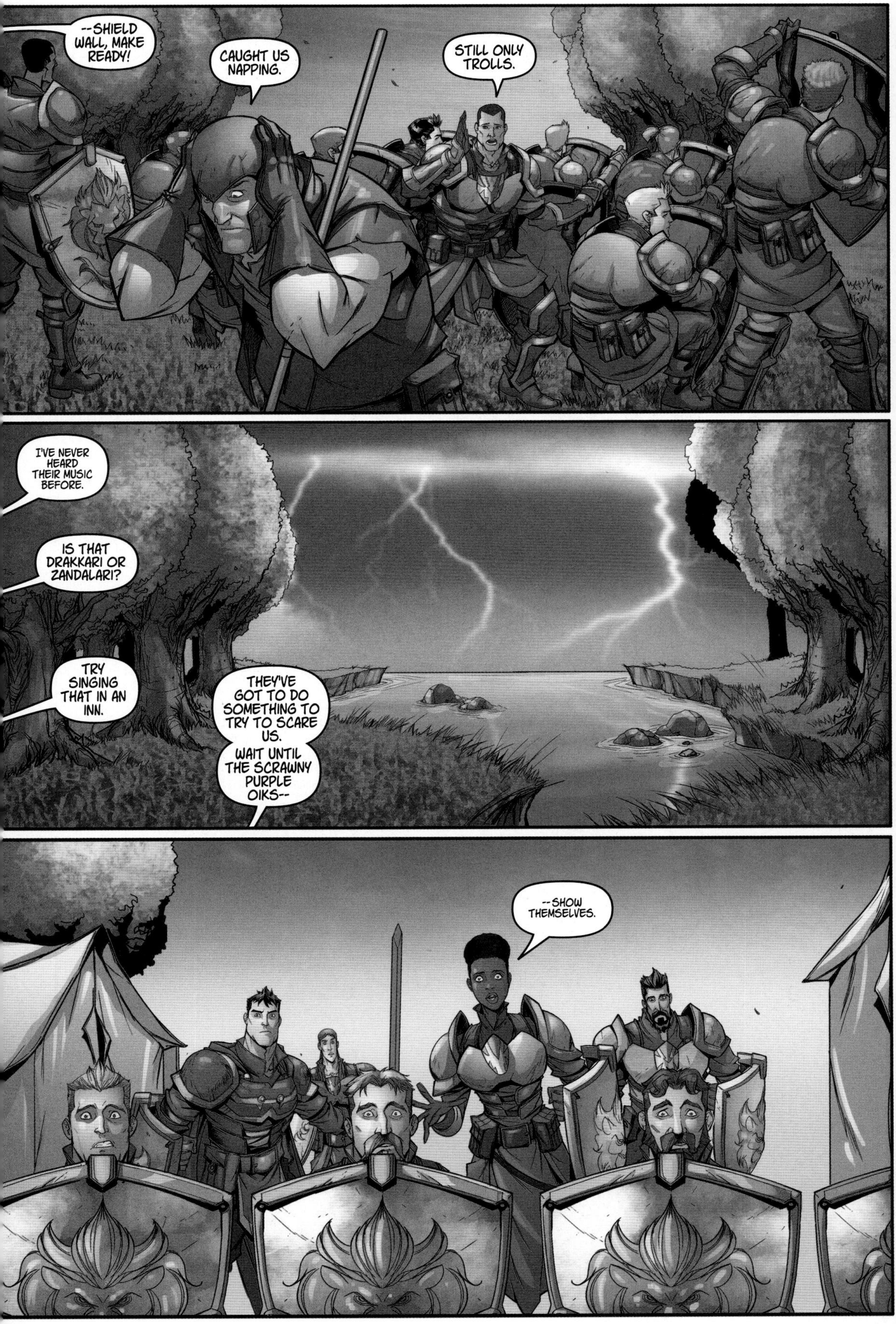
--SHIELD WALL, MAKE READY!
CAUGHT US NAPPING.
STILL ONLY TROLLS.
I'VE NEVER HEARD THEIR MUSIC BEFORE.
IS THAT DRAKKARI OR ZANDALARI?
TRY SINGING THAT IN AN INN.
THEY'VE GOT TO DO SOMETHING TO TRY TO SCARE US.
WAIT UNTIL THE SCRAWNY PURPLE OIKS--
--SHOW THEMSELVES.

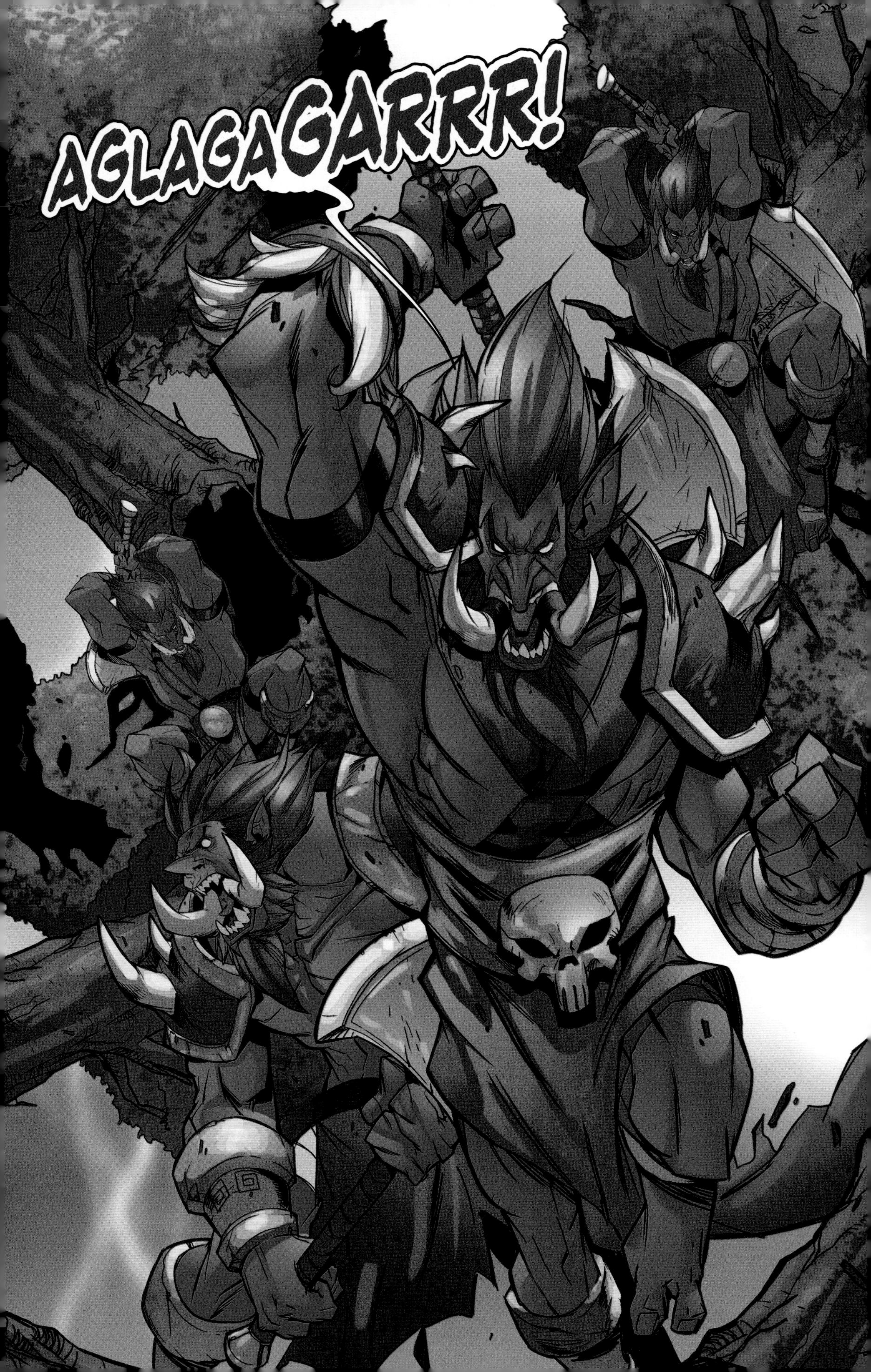
AGLAGAGARRR!

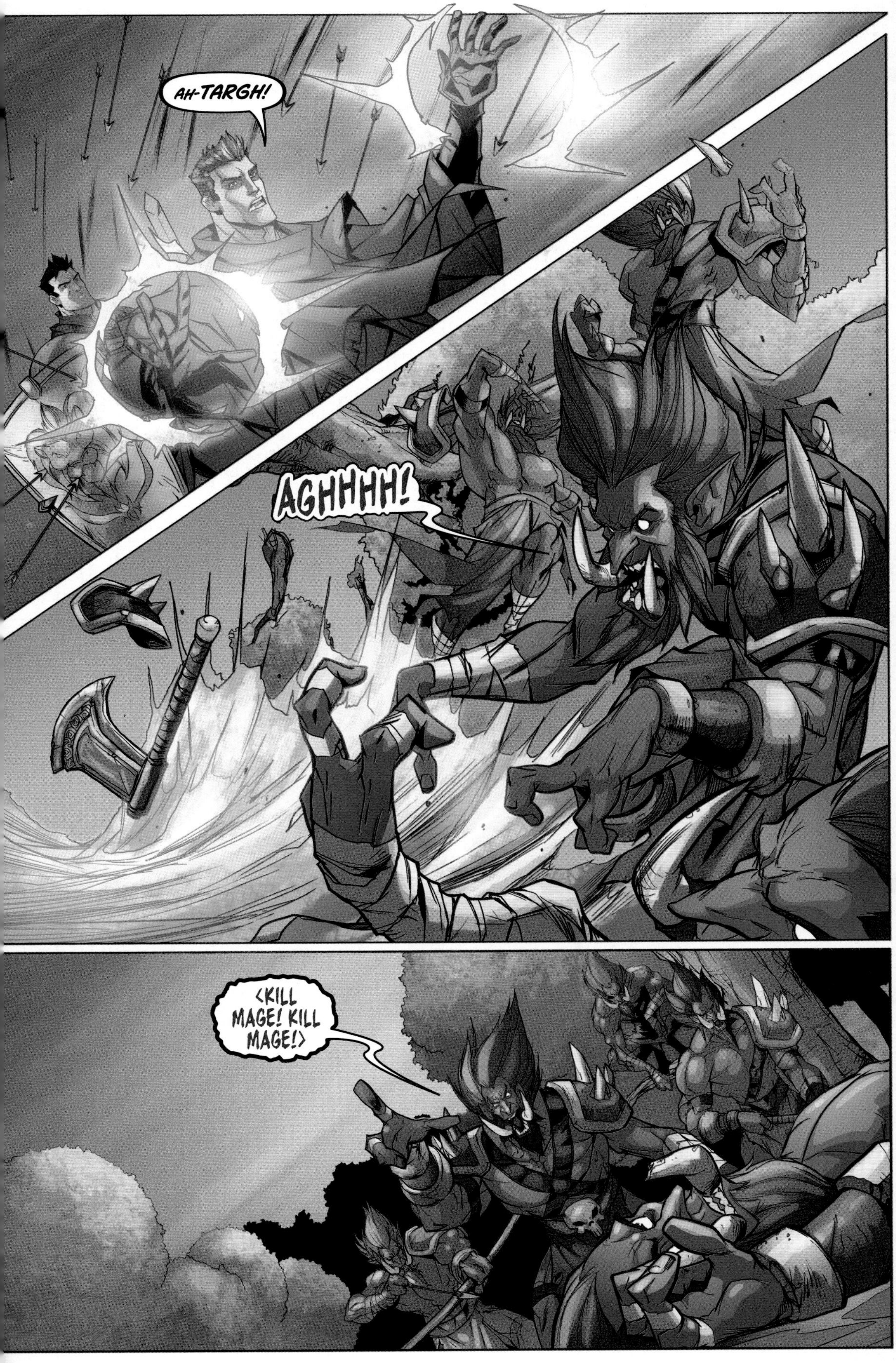
AH-TARGH!
AGHHHH!
<KILL MAGE! KILL MAGE!>

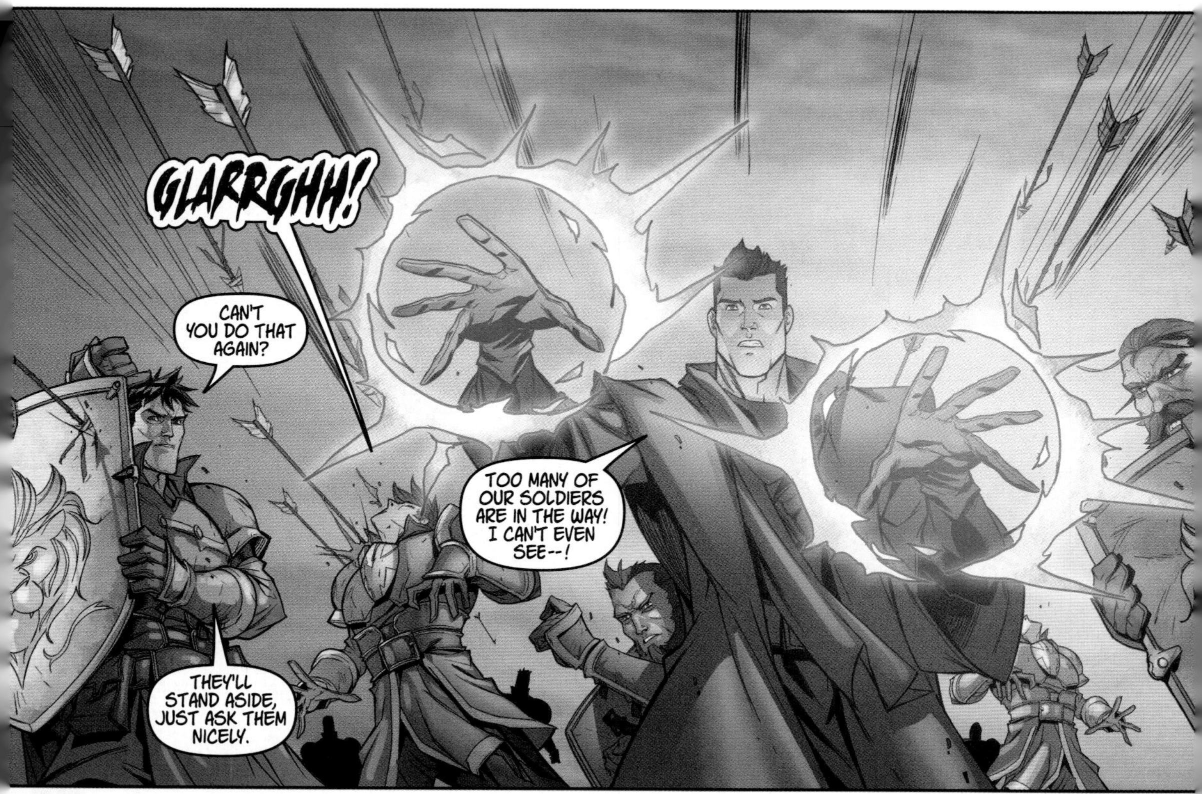
GLARRGHH!
CAN'T YOU DO THAT AGAIN?
TOO MANY OF OUR SOLDIERS ARE IN THE WAY! I CAN'T EVEN SEE--!
THEY'LL STAND ASIDE, JUST ASK THEM NICELY.
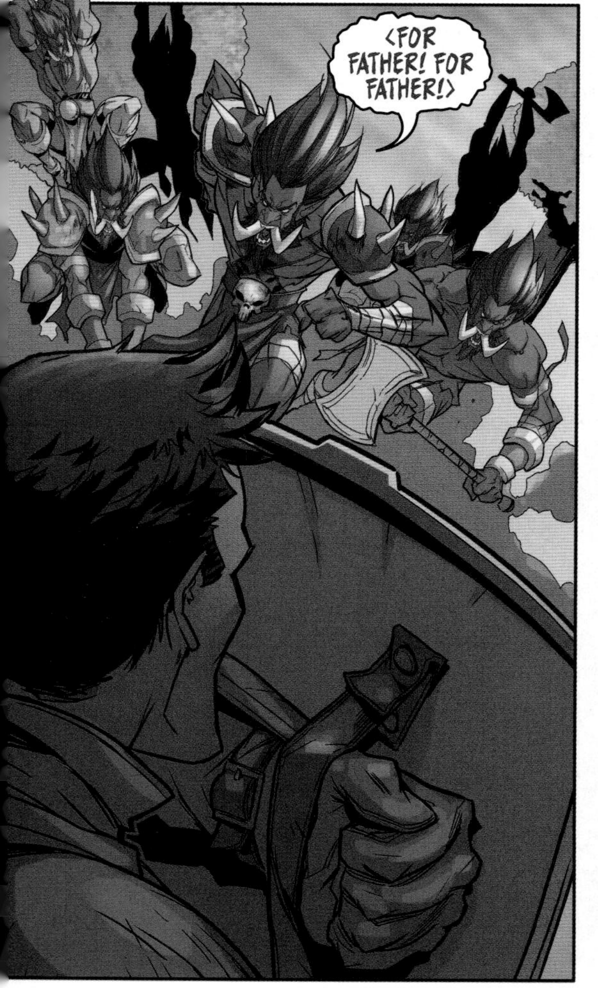
<FOR FATHER! FOR FATHER!>
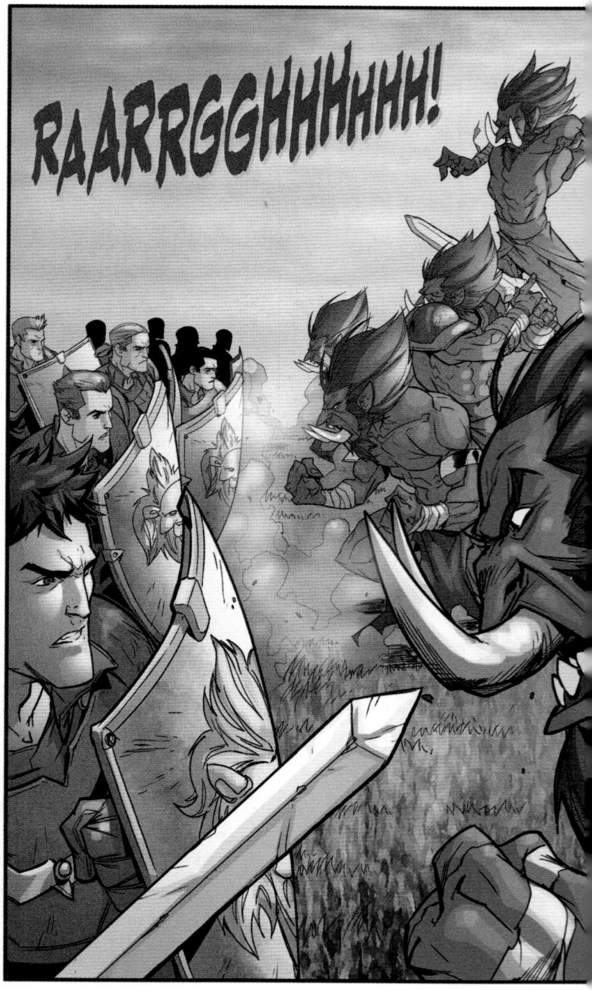
RAARRGGHHHHHH!

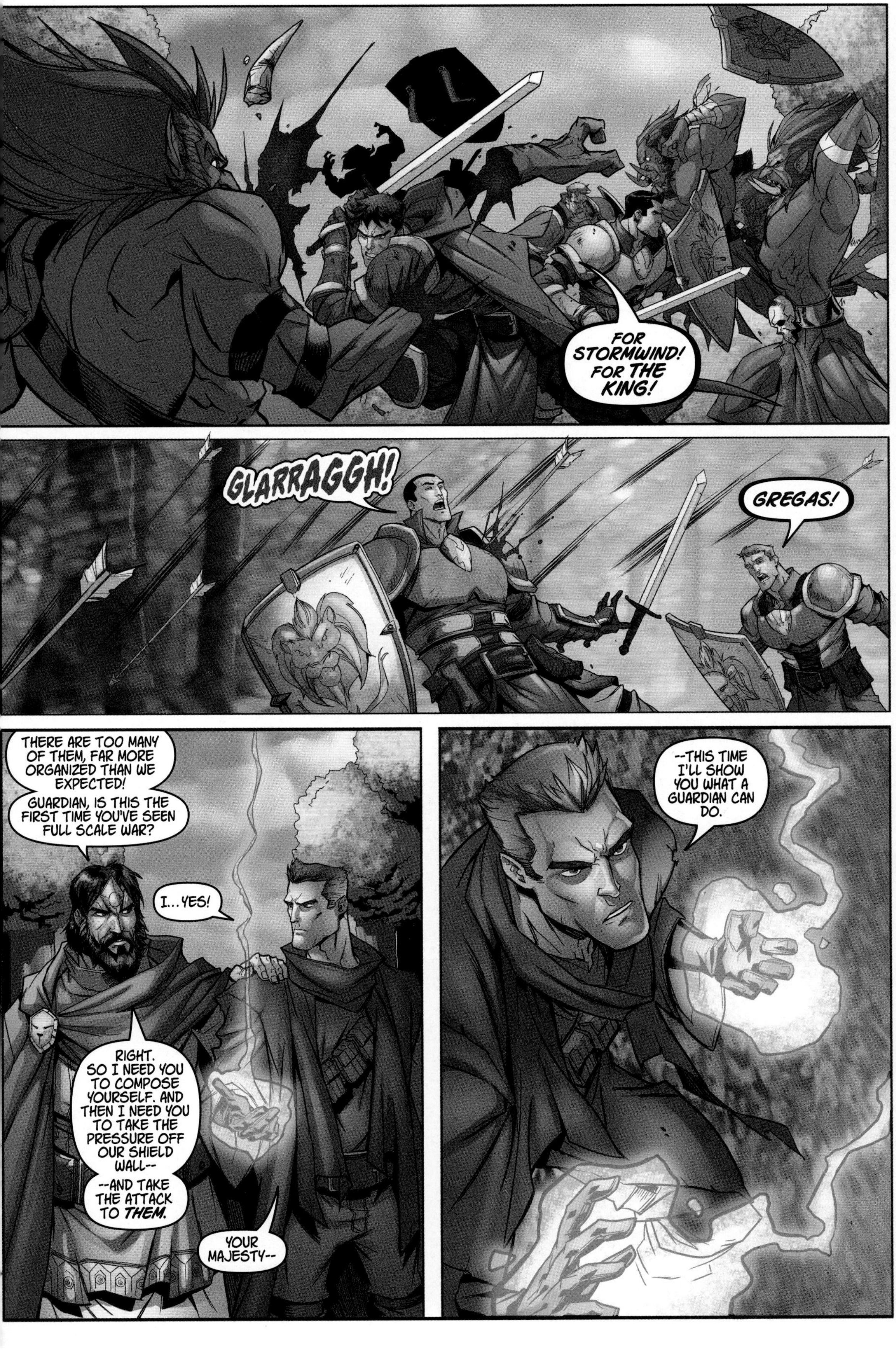
FOR STORMWIND! FOR THE KING!
GLARRAGGH!
GREGAS!
THERE ARE TOO MANY OF THEM, FAR MORE ORGANIZED THAN WE EXPECTED!
GUARDIAN, IS THIS THE FIRST TIME YOU'VE SEEN FULL SCALE WAR?
I... YES!
RIGHT. SO I NEED YOU TO COMPOSE YOURSELF. AND THEN I NEED YOU TO TAKE THE PRESSURE OFF OUR SHIELD WALL--
--AND TAKE THE ATTACK TO *THEM*.
YOUR MAJESTY--
--THIS TIME I'LL SHOW YOU WHAT A GUARDIAN CAN DO.

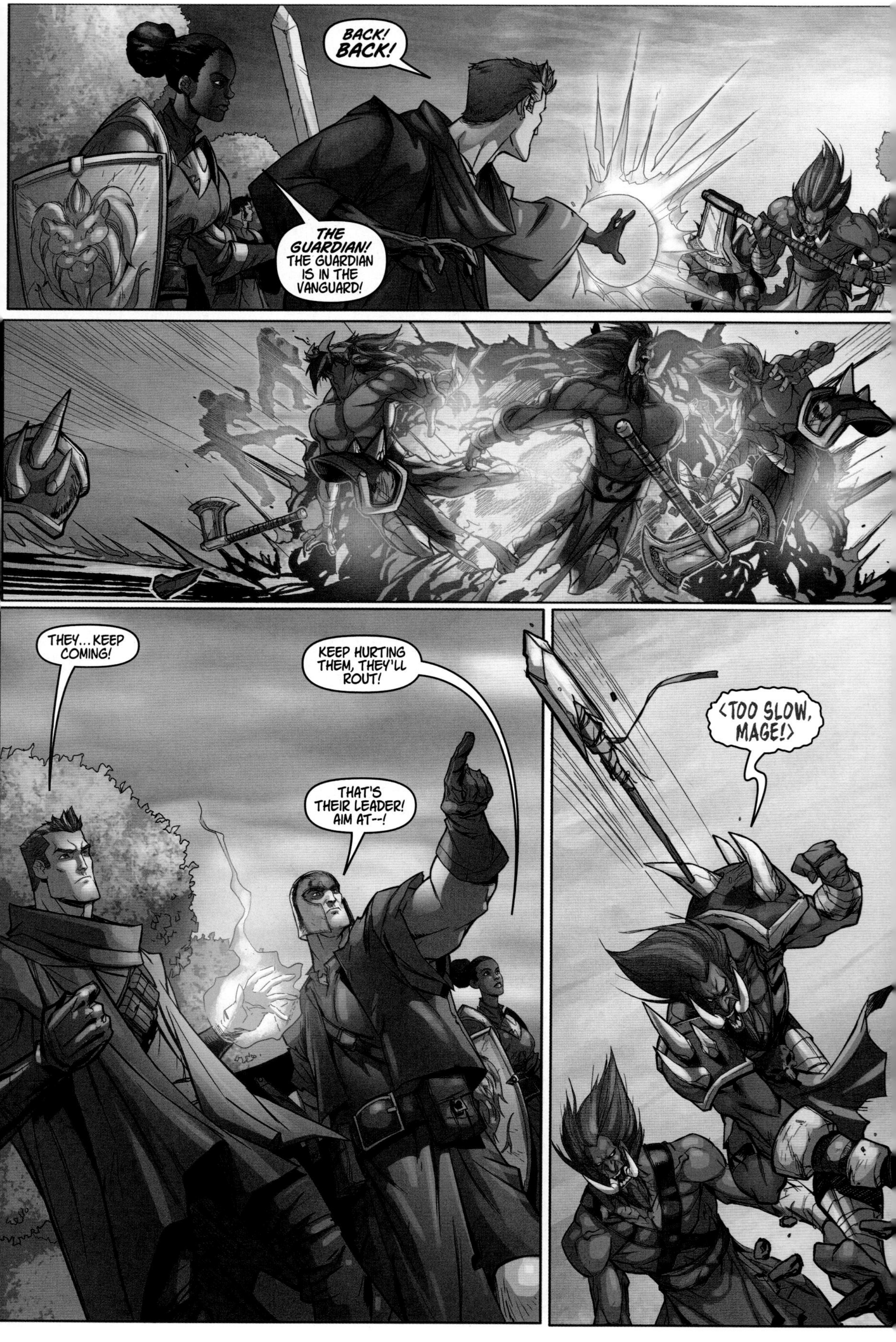
BACK! BACK!
THE GUARDIAN! THE GUARDIAN IS IN THE VANGUARD!
THEY...KEEP COMING!
KEEP HURTING THEM, THEY'LL ROUT!
THAT'S THEIR LEADER! AIM AT--!
<TOO SLOW, MAGE!>

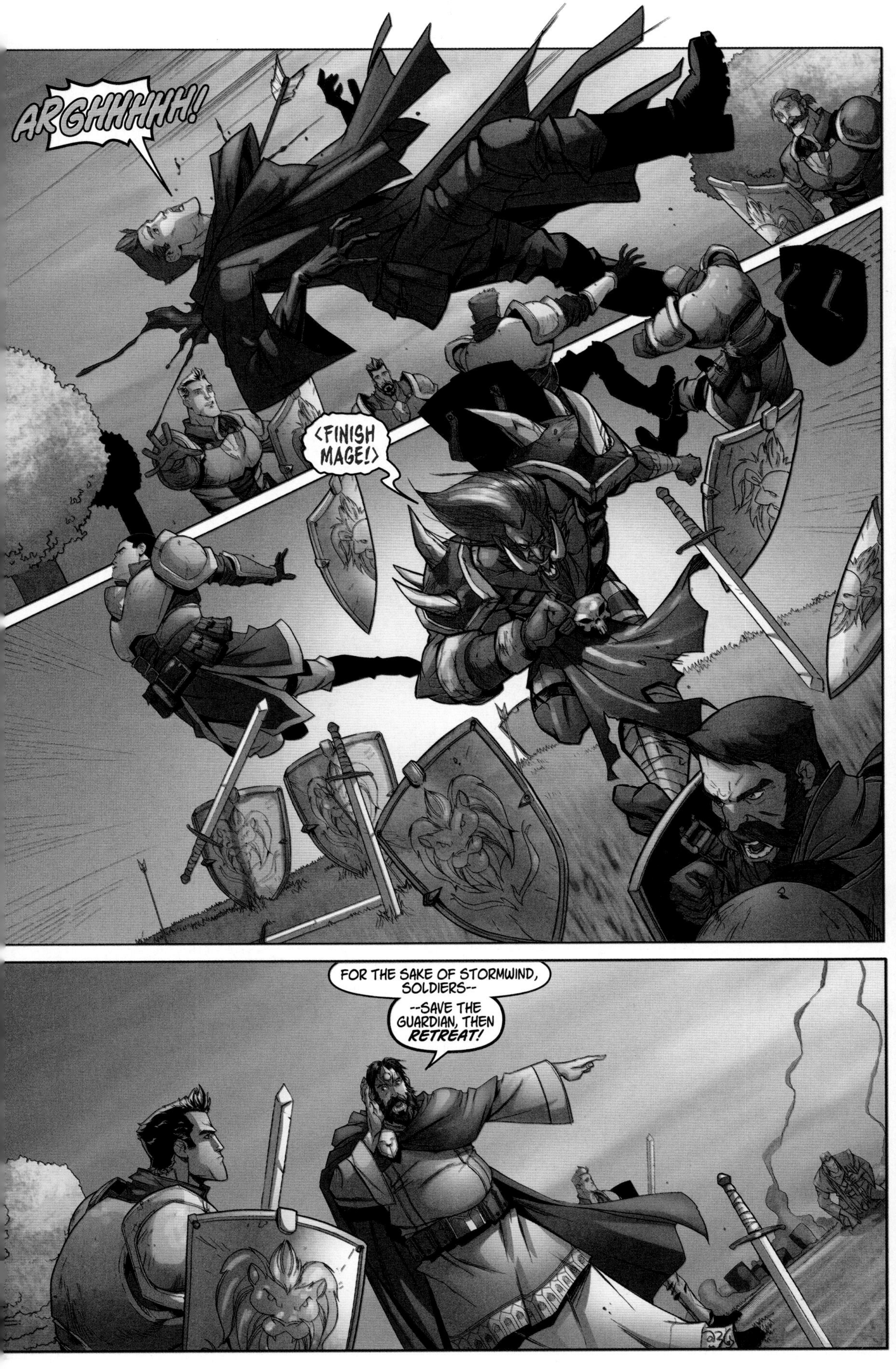
ARGHHHHH!
<FINISH MAGE!>
FOR THE SAKE OF STORMWIND, SOLDIERS--
--SAVE THE GUARDIAN, THEN *RETREAT!*

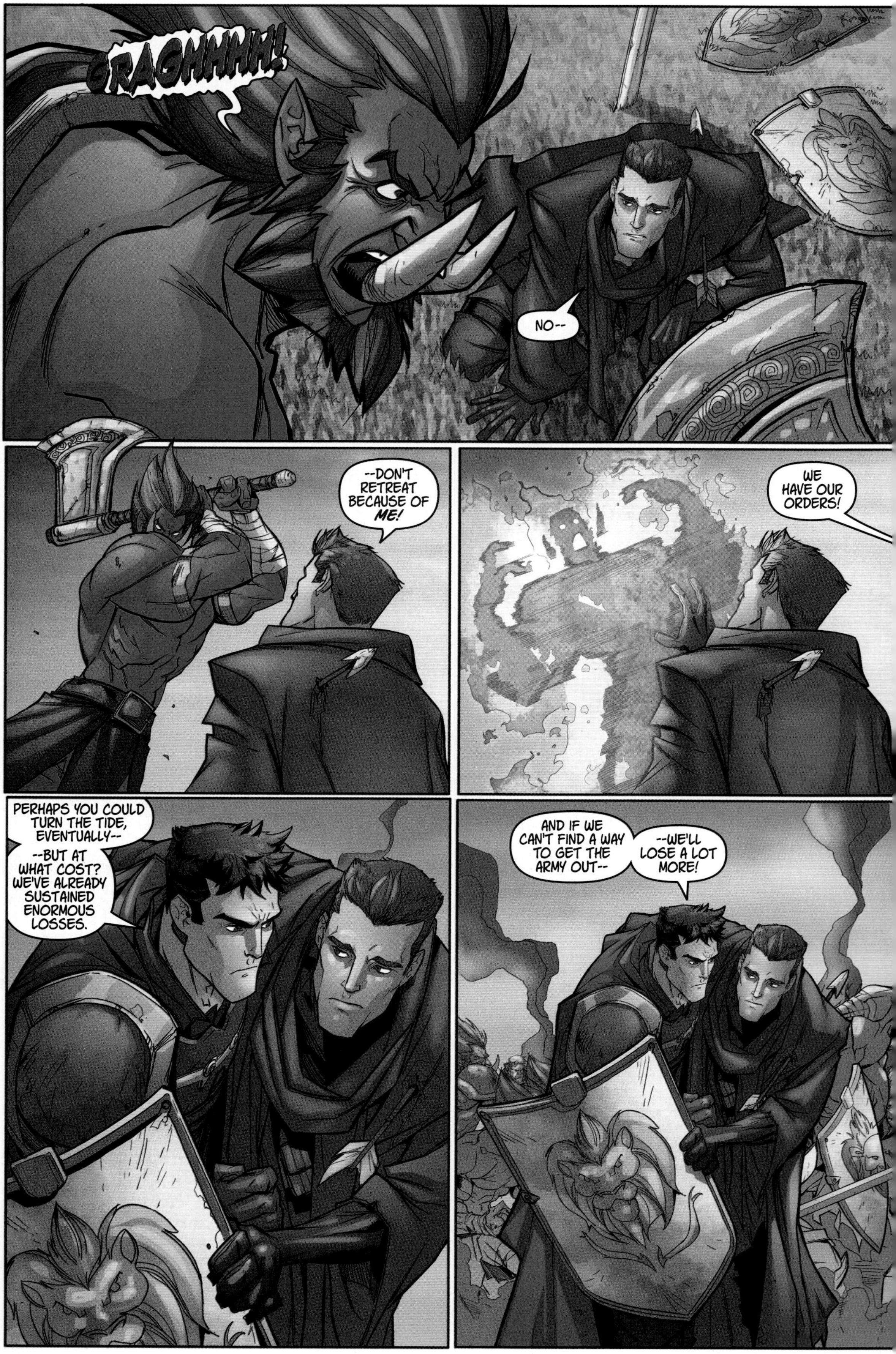
GRAGHHHH!
NO--
--DON'T RETREAT BECAUSE OF ME!
WE HAVE OUR ORDERS!
PERHAPS YOU COULD TURN THE TIDE, EVENTUALLY--
--BUT AT WHAT COST? WE'VE ALREADY SUSTAINED ENORMOUS LOSSES.
AND IF WE CAN'T FIND A WAY TO GET THE ARMY OUT--
--WE'LL LOSE A LOT MORE!

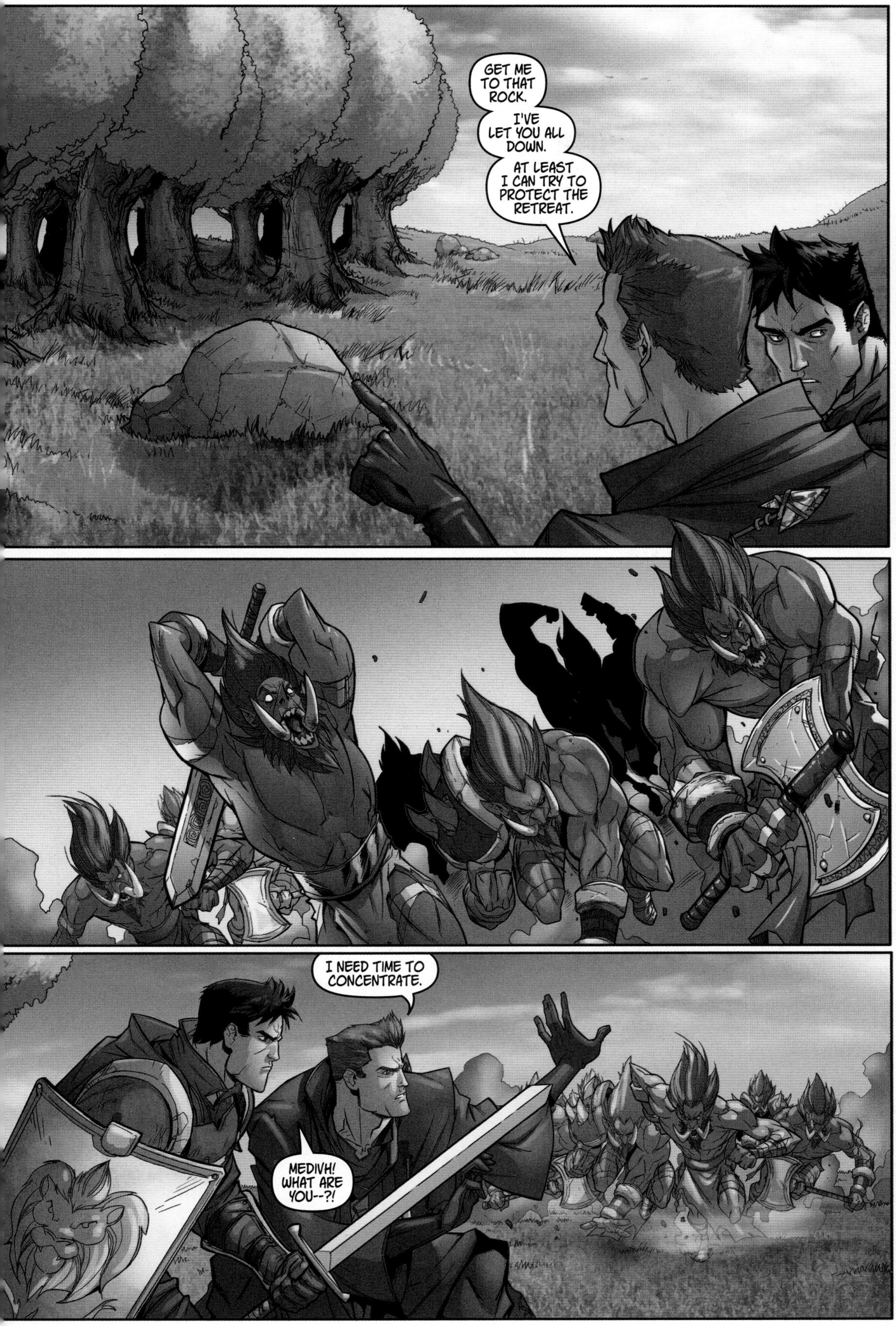
GET ME TO THAT ROCK.
I'VE LET YOU ALL DOWN.
AT LEAST I CAN TRY TO PROTECT THE RETREAT.
I NEED TIME TO CONCENTRATE.
MEDIVH! WHAT ARE YOU--?!

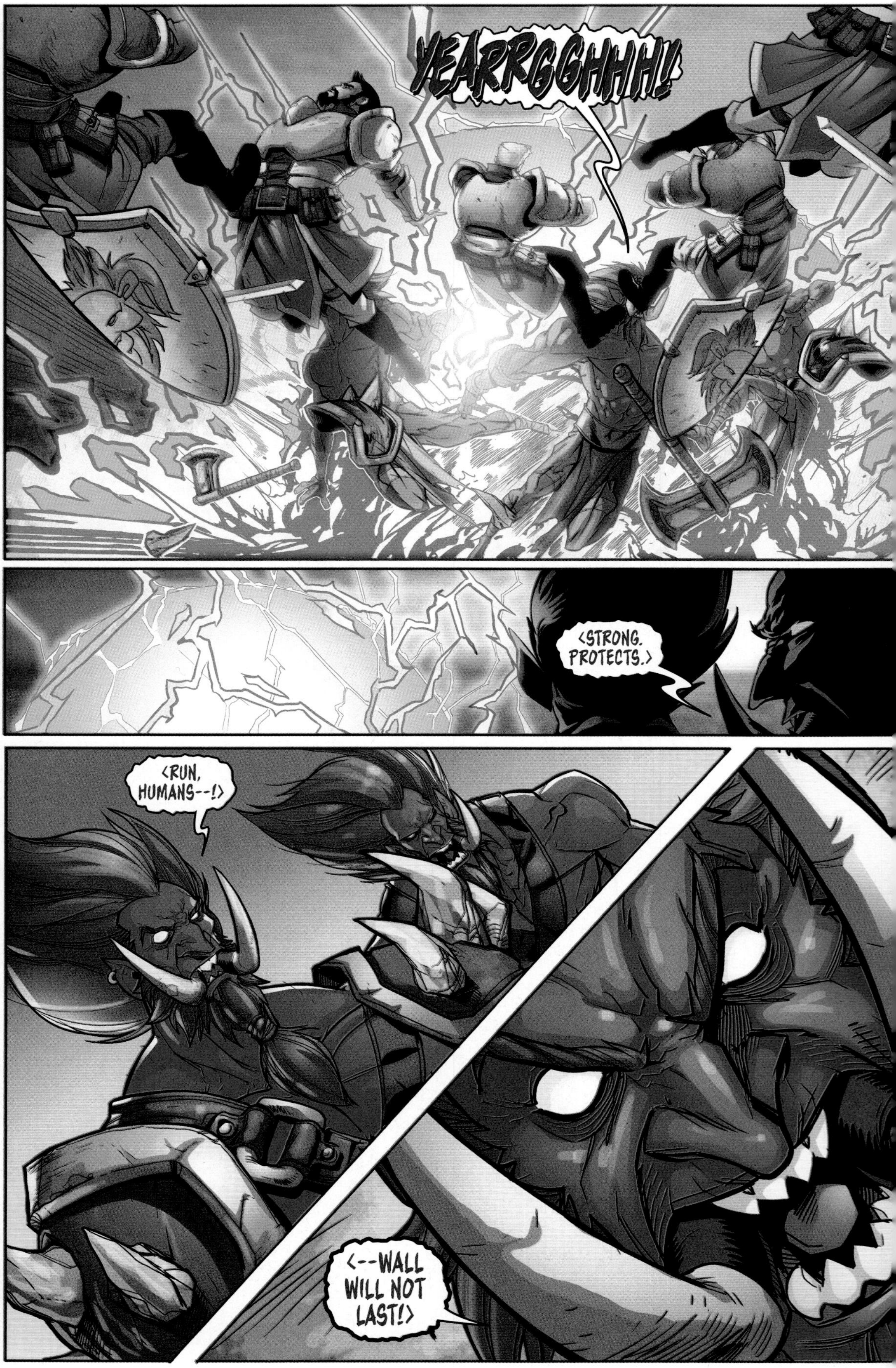
YEARRGGHHH!
<STRONG. PROTECTS.>
<RUN, HUMANS--!>
<--WALL WILL NOT LAST!>

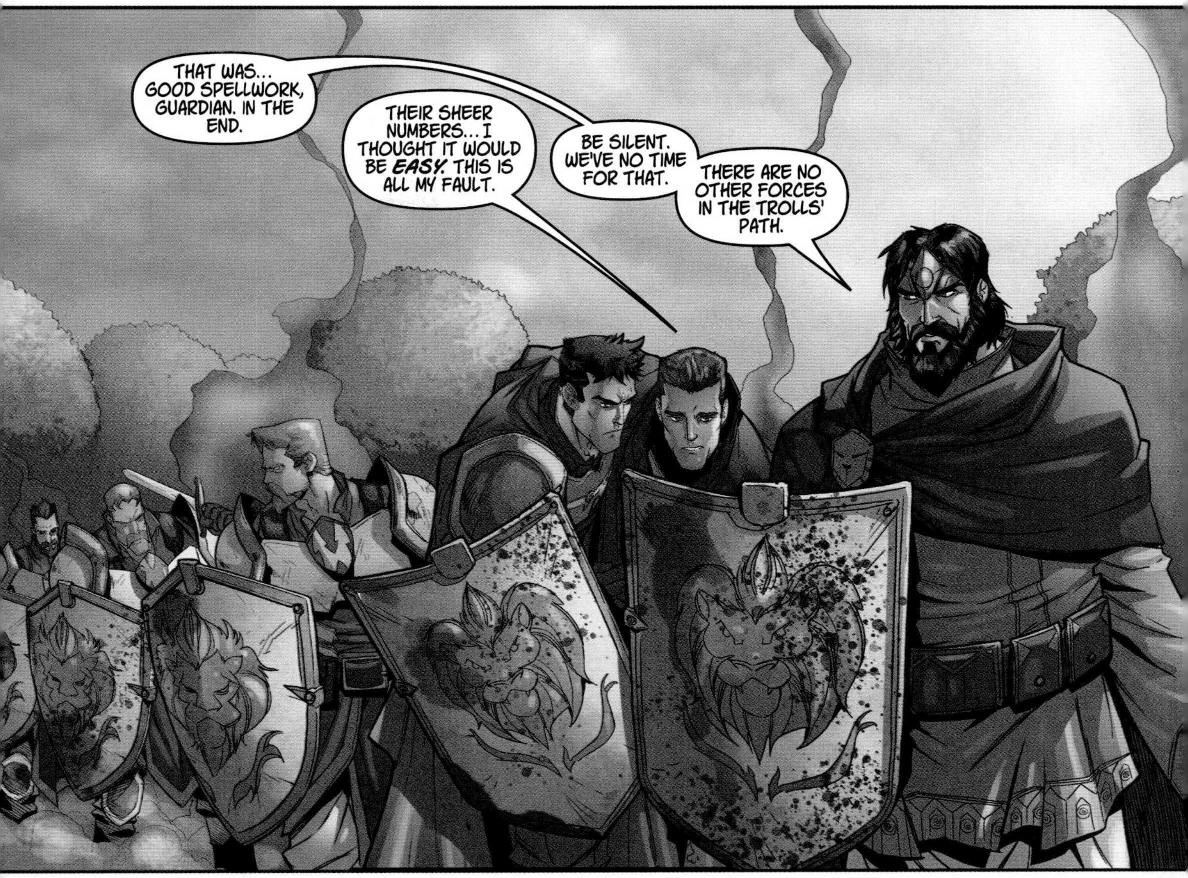
THAT WAS... GOOD SPELLWORK, GUARDIAN. IN THE END.
THEIR SHEER NUMBERS... I THOUGHT IT WOULD BE EASY. THIS IS ALL MY FAULT.
BE SILENT. WE'VE NO TIME FOR THAT.
THERE ARE NO OTHER FORCES IN THE TROLLS' PATH.

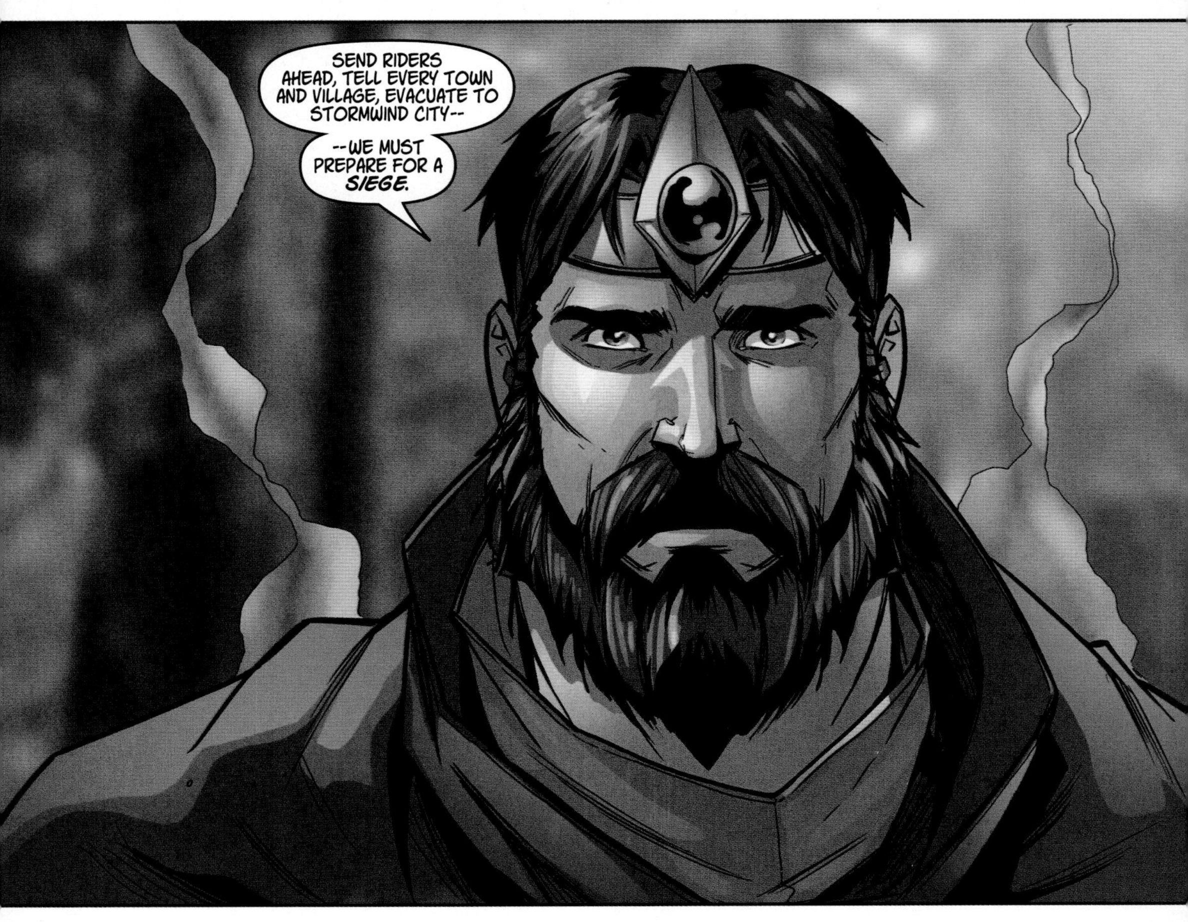
SEND RIDERS AHEAD, TELL EVERY TOWN AND VILLAGE, EVACUATE TO STORMWIND CITY--
--WE MUST PREPARE FOR A SIEGE.

CHAPTER FOUR

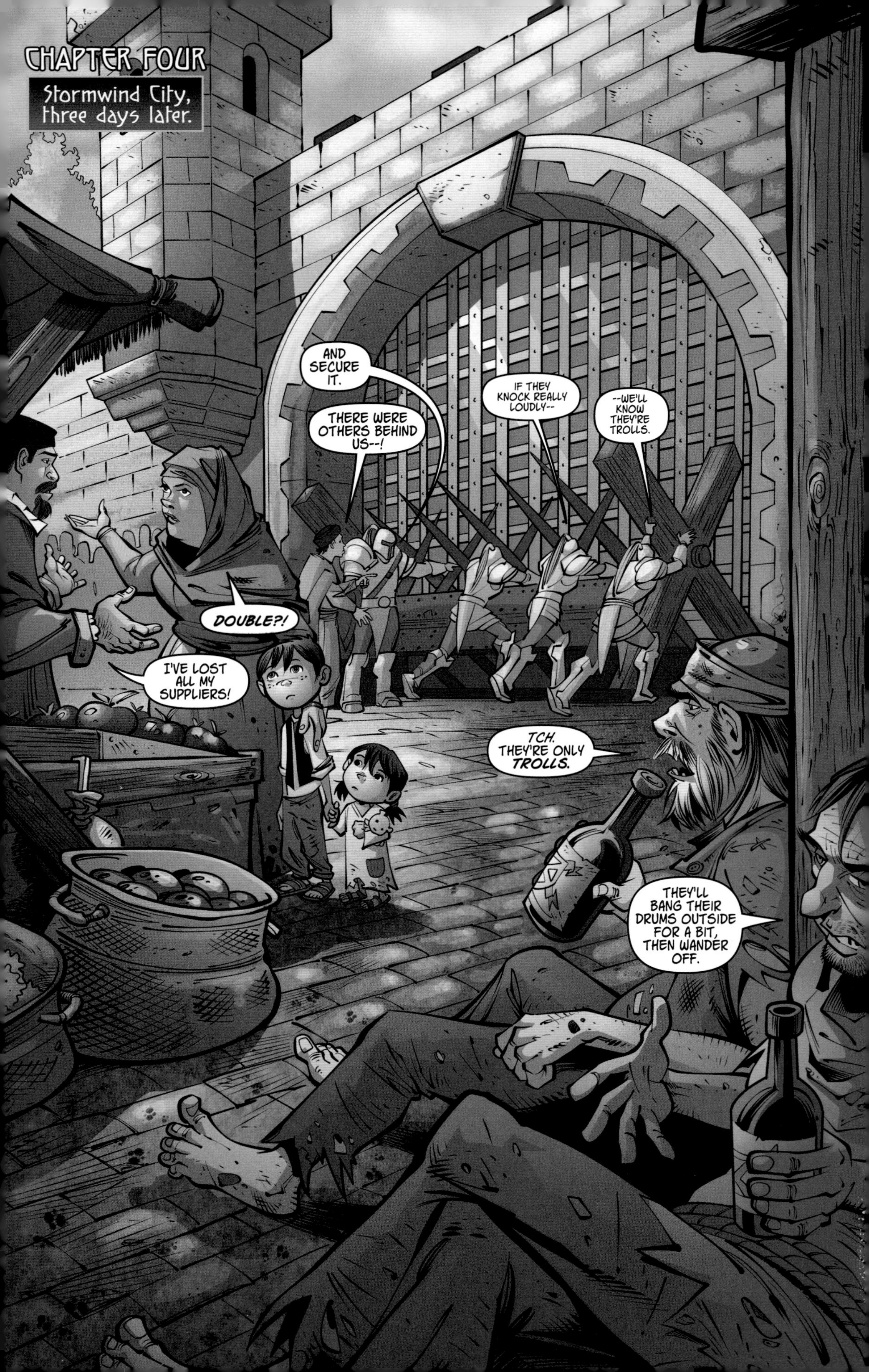
Stormwind City, three days later.
AND SECURE IT.
THERE WERE OTHERS BEHIND US--!
IF THEY KNOCK REALLY LOUDLY--
--WE'LL KNOW THEY'RE TROLLS.
DOUBLE?!
I'VE LOST ALL MY SUPPLIERS!
TCH. THEY'RE ONLY TROLLS.
THEY'LL BANG THEIR DRUMS OUTSIDE FOR A BIT, THEN WANDER OFF.

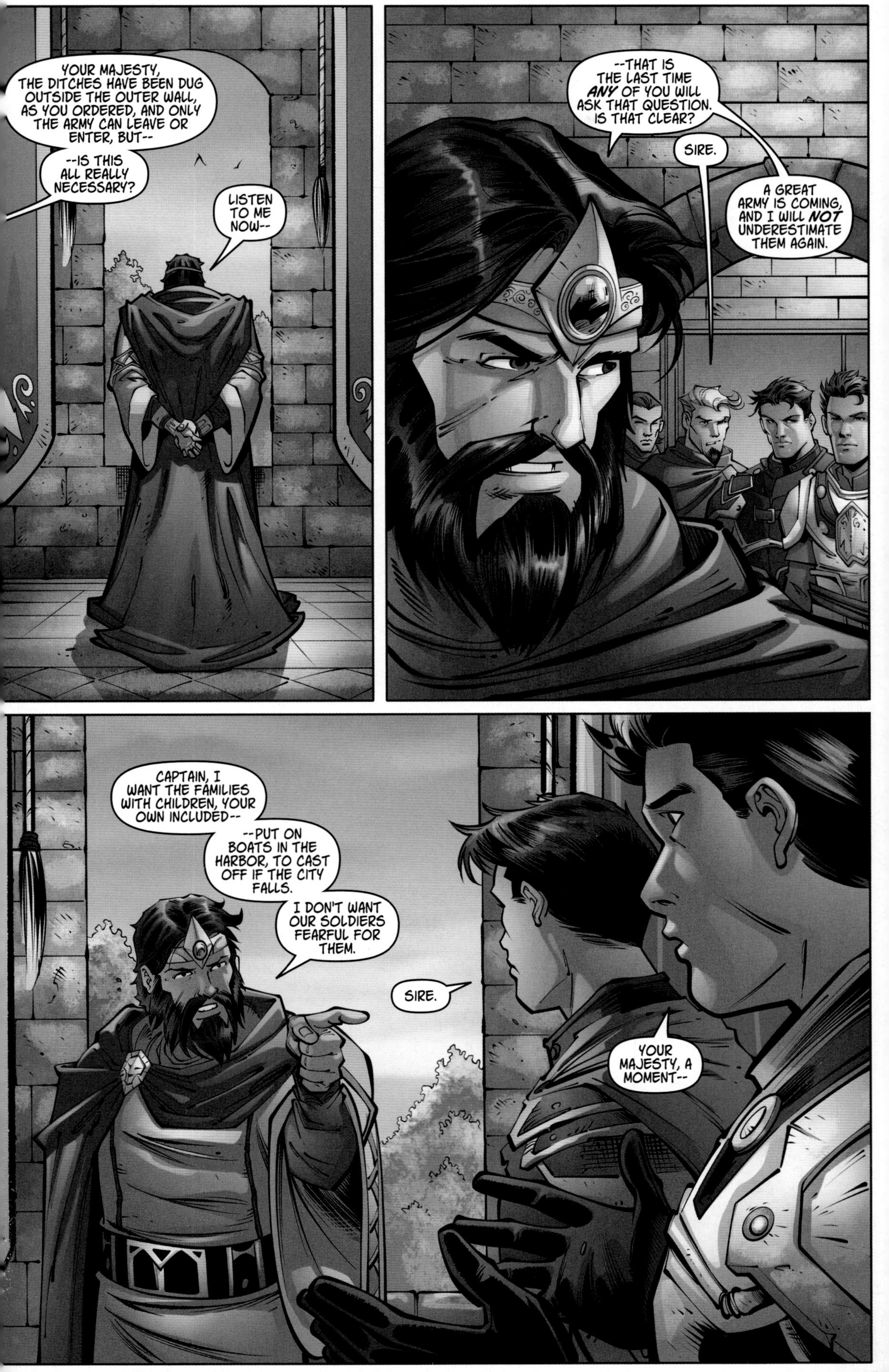
YOUR MAJESTY, THE DITCHES HAVE BEEN DUG OUTSIDE THE OUTER WALL, AS YOU ORDERED, AND ONLY THE ARMY CAN LEAVE OR ENTER, BUT--
--IS THIS ALL REALLY NECESSARY?
LISTEN TO ME NOW--
--THAT IS THE LAST TIME *ANY* OF YOU WILL ASK THAT QUESTION. IS THAT CLEAR?
SIRE.
A GREAT ARMY IS COMING, AND I WILL *NOT* UNDERESTIMATE THEM AGAIN.
CAPTAIN, I WANT THE FAMILIES WITH CHILDREN, YOUR OWN INCLUDED--
--PUT ON BOATS IN THE HARBOR, TO CAST OFF IF THE CITY FALLS.
I DON'T WANT OUR SOLDIERS FEARFUL FOR THEM.
SIRE.
YOUR MAJESTY, A MOMENT--

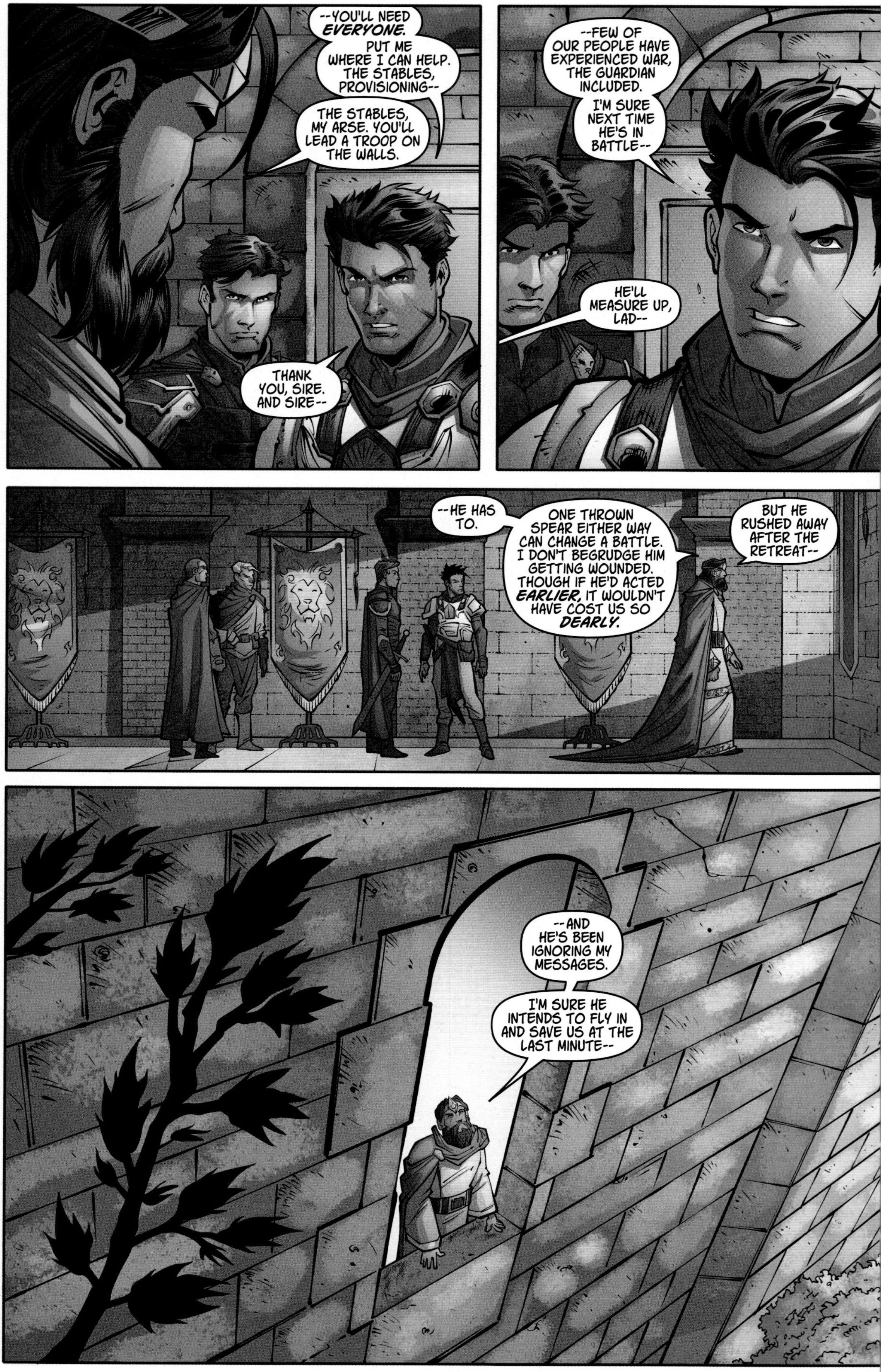

--YOU'LL NEED EVERYONE.
PUT ME WHERE I CAN HELP. THE STABLES, PROVISIONING--
THE STABLES, MY ARSE. YOU'LL LEAD A TROOP ON THE WALLS.
THANK YOU, SIRE. AND SIRE--
--FEW OF OUR PEOPLE HAVE EXPERIENCED WAR, THE GUARDIAN INCLUDED.
I'M SURE NEXT TIME HE'S IN BATTLE--
HE'LL MEASURE UP, LAD--
--HE HAS TO.
ONE THROWN SPEAR EITHER WAY CAN CHANGE A BATTLE. I DON'T BEGRUDGE HIM GETTING WOUNDED. THOUGH IF HE'D ACTED EARLIER, IT WOULDN'T HAVE COST US SO DEARLY.
BUT HE RUSHED AWAY AFTER THE RETREAT--
--AND HE'S BEEN IGNORING MY MESSAGES.
I'M SURE HE INTENDS TO FLY IN AND SAVE US AT THE LAST MINUTE--

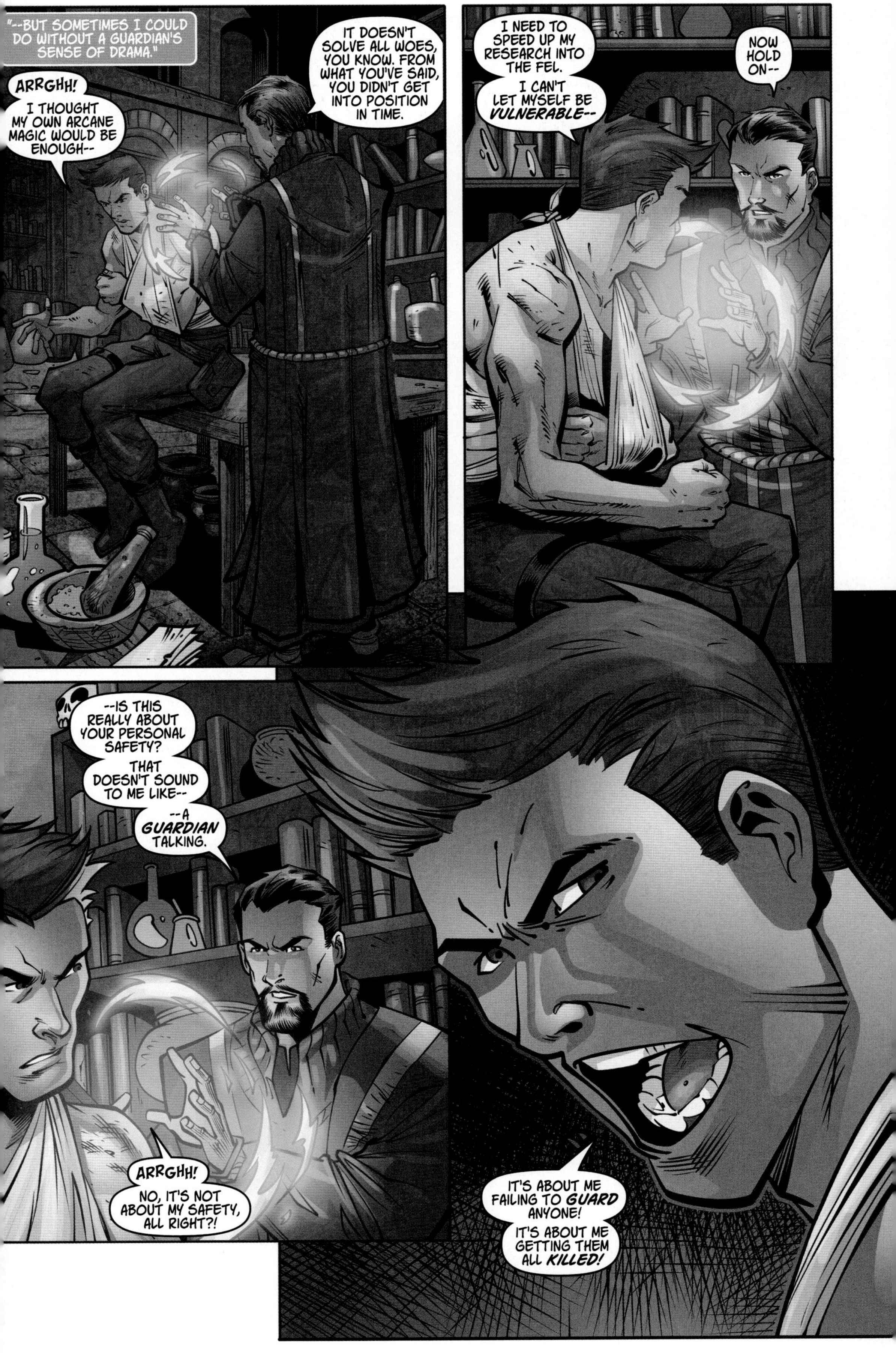
"--BUT SOMETIMES I COULD DO WITHOUT A GUARDIAN'S SENSE OF DRAMA."
ARRGHH!
I THOUGHT MY OWN ARCANE MAGIC WOULD BE ENOUGH--
IT DOESN'T SOLVE ALL WOES, YOU KNOW. FROM WHAT YOU'VE SAID, YOU DIDN'T GET INTO POSITION IN TIME.
I NEED TO SPEED UP MY RESEARCH INTO THE FEL.
I CAN'T LET MYSELF BE VULNERABLE--
NOW HOLD ON--
--IS THIS REALLY ABOUT YOUR PERSONAL SAFETY?
THAT DOESN'T SOUND TO ME LIKE--
--A GUARDIAN TALKING.
ARRGHH!
NO, IT'S NOT ABOUT MY SAFETY, ALL RIGHT?!
IT'S ABOUT ME FAILING TO GUARD ANYONE!
IT'S ABOUT ME GETTING THEM ALL KILLED!

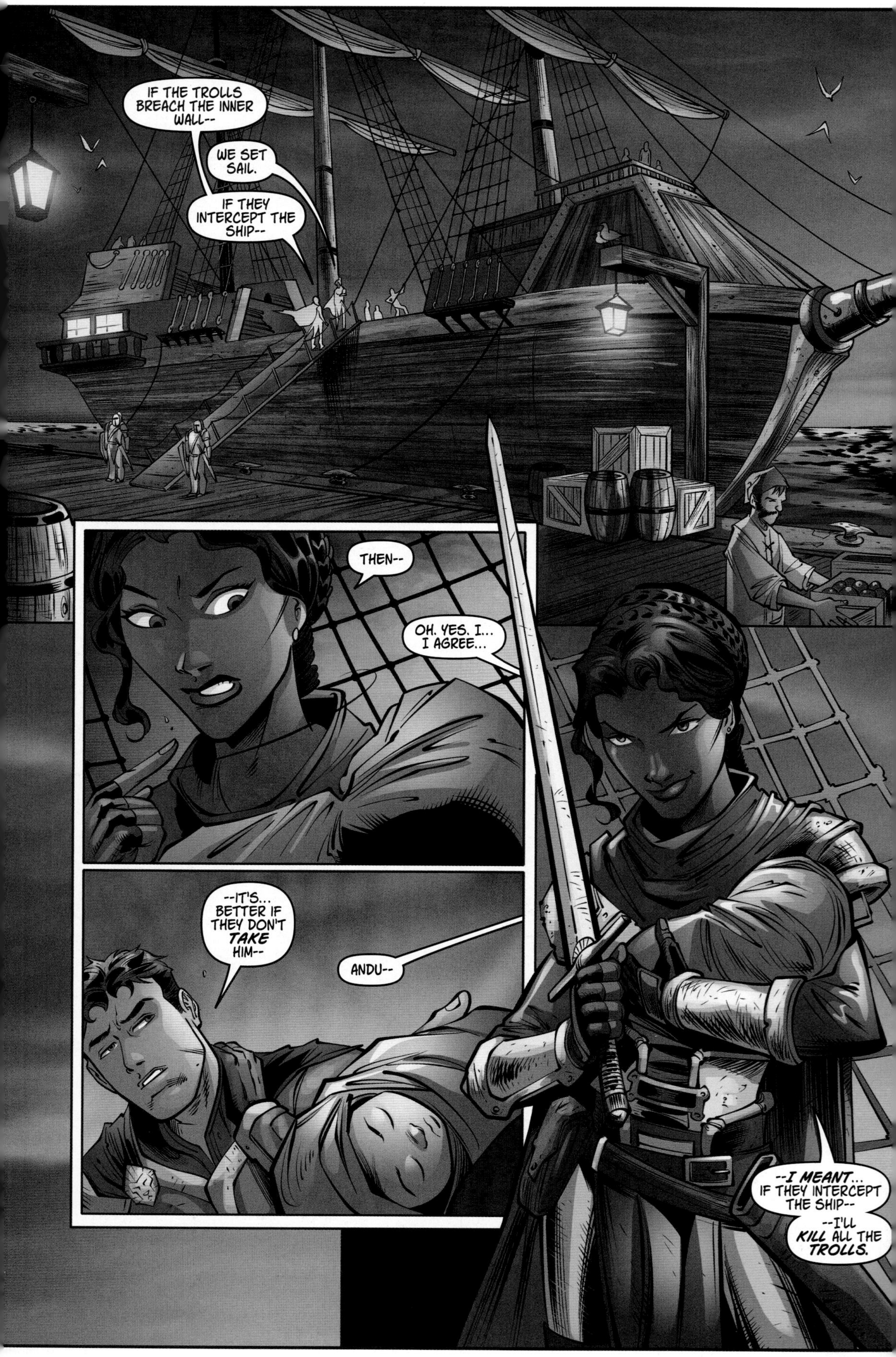
IF THE TROLLS BREACH THE INNER WALL--
WE SET SAIL.
IF THEY INTERCEPT THE SHIP--
THEN--
OH. YES. I... I AGREE...
--IT'S... BETTER IF THEY DON'T *TAKE* HIM--
ANDU--
--*I MEANT*... IF THEY INTERCEPT THE SHIP--
--I'LL *KILL* ALL THE *TROLLS*.

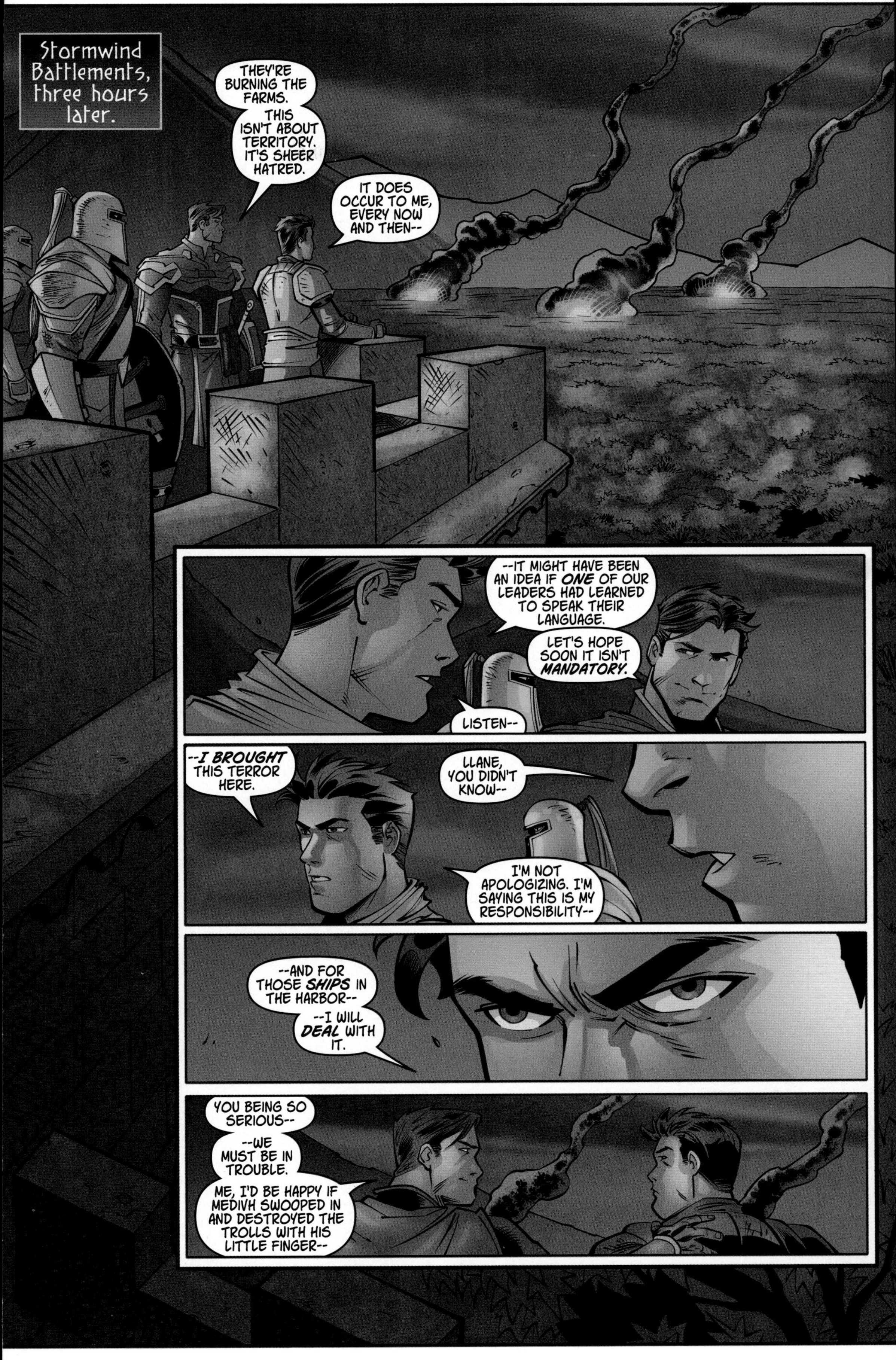
Stormwind Battlements, three hours later.
THEY'RE BURNING THE FARMS.
THIS ISN'T ABOUT TERRITORY. IT'S SHEER HATRED.
IT DOES OCCUR TO ME, EVERY NOW AND THEN--
--IT MIGHT HAVE BEEN AN IDEA IF ONE OF OUR LEADERS HAD LEARNED TO SPEAK THEIR LANGUAGE.
LET'S HOPE SOON IT ISN'T MANDATORY.
LISTEN--
--I BROUGHT THIS TERROR HERE.
LLANE, YOU DIDN'T KNOW--
I'M NOT APOLOGIZING. I'M SAYING THIS IS MY RESPONSIBILITY--
--AND FOR THOSE SHIPS IN THE HARBOR--
--I WILL DEAL WITH IT.
YOU BEING SO SERIOUS--
--WE MUST BE IN TROUBLE.
ME, I'D BE HAPPY IF MEDIVH SWOOPED IN AND DESTROYED THE TROLLS WITH HIS LITTLE FINGER--

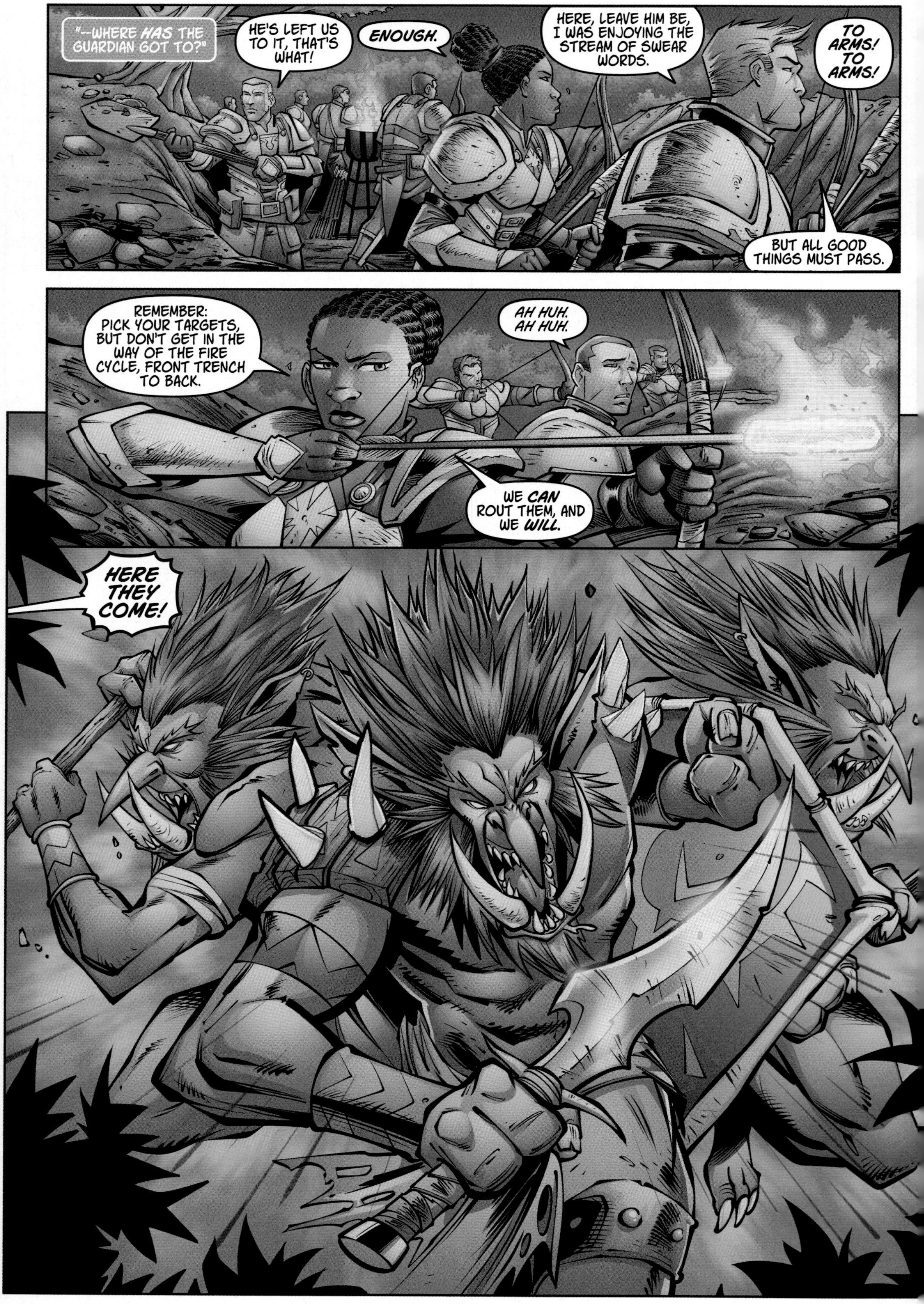
"--WHERE *HAS* THE GUARDIAN GOT TO?"
HE'S LEFT US TO IT, THAT'S WHAT!
ENOUGH.
HERE, LEAVE HIM BE, I WAS ENJOYING THE STREAM OF SWEAR WORDS.
TO ARMS! TO ARMS!
BUT ALL GOOD THINGS MUST PASS.
REMEMBER: PICK YOUR TARGETS, BUT DON'T GET IN THE WAY OF THE FIRE CYCLE, FRONT TRENCH TO BACK.
AH HUH. AH HUH.
WE *CAN* ROUT THEM, AND WE *WILL*.
HERE THEY COME!

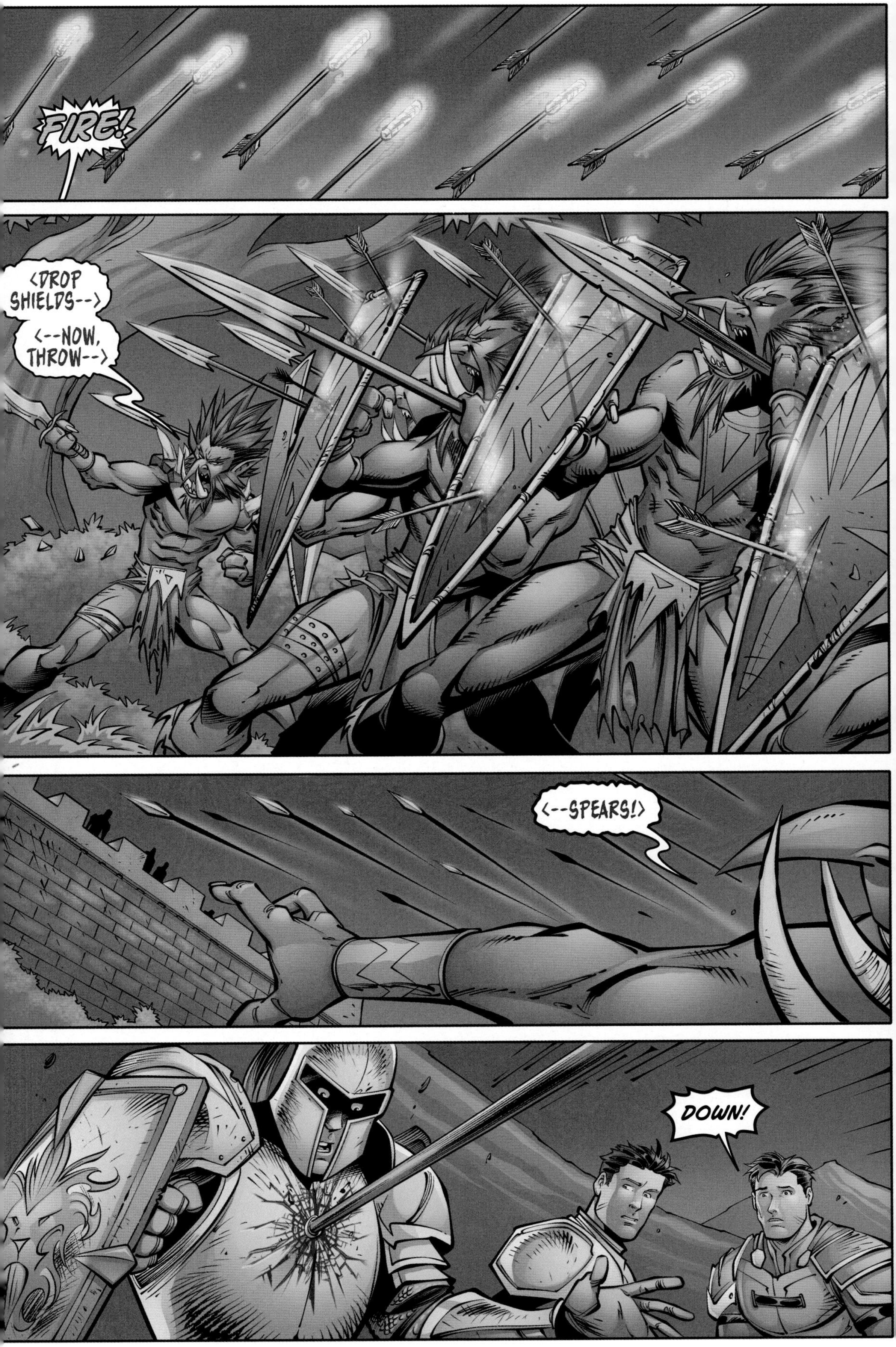
FIRE!
<DROP SHIELDS-->
<--NOW, THROW-->
<--SPEARS!>
DOWN!

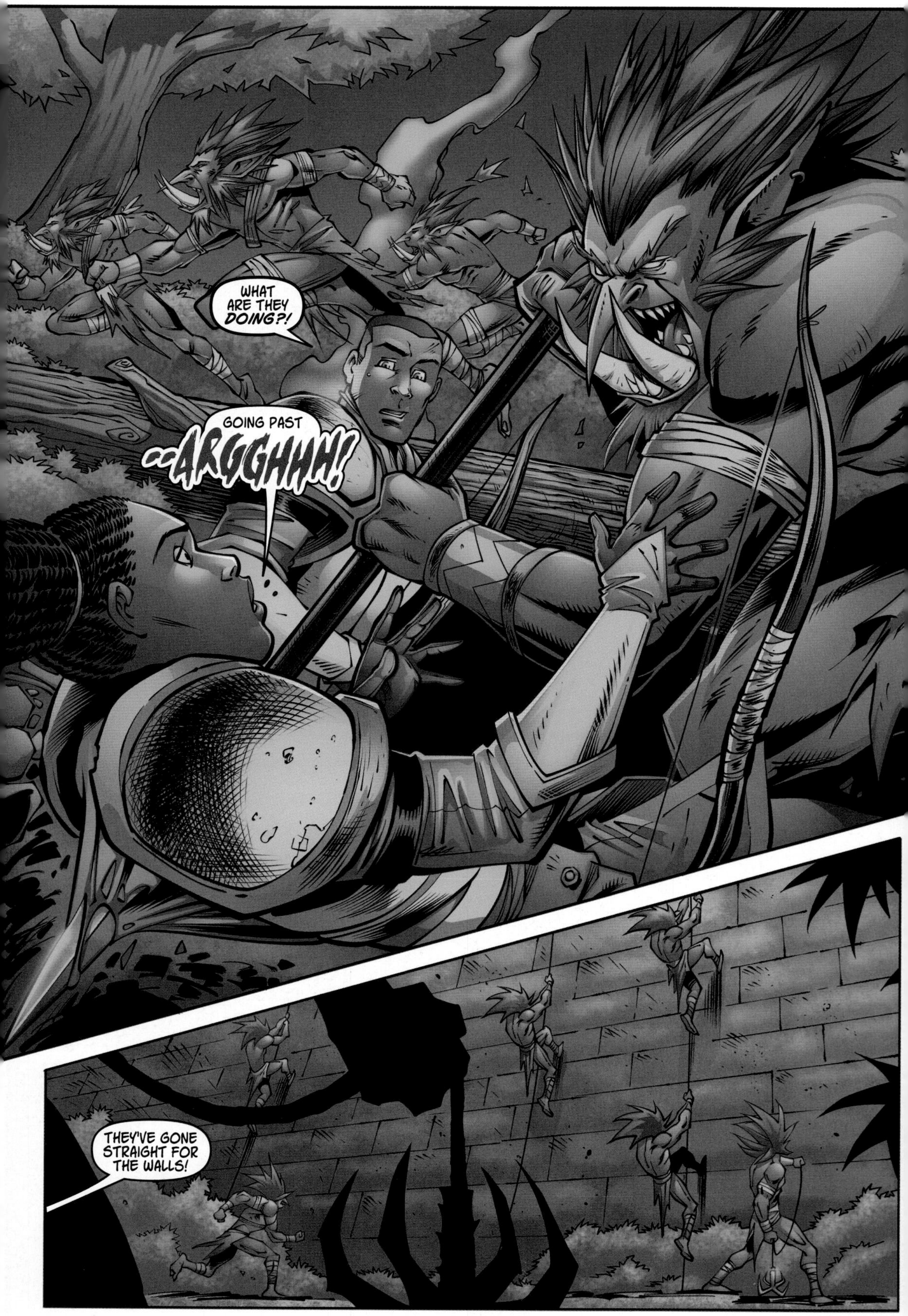
WHAT ARE THEY DOING?!
GOING PAST
--ARGGHHH!
THEY'VE GONE STRAIGHT FOR THE WALLS!

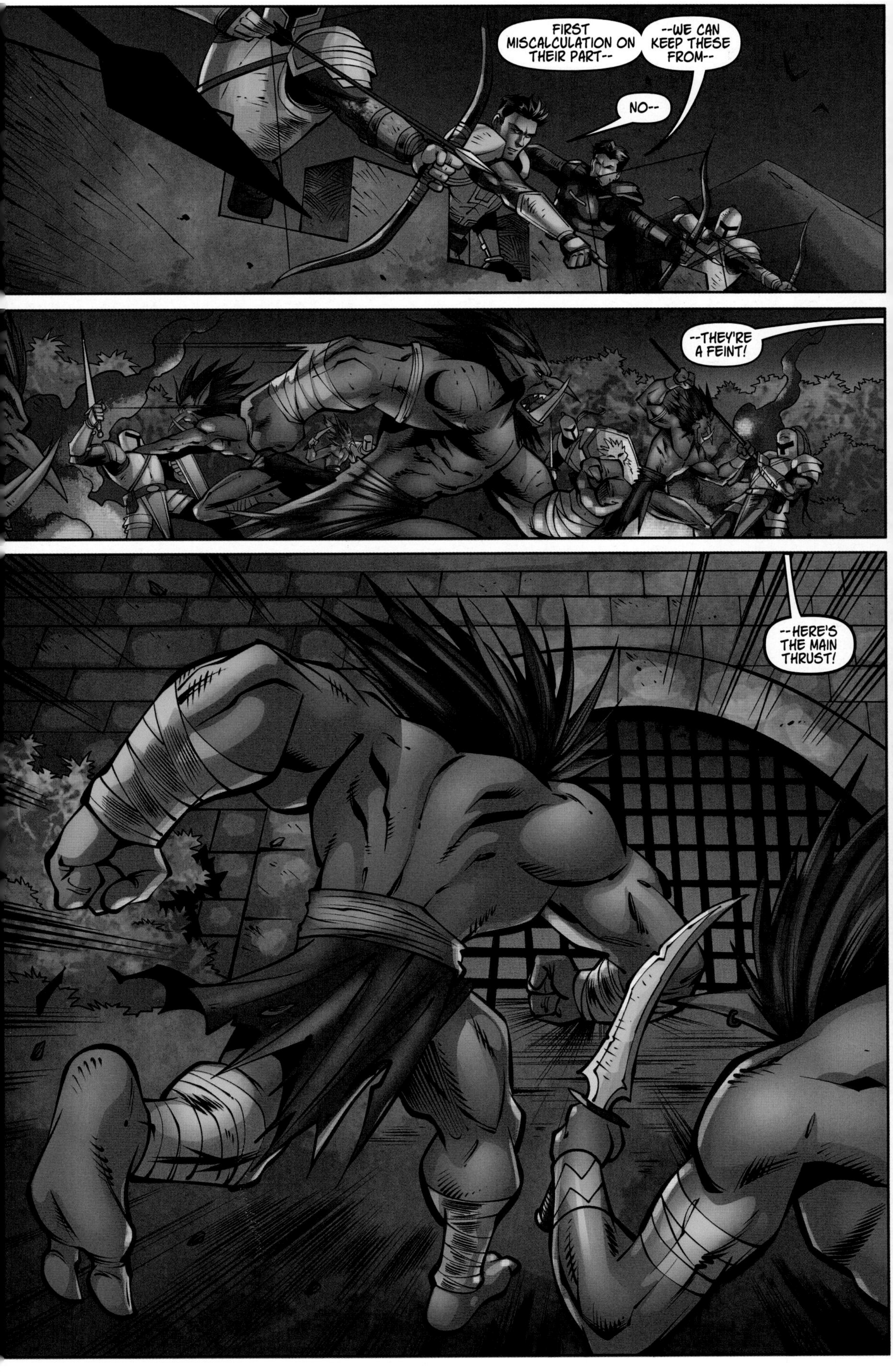
FIRST MISCALCULATION ON THEIR PART--
--WE CAN KEEP THESE FROM--
NO--
--THEY'RE A FEINT!
--HERE'S THE MAIN THRUST!

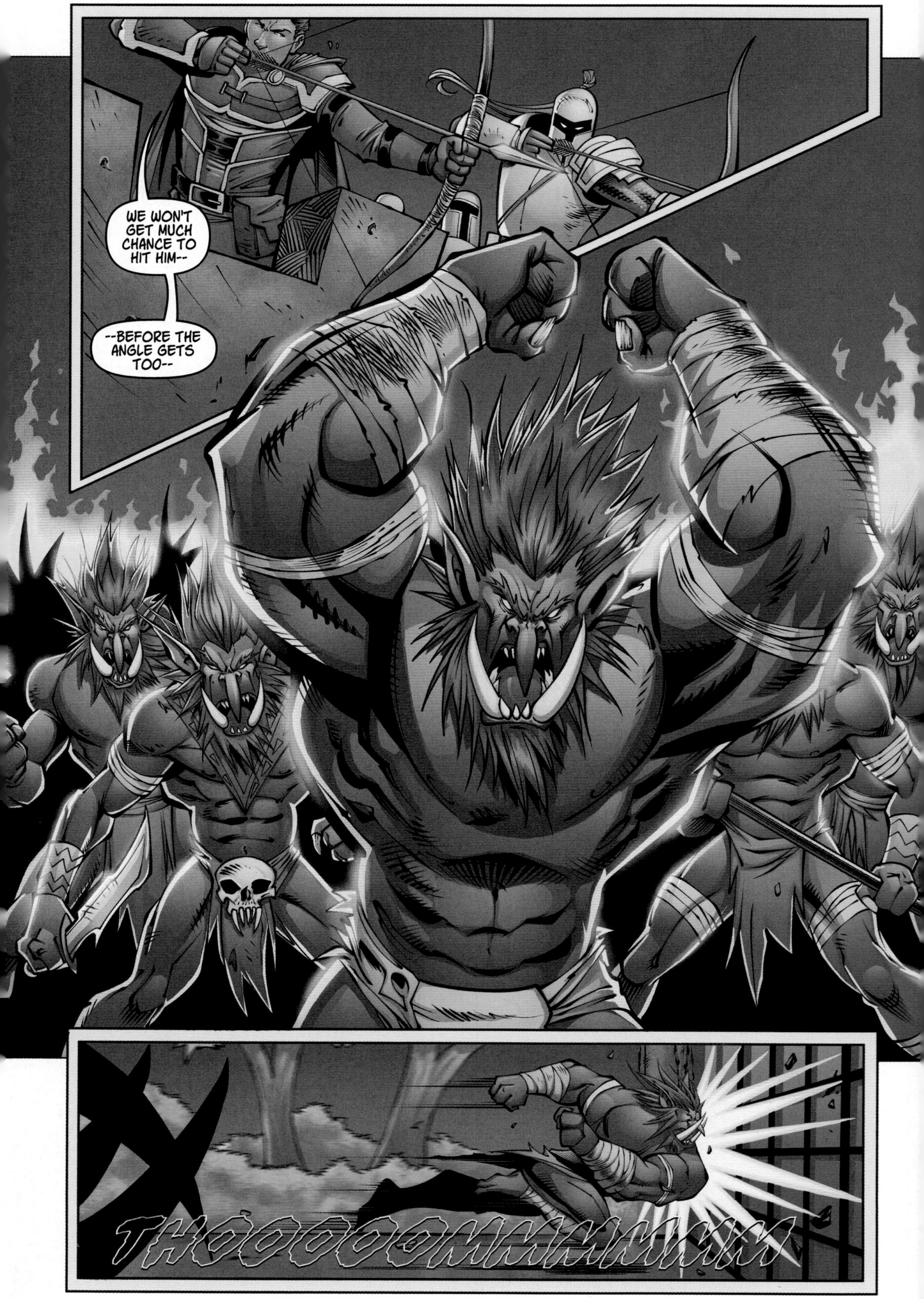
WE WON'T GET MUCH CHANCE TO HIT HIM--
--BEFORE THE ANGLE GETS TOO--
THOOOOOOMMMMMMM

GARRRGHHHHHHHHHH!

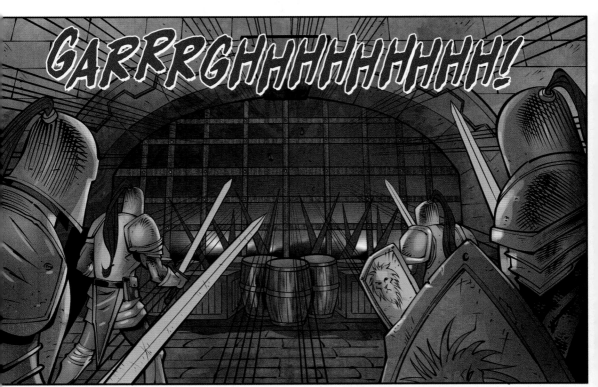

IT'S...IT'S MONSTROUS.

IT'LL BE THROUGH IN A SEC.

IF THE GUARDIAN'S GOING TO SHOW UP--

--NOW WOULD BE A GOOD TIME.

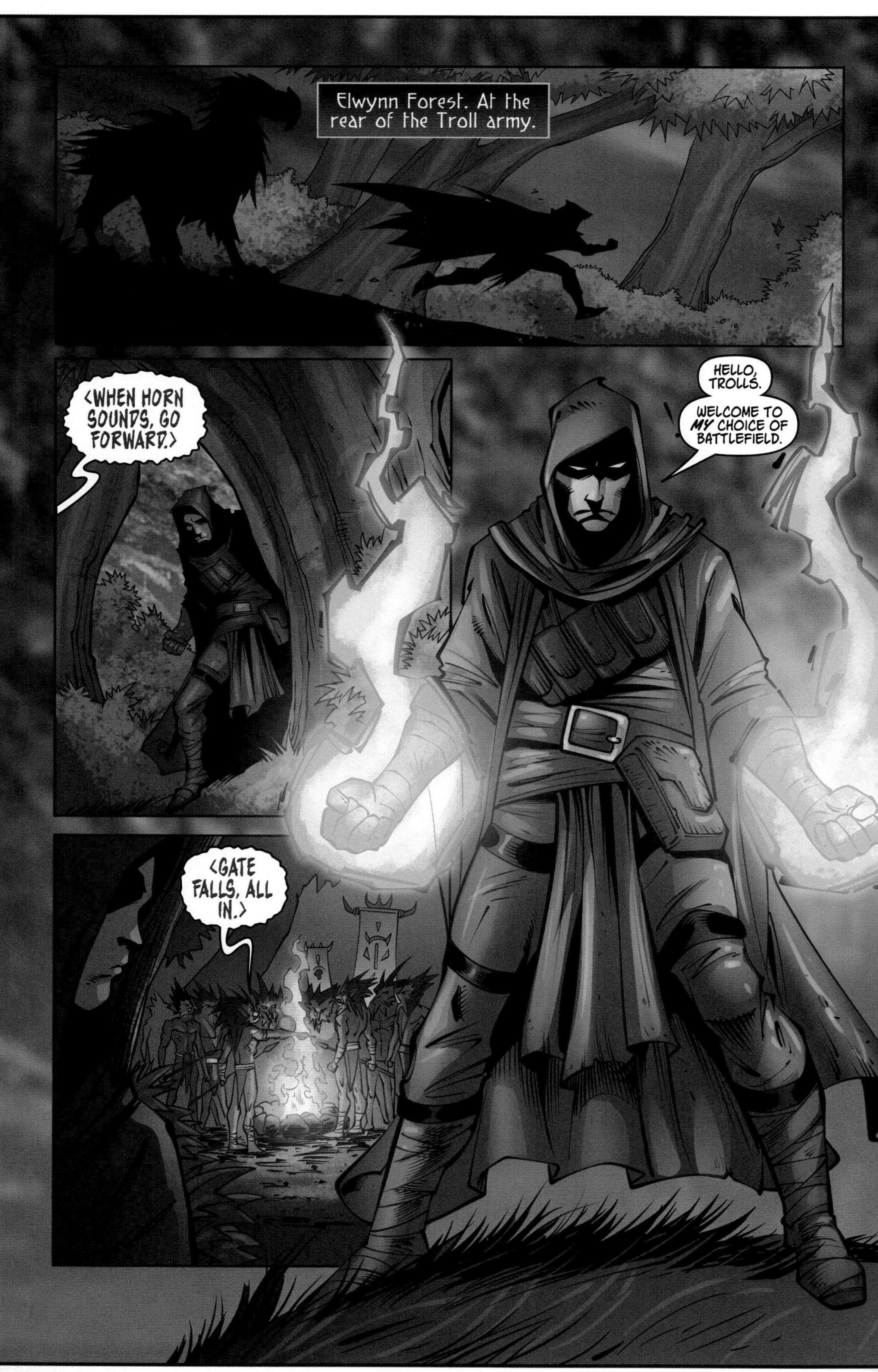
Elwynn Forest. At the rear of the Troll army.
<WHEN HORN SOUNDS, GO FORWARD.>
HELLO, TROLLS.
WELCOME TO MY CHOICE OF BATTLEFIELD.
<GATE FALLS, ALL IN.>

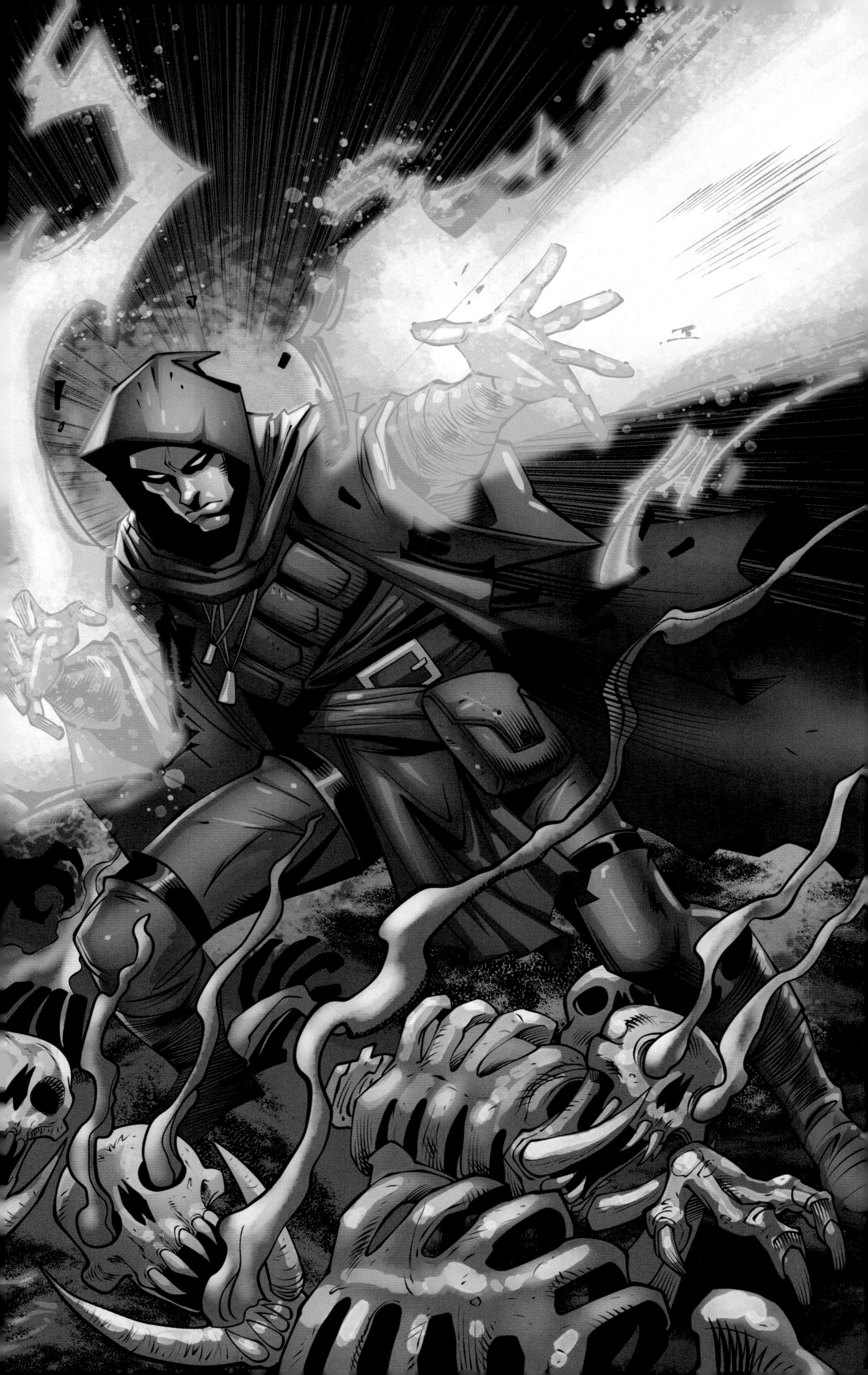

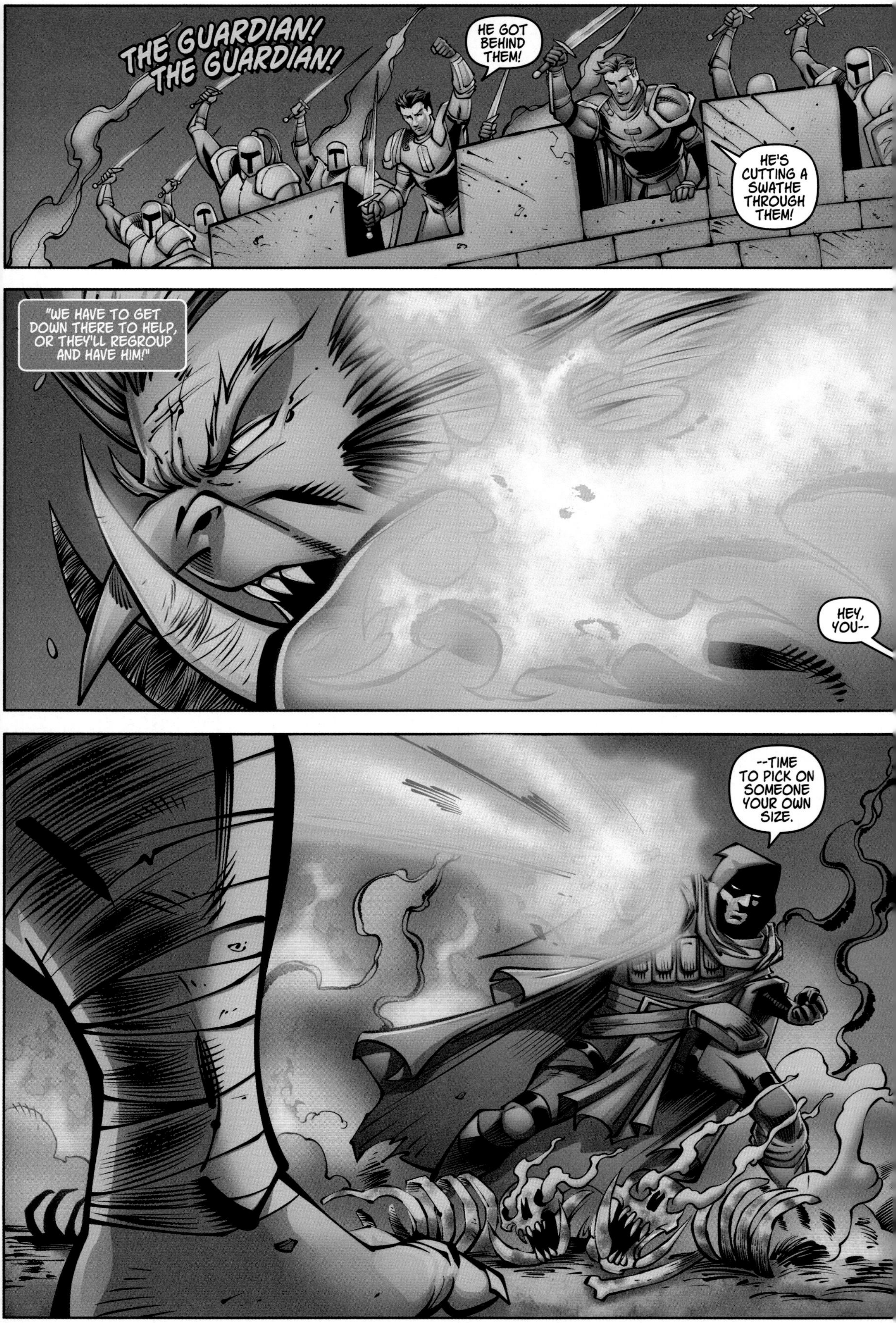
THE GUARDIAN! THE GUARDIAN!
HE GOT BEHIND THEM!
HE'S CUTTING A SWATHE THROUGH THEM!
"WE HAVE TO GET DOWN THERE TO HELP, OR THEY'LL REGROUP AND HAVE HIM!"
HEY, YOU--
--TIME TO PICK ON SOMEONE YOUR OWN SIZE.

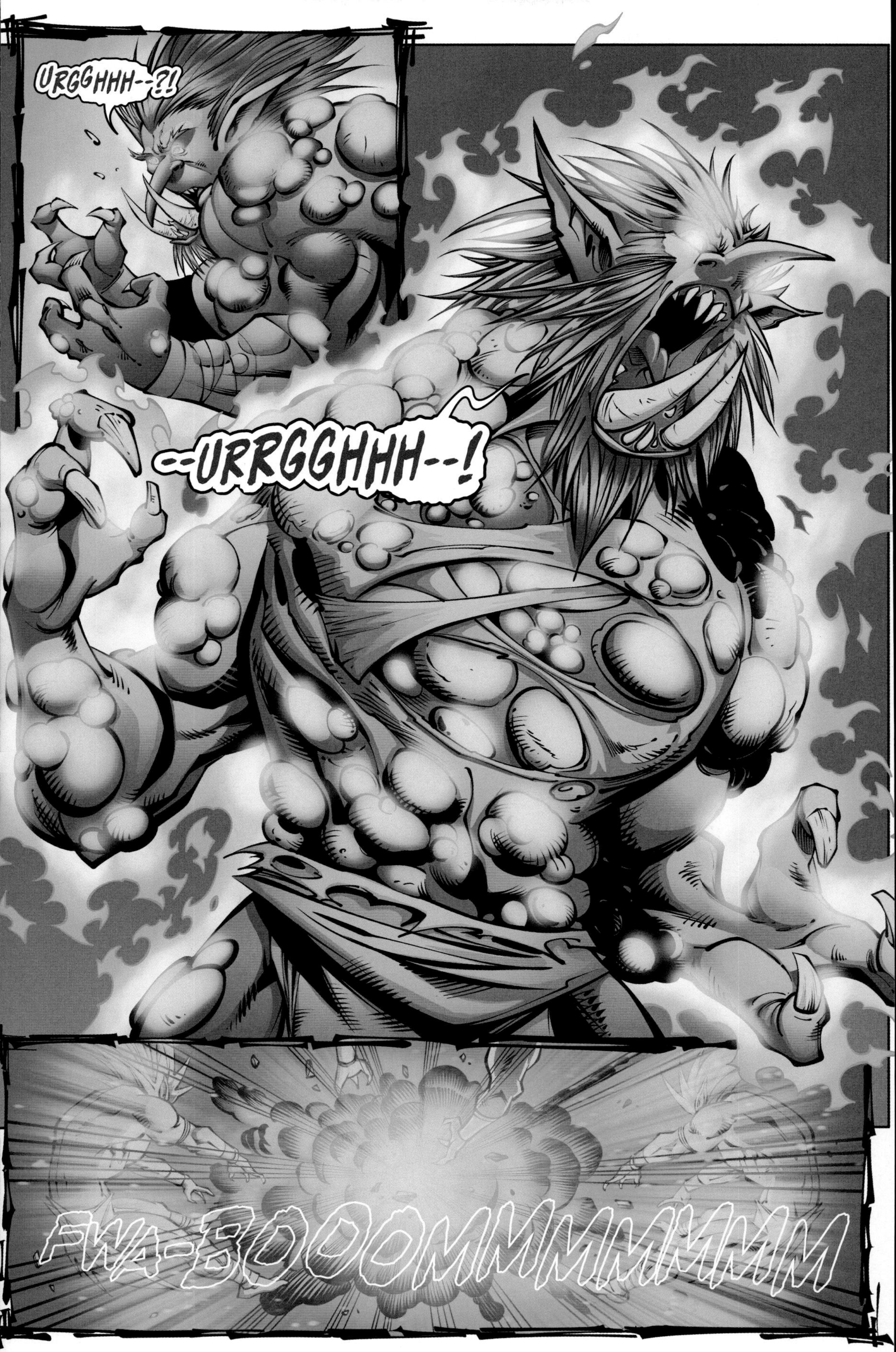
URGGHHH--?!
--URRGGHHH--!
FWA-BOOOMMMMMMMM

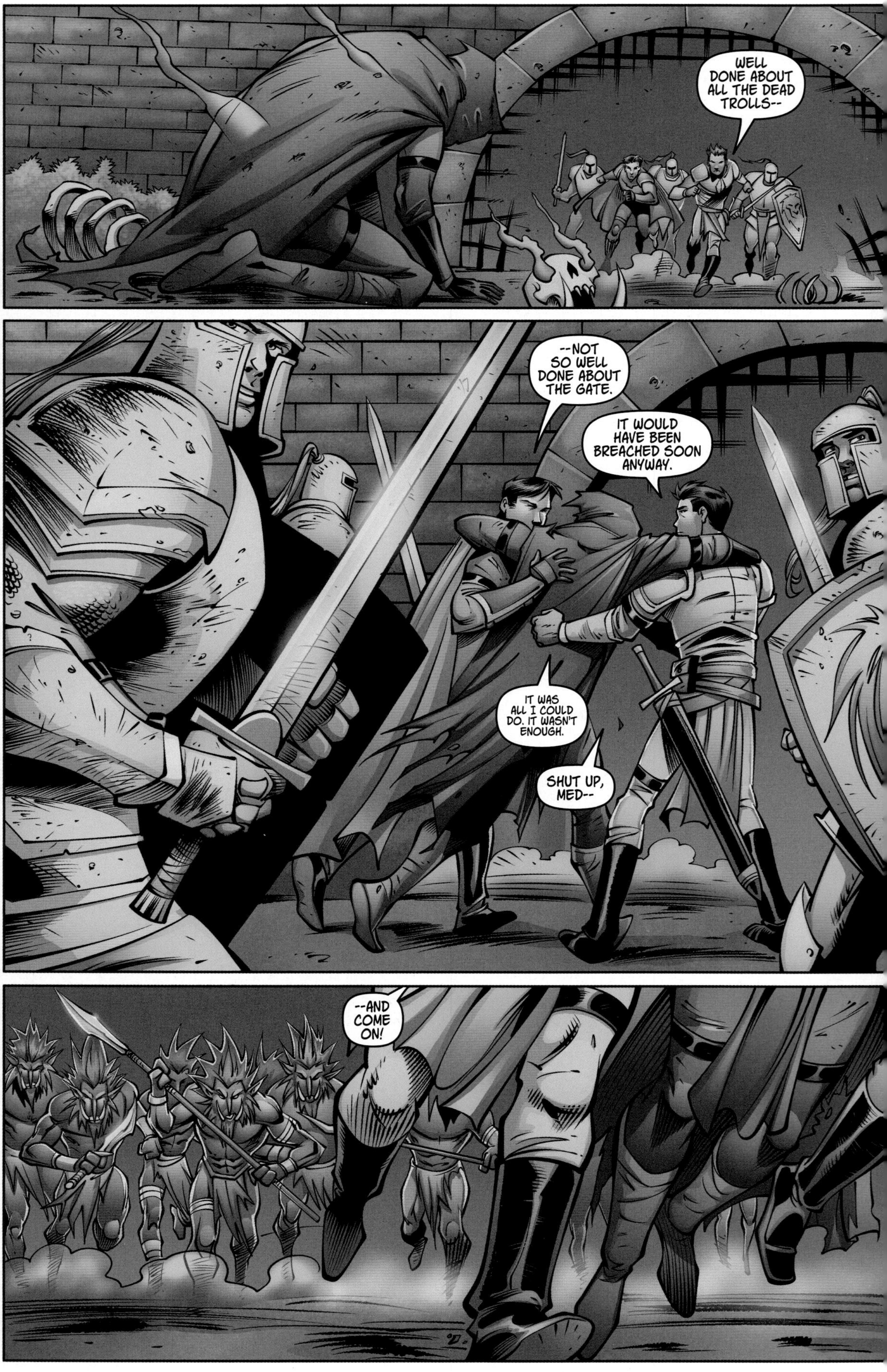
WELL DONE ABOUT ALL THE DEAD TROLLS--
--NOT SO WELL DONE ABOUT THE GATE.
IT WOULD HAVE BEEN BREACHED SOON ANYWAY.
IT WAS ALL I COULD DO. IT WASN'T ENOUGH.
SHUT UP, MED--
--AND COME ON!

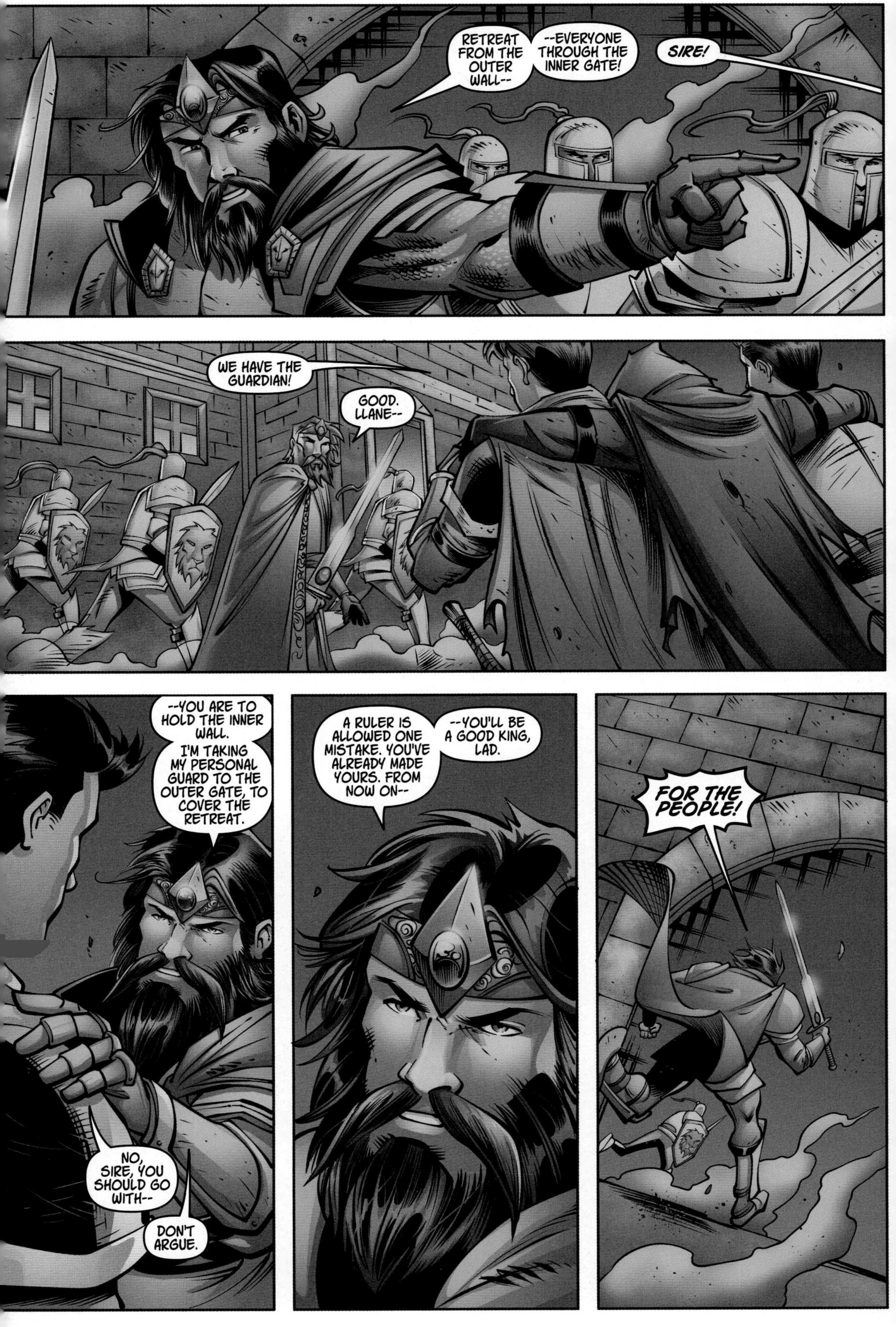

RETREAT FROM THE OUTER WALL--
--EVERYONE THROUGH THE INNER GATE!
SIRE!
WE HAVE THE GUARDIAN!
GOOD. LLANE--
--YOU ARE TO HOLD THE INNER WALL.
I'M TAKING MY PERSONAL GUARD TO THE OUTER GATE, TO COVER THE RETREAT.
NO, SIRE, YOU SHOULD GO WITH--
DON'T ARGUE.
A RULER IS ALLOWED ONE MISTAKE. YOU'VE ALREADY MADE YOURS. FROM NOW ON--
--YOU'LL BE A GOOD KING, LAD.
FOR THE PEOPLE!

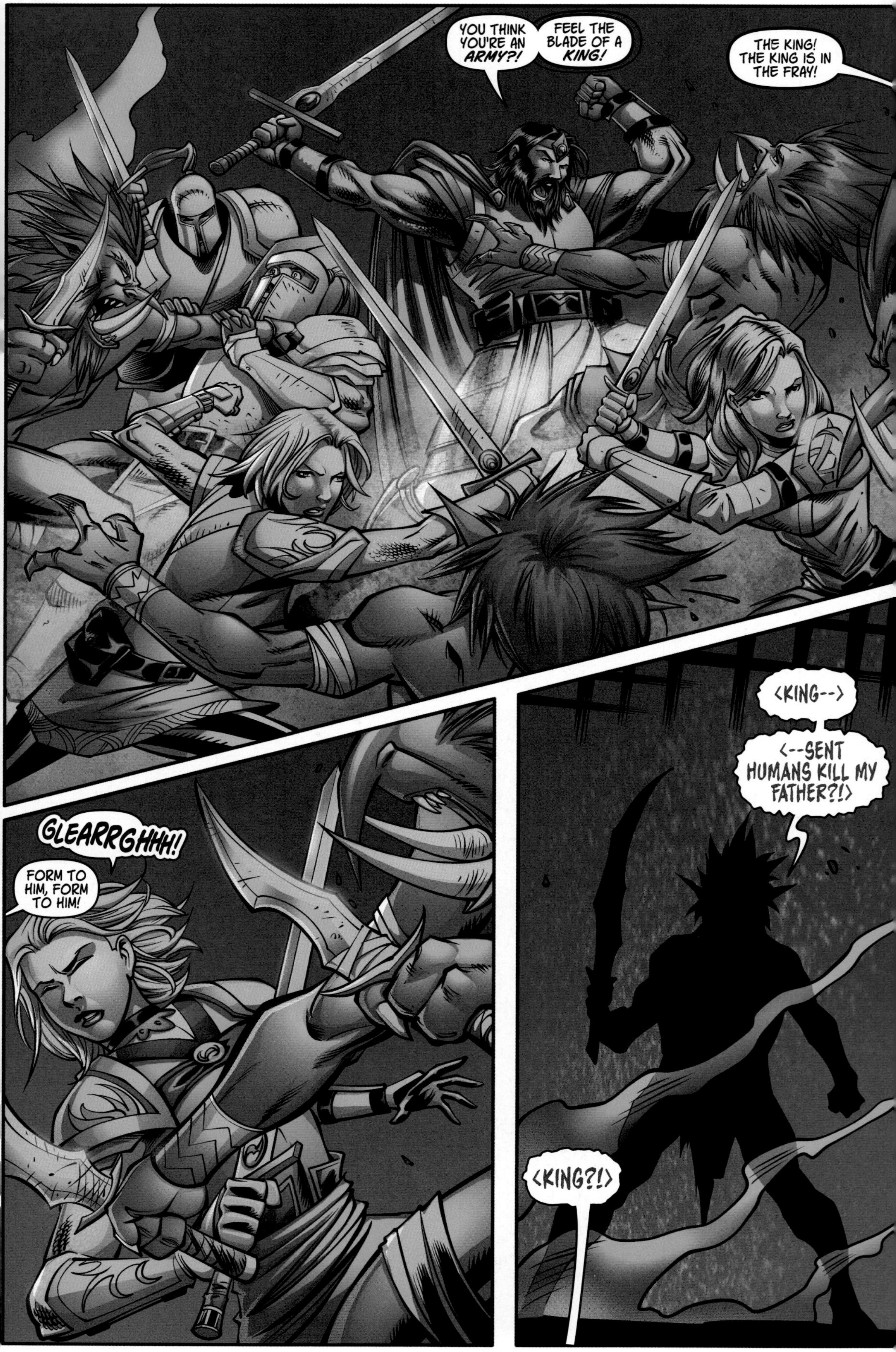
YOU THINK YOU'RE AN ARMY?!
FEEL THE BLADE OF A KING!
THE KING! THE KING IS IN THE FRAY!
GLEARRGHHH!
FORM TO HIM, FORM TO HIM!
<KING-->
<--SENT HUMANS KILL MY FATHER?!>
<KING?!>

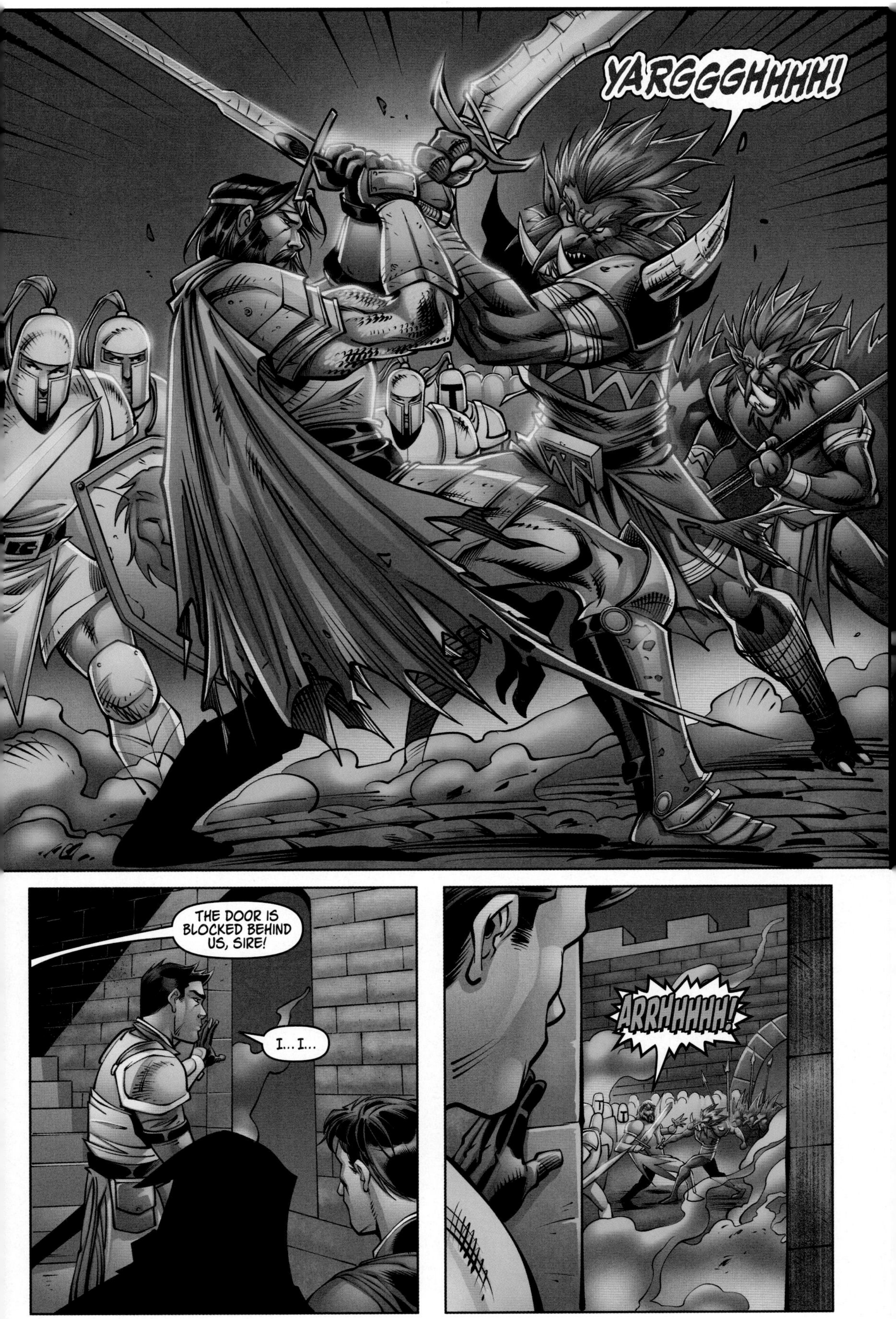
YARGGGHHHH!
THE DOOR IS BLOCKED BEHIND US, SIRE!
I... I...
ARRHHHHH!

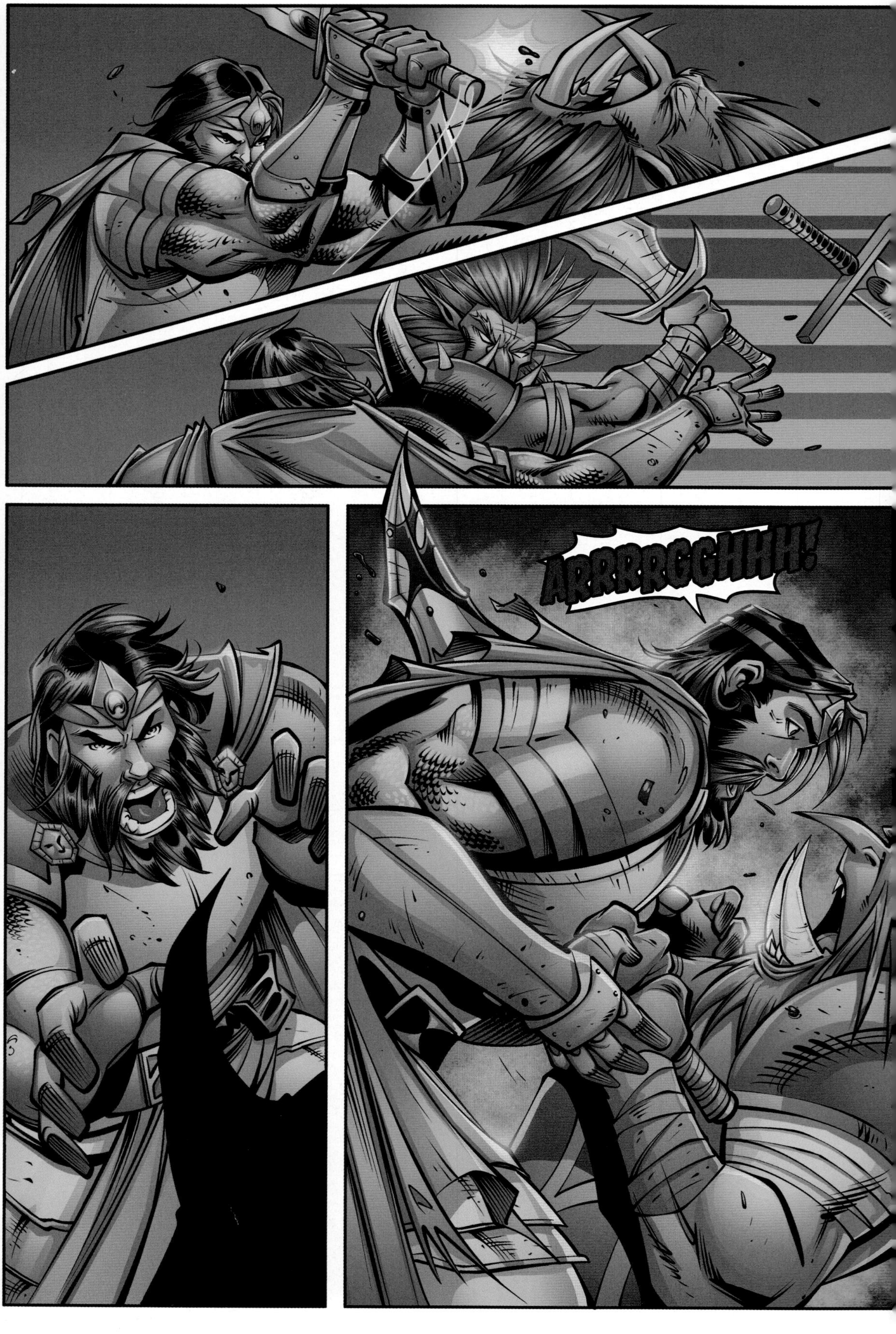
ARRRRGGHHH!

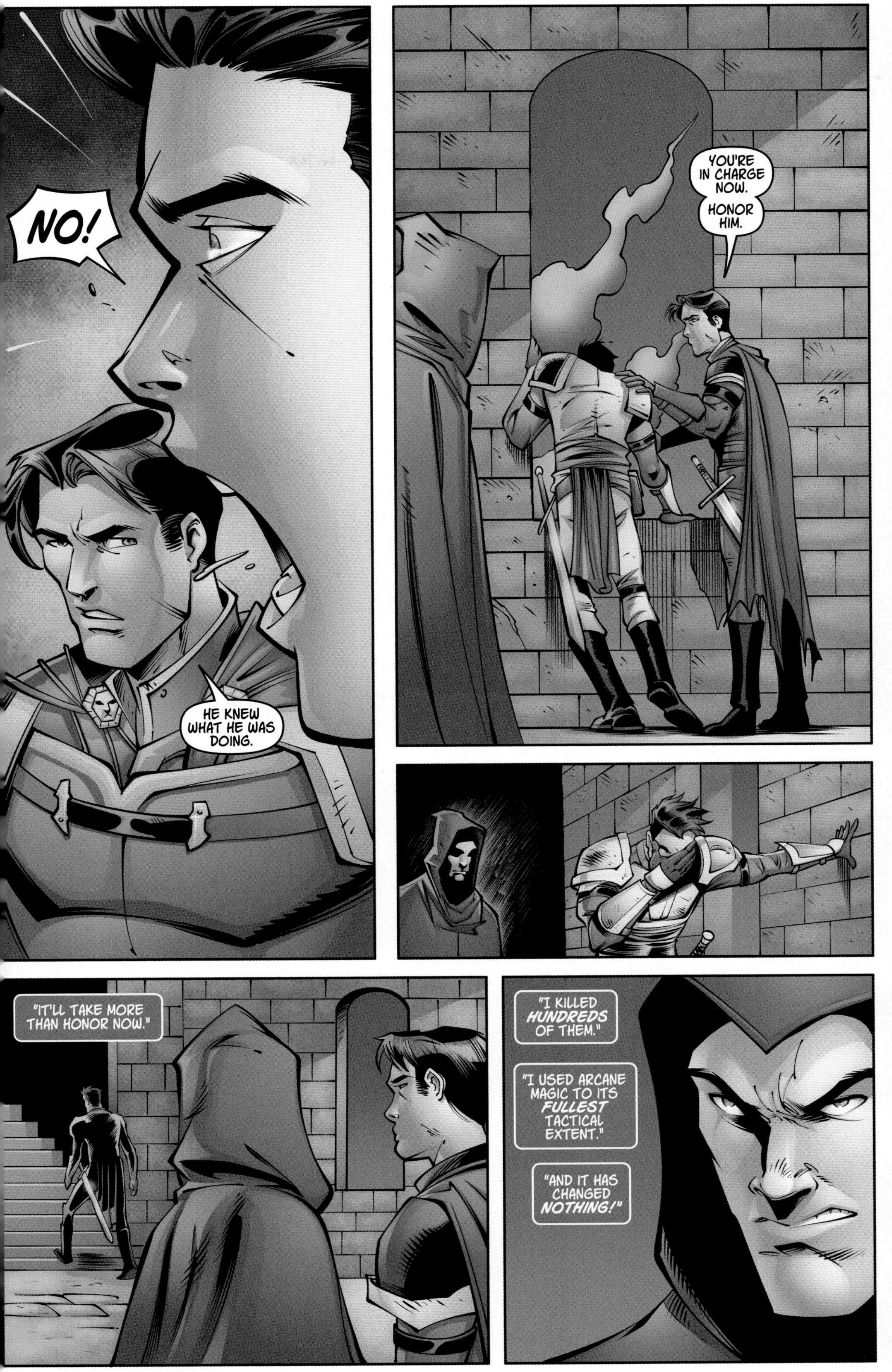
NO!
HE KNEW WHAT HE WAS DOING.
YOU'RE IN CHARGE NOW.
HONOR HIM.
"IT'LL TAKE MORE THAN HONOR NOW."
"I KILLED HUNDREDS OF THEM."
"I USED ARCANE MAGIC TO ITS FULLEST TACTICAL EXTENT."
"AND IT HAS CHANGED NOTHING!"

CHAPTER FIVE

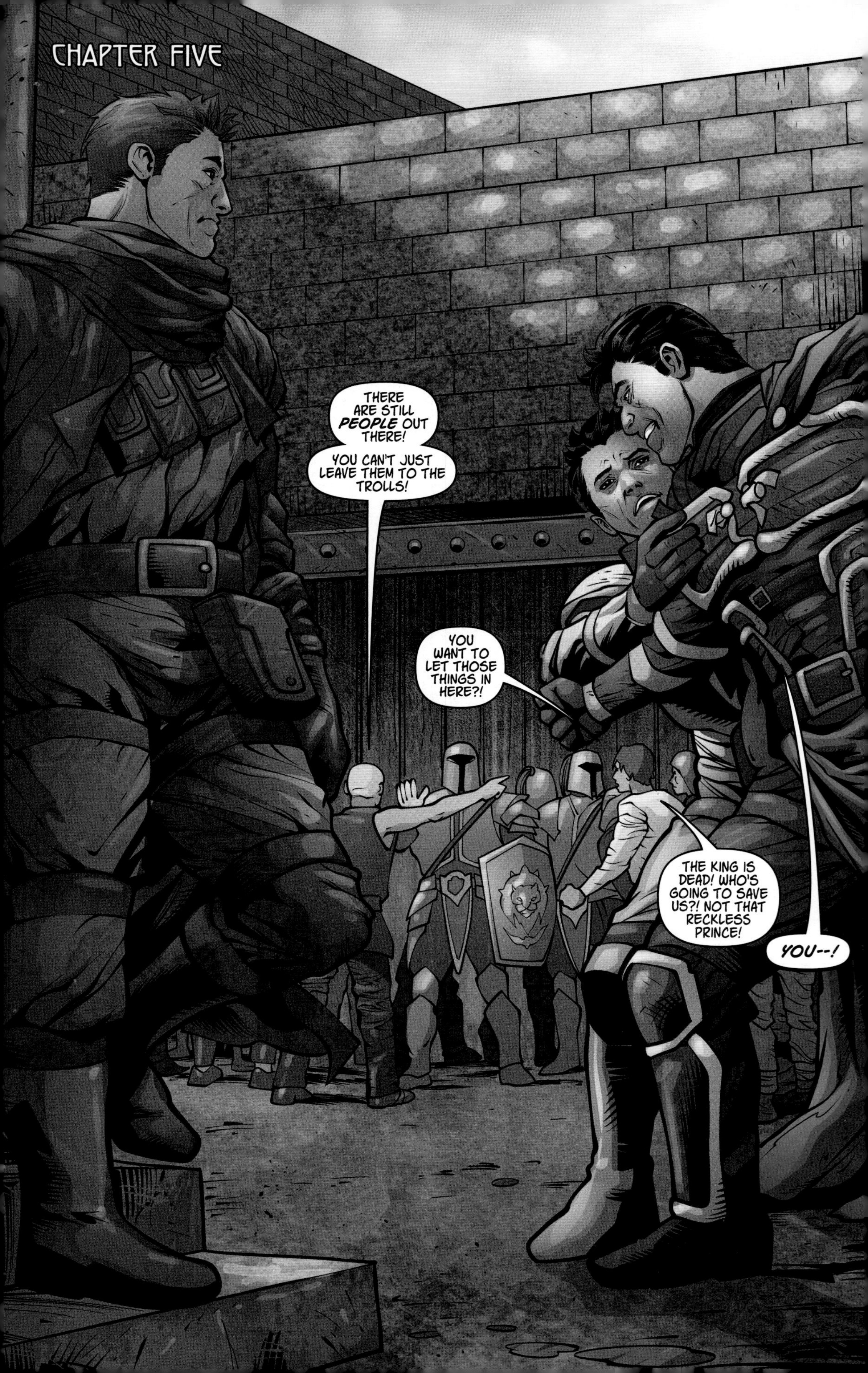
THERE ARE STILL *PEOPLE* OUT THERE!
YOU CAN'T JUST LEAVE THEM TO THE TROLLS!
YOU WANT TO LET THOSE THINGS IN HERE?!
THE KING IS DEAD! WHO'S GOING TO SAVE US?! NOT THAT RECKLESS PRINCE!
YOU--!

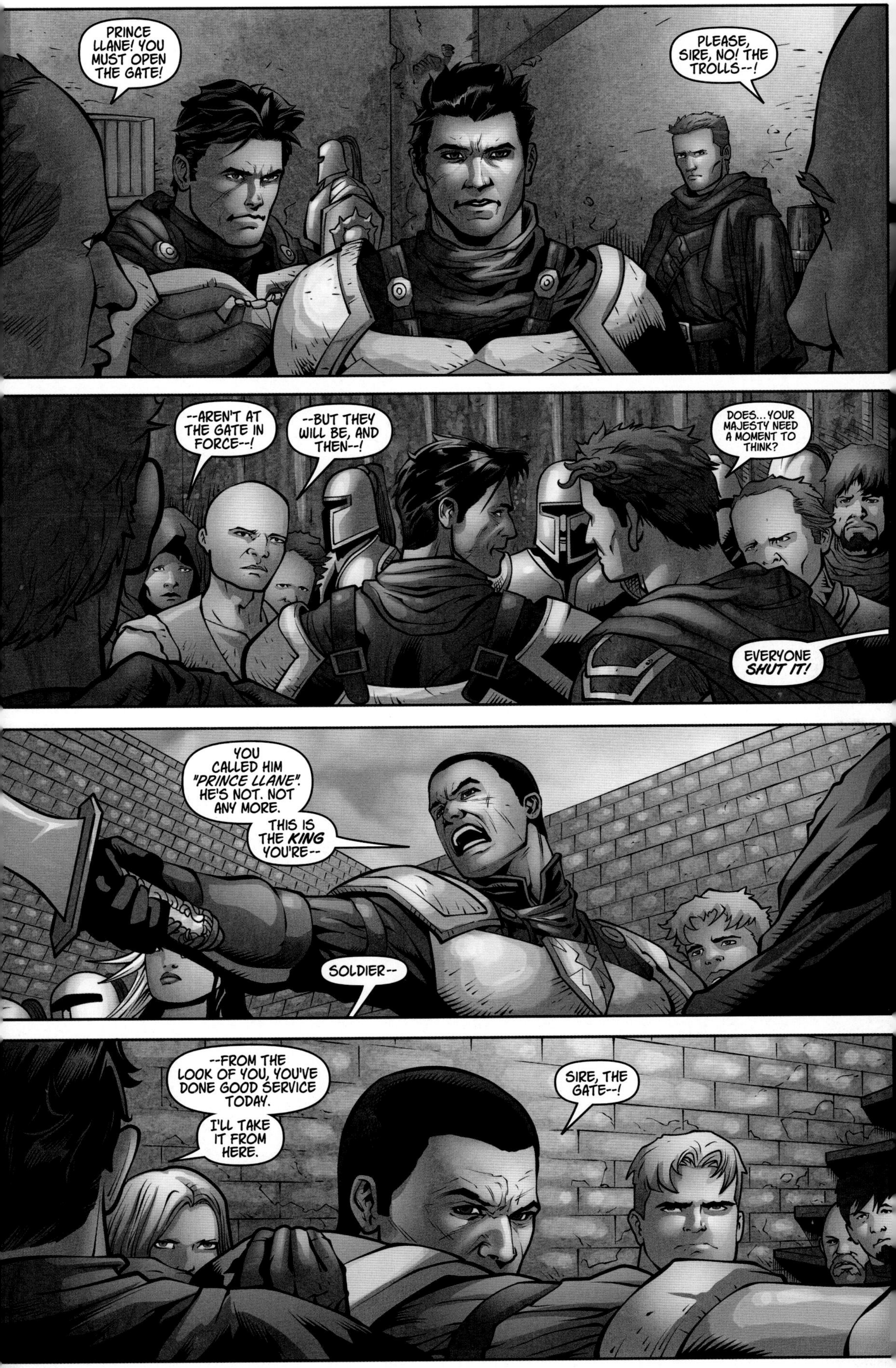
PRINCE LLANE! YOU MUST OPEN THE GATE!
PLEASE, SIRE, NO! THE TROLLS--!
--AREN'T AT THE GATE IN FORCE--!
--BUT THEY WILL BE, AND THEN--!
DOES... YOUR MAJESTY NEED A MOMENT TO THINK?
EVERYONE *SHUT IT!*
YOU CALLED HIM *"PRINCE LLANE"*. HE'S NOT. NOT ANY MORE.
THIS IS THE *KING* YOU'RE--
SOLDIER--
--FROM THE LOOK OF YOU, YOU'VE DONE GOOD SERVICE TODAY.
I'LL TAKE IT FROM HERE.
SIRE, THE GATE--!

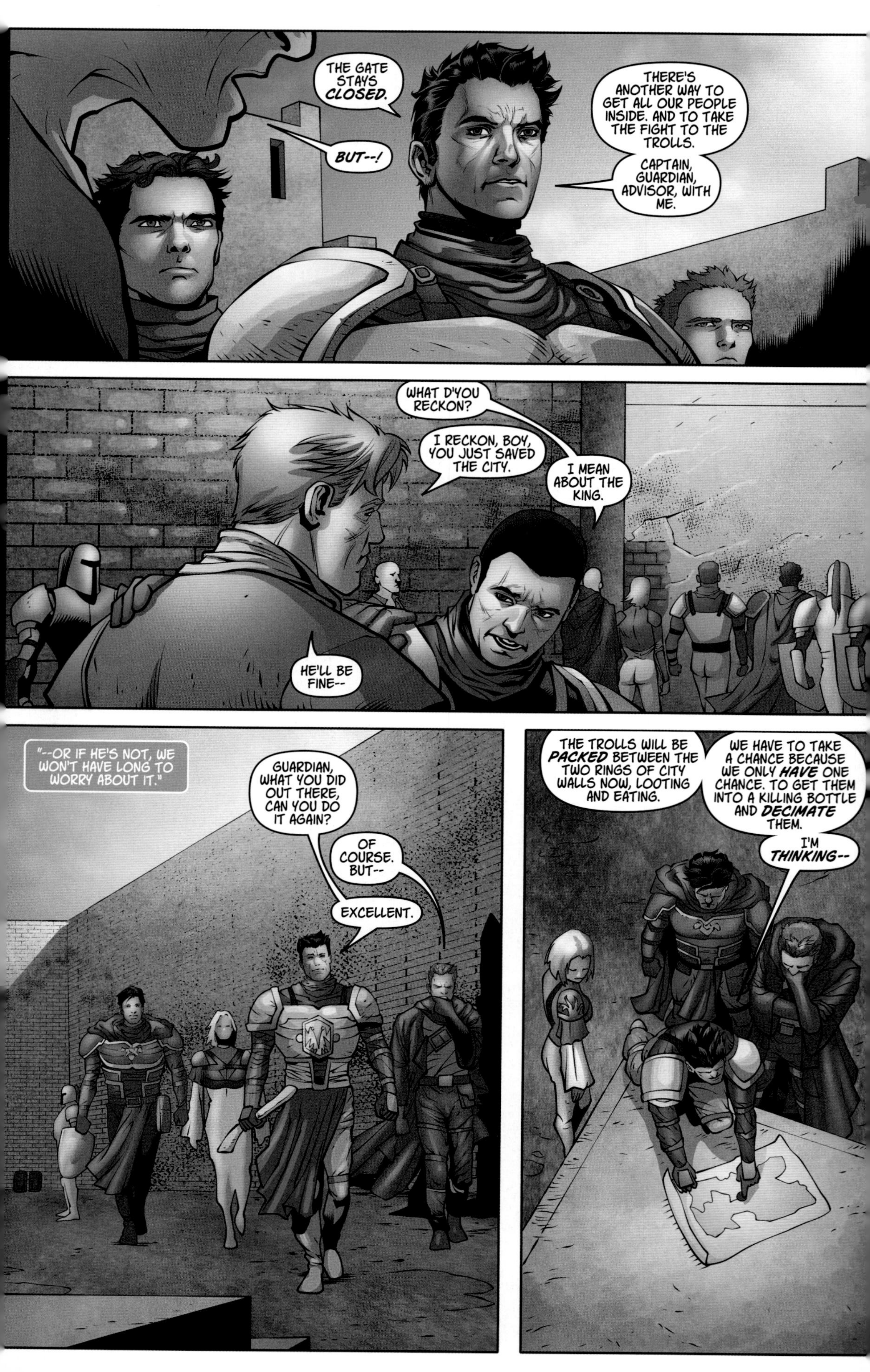
THE GATE STAYS *CLOSED.*
BUT--!
THERE'S ANOTHER WAY TO GET ALL OUR PEOPLE INSIDE. AND TO TAKE THE FIGHT TO THE TROLLS.
CAPTAIN, GUARDIAN, ADVISOR, WITH ME.
WHAT D'YOU RECKON?
I RECKON, BOY, YOU JUST SAVED THE CITY.
I MEAN ABOUT THE KING.
HE'LL BE FINE--
"--OR IF HE'S NOT, WE WON'T HAVE LONG TO WORRY ABOUT IT."
GUARDIAN, WHAT YOU DID OUT THERE, CAN YOU DO IT AGAIN?
OF COURSE. BUT--
EXCELLENT.
THE TROLLS WILL BE ***PACKED*** BETWEEN THE TWO RINGS OF CITY WALLS NOW, LOOTING AND EATING.
WE HAVE TO TAKE A CHANCE BECAUSE WE ONLY ***HAVE*** ONE CHANCE. TO GET THEM INTO A KILLING BOTTLE AND ***DECIMATE*** THEM.
I'M ***THINKING--***

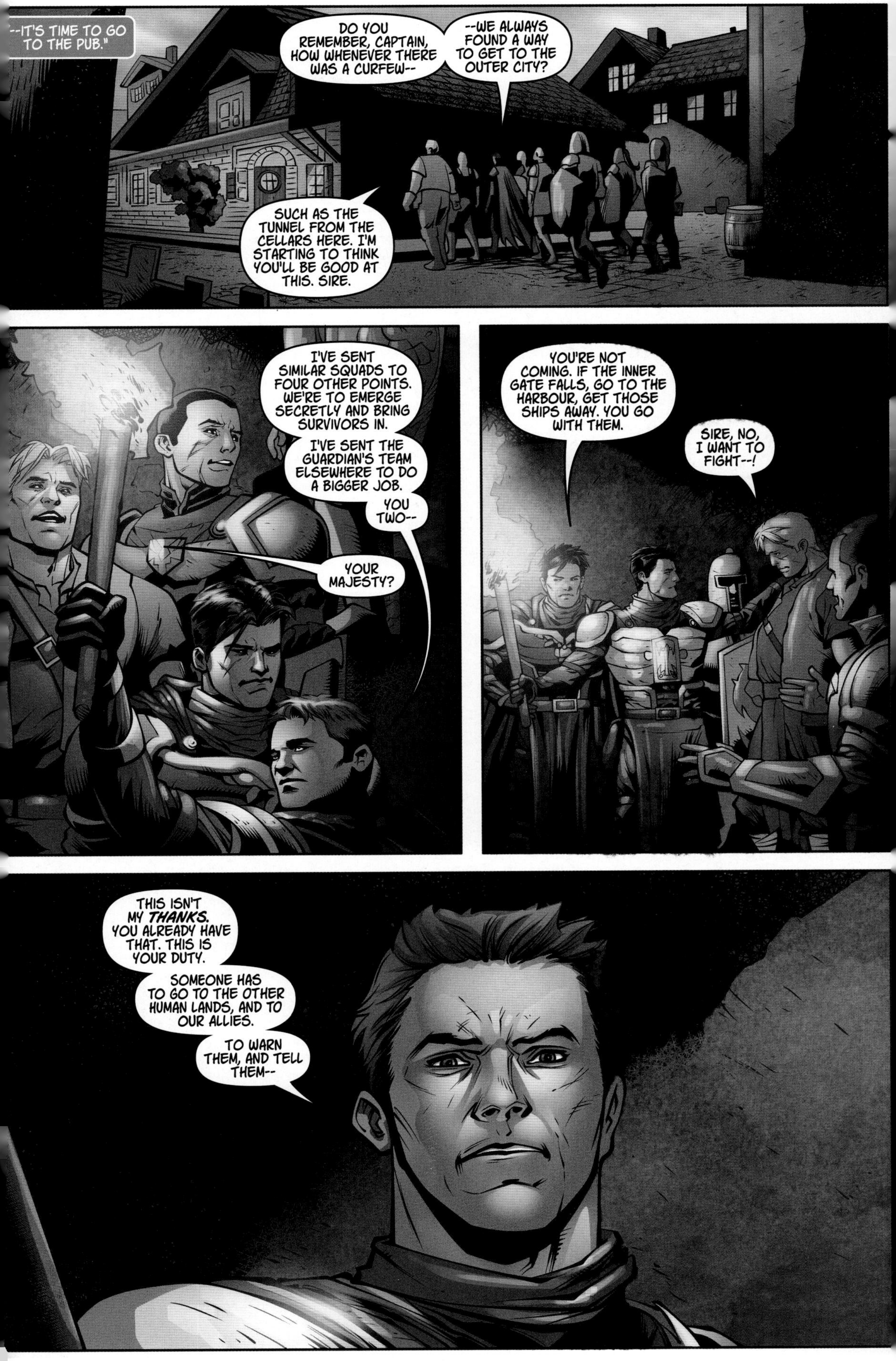

--IT'S TIME TO GO TO THE PUB."
DO YOU REMEMBER, CAPTAIN, HOW WHENEVER THERE WAS A CURFEW--
--WE ALWAYS FOUND A WAY TO GET TO THE OUTER CITY?
SUCH AS THE TUNNEL FROM THE CELLARS HERE. I'M STARTING TO THINK YOU'LL BE GOOD AT THIS. SIRE.
I'VE SENT SIMILAR SQUADS TO FOUR OTHER POINTS. WE'RE TO EMERGE SECRETLY AND BRING SURVIVORS IN.
I'VE SENT THE GUARDIAN'S TEAM ELSEWHERE TO DO A BIGGER JOB.
YOU TWO--
YOUR MAJESTY?
YOU'RE NOT COMING. IF THE INNER GATE FALLS, GO TO THE HARBOUR, GET THOSE SHIPS AWAY. YOU GO WITH THEM.
SIRE, NO, I WANT TO FIGHT--!
THIS ISN'T MY *THANKS*. YOU ALREADY HAVE THAT. THIS IS YOUR DUTY.
SOMEONE HAS TO GO TO THE OTHER HUMAN LANDS, AND TO OUR ALLIES.
TO WARN THEM, AND TELL THEM--

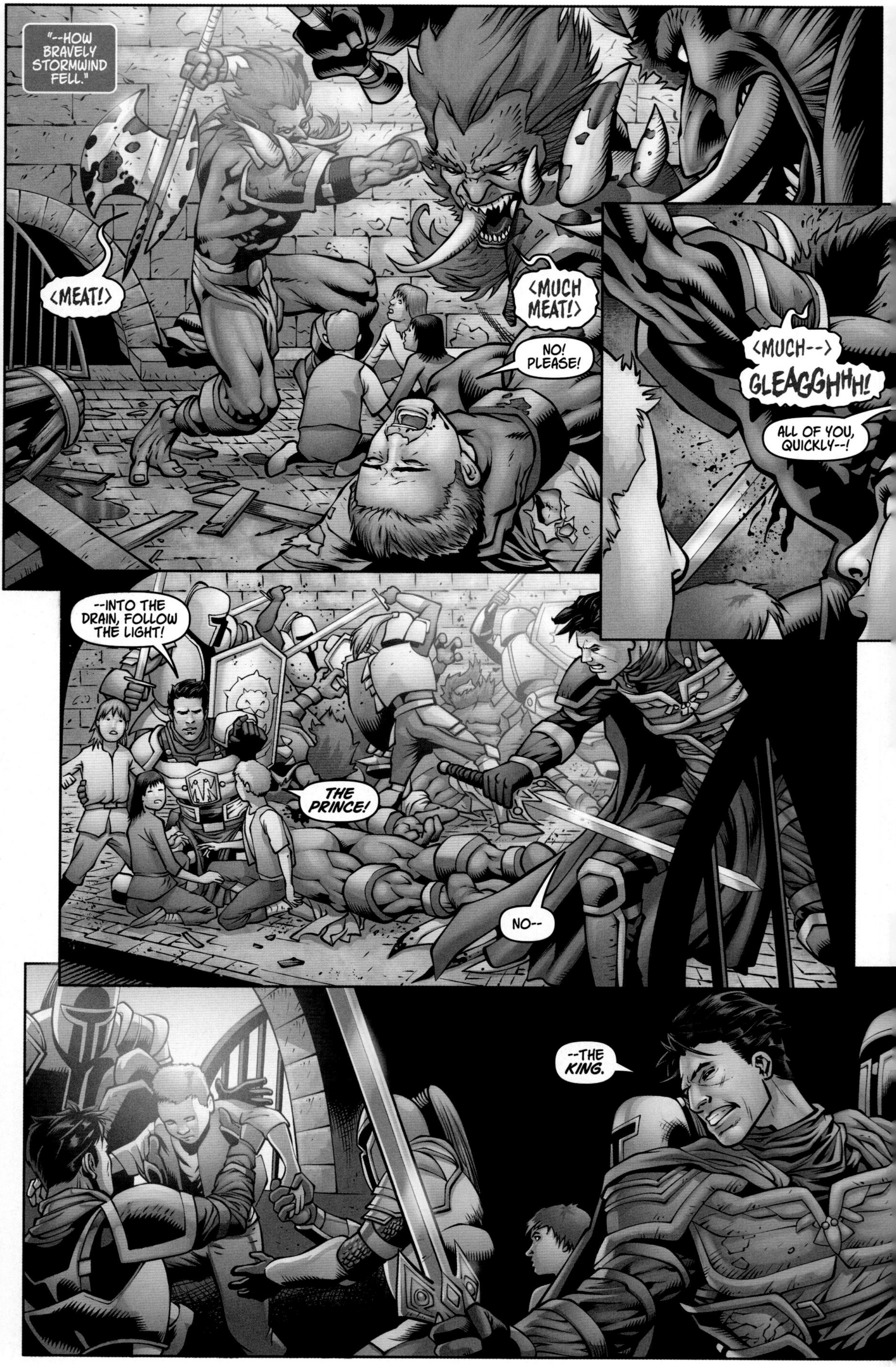
"--HOW BRAVELY STORMWIND FELL."
<MEAT!>
<MUCH MEAT!>
NO! PLEASE!
<MUCH-->
GLEAGGHHH!
ALL OF YOU, QUICKLY--!
--INTO THE DRAIN, FOLLOW THE LIGHT!
THE PRINCE!
NO--
--THE KING.

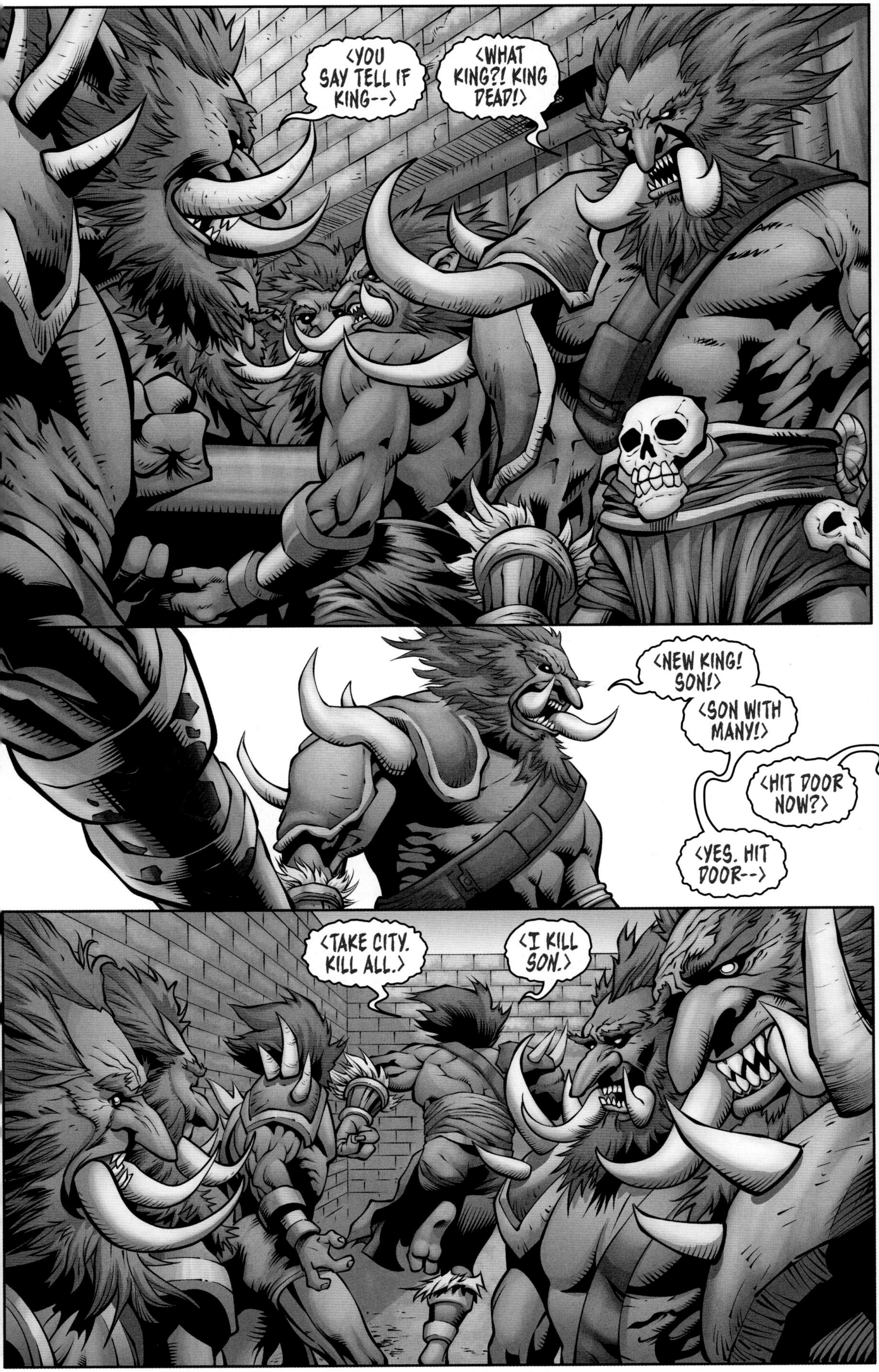
<YOU SAY TELL IF KING-->
<WHAT KING?! KING DEAD!>
<NEW KING! SON!>
<SON WITH MANY!>
<HIT DOOR NOW?>
<YES. HIT DOOR-->
<TAKE CITY. KILL ALL.>
<I KILL SON.>

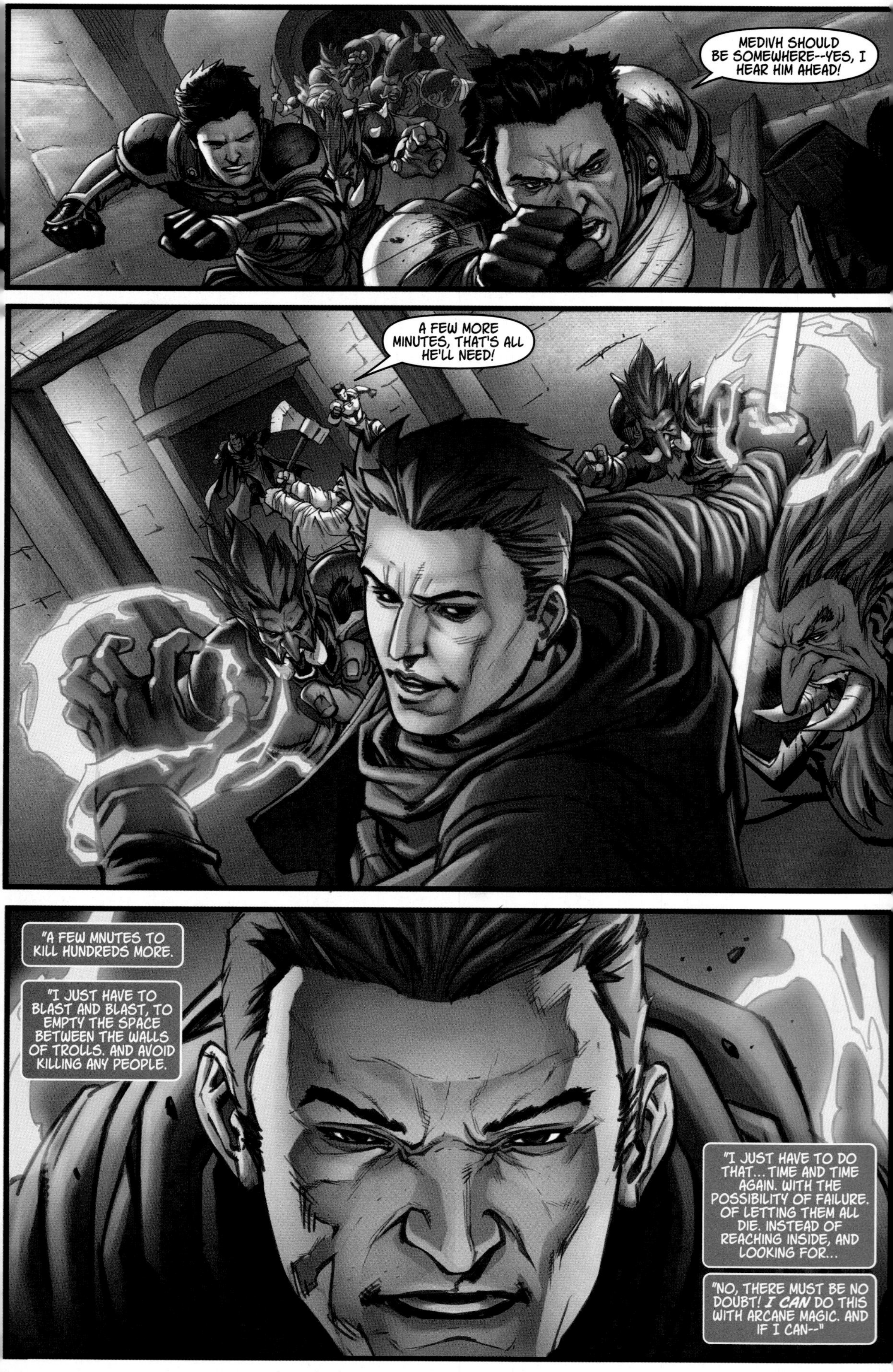
MEDIVH SHOULD BE SOMEWHERE--YES, I HEAR HIM AHEAD!
A FEW MORE MINUTES, THAT'S ALL HE'LL NEED!
"A FEW MNUTES TO KILL HUNDREDS MORE.
"I JUST HAVE TO BLAST AND BLAST, TO EMPTY THE SPACE BETWEEN THE WALLS OF TROLLS. AND AVOID KILLING ANY PEOPLE.
"I JUST HAVE TO DO THAT...TIME AND TIME AGAIN. WITH THE POSSIBILITY OF FAILURE. OF LETTING THEM ALL DIE. INSTEAD OF REACHING INSIDE, AND LOOKING FOR...
"NO, THERE MUST BE NO DOUBT! *I CAN* DO THIS WITH ARCANE MAGIC. AND IF I CAN--"

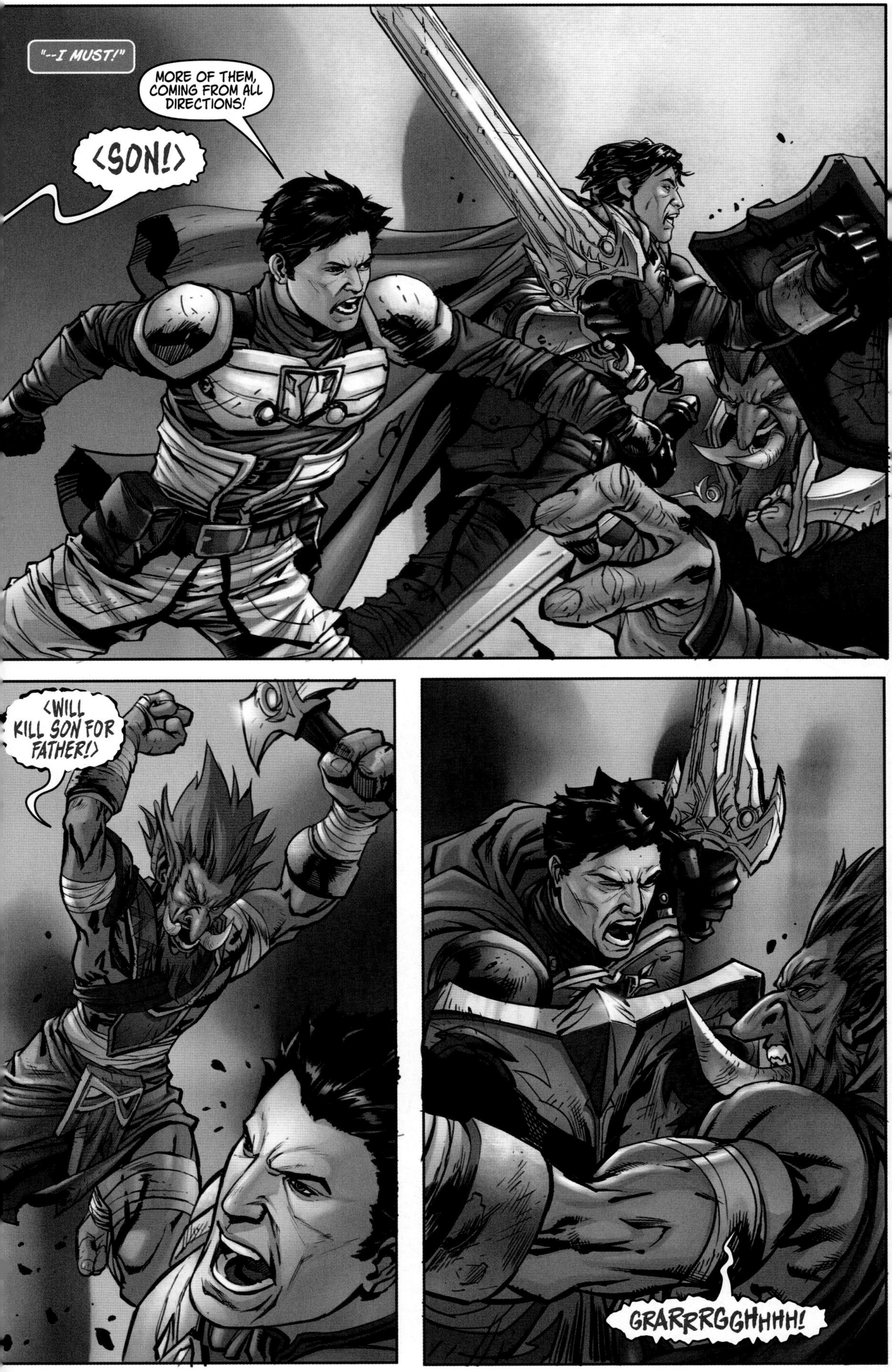
"--I MUST!"
MORE OF THEM, COMING FROM ALL DIRECTIONS!
<SON!>
<WILL KILL SON FOR FATHER!>
GRARRRGGHHHH!

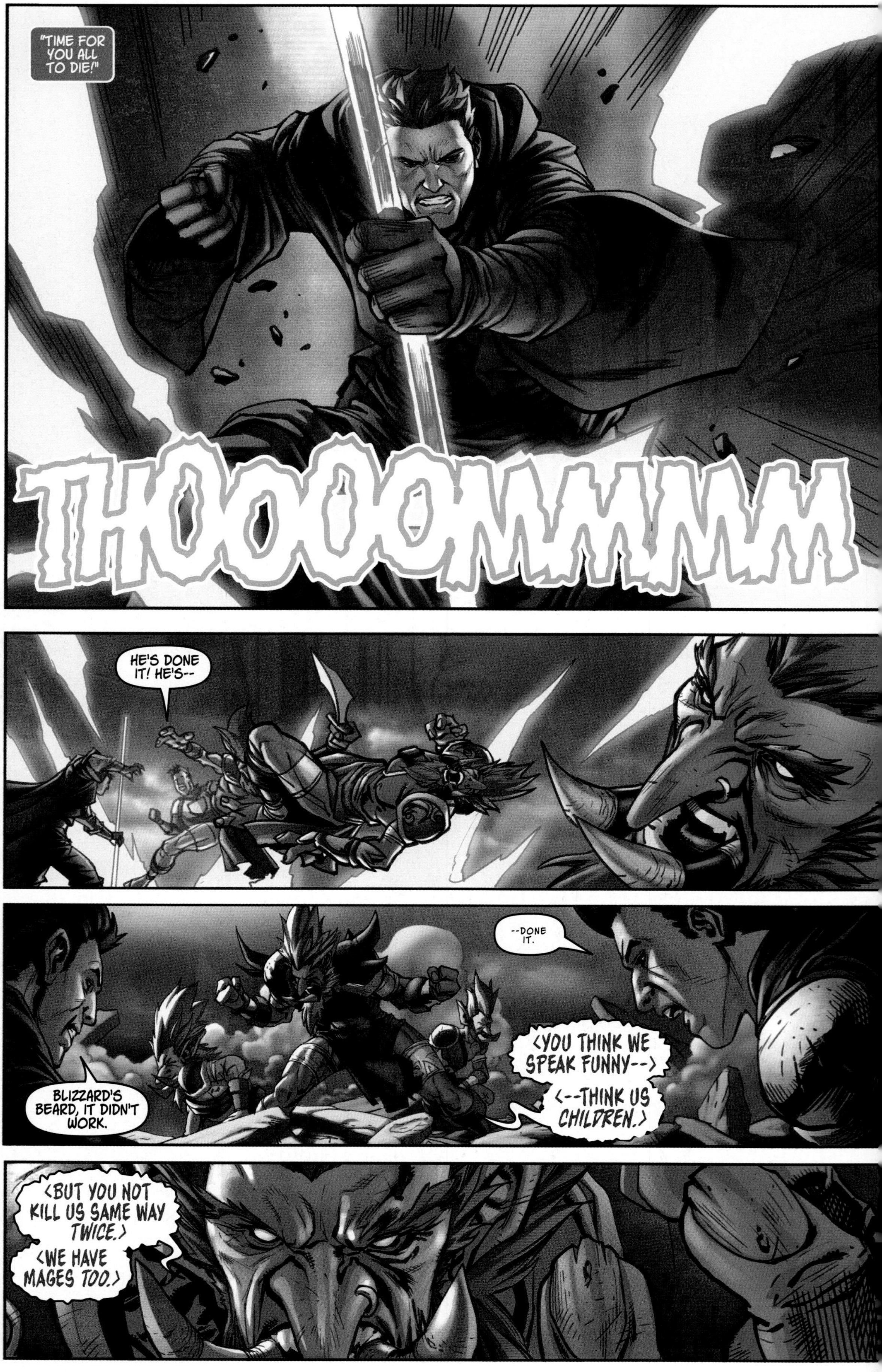
"TIME FOR YOU ALL TO DIE!"
THOOOOMMMM
HE'S DONE IT! HE'S--
--DONE IT.
BLIZZARD'S BEARD, IT DIDN'T WORK.
<YOU THINK WE SPEAK FUNNY-->
<--THINK US CHILDREN.>
<BUT YOU NOT KILL US SAME WAY TWICE.>
<WE HAVE MAGES TOO.>

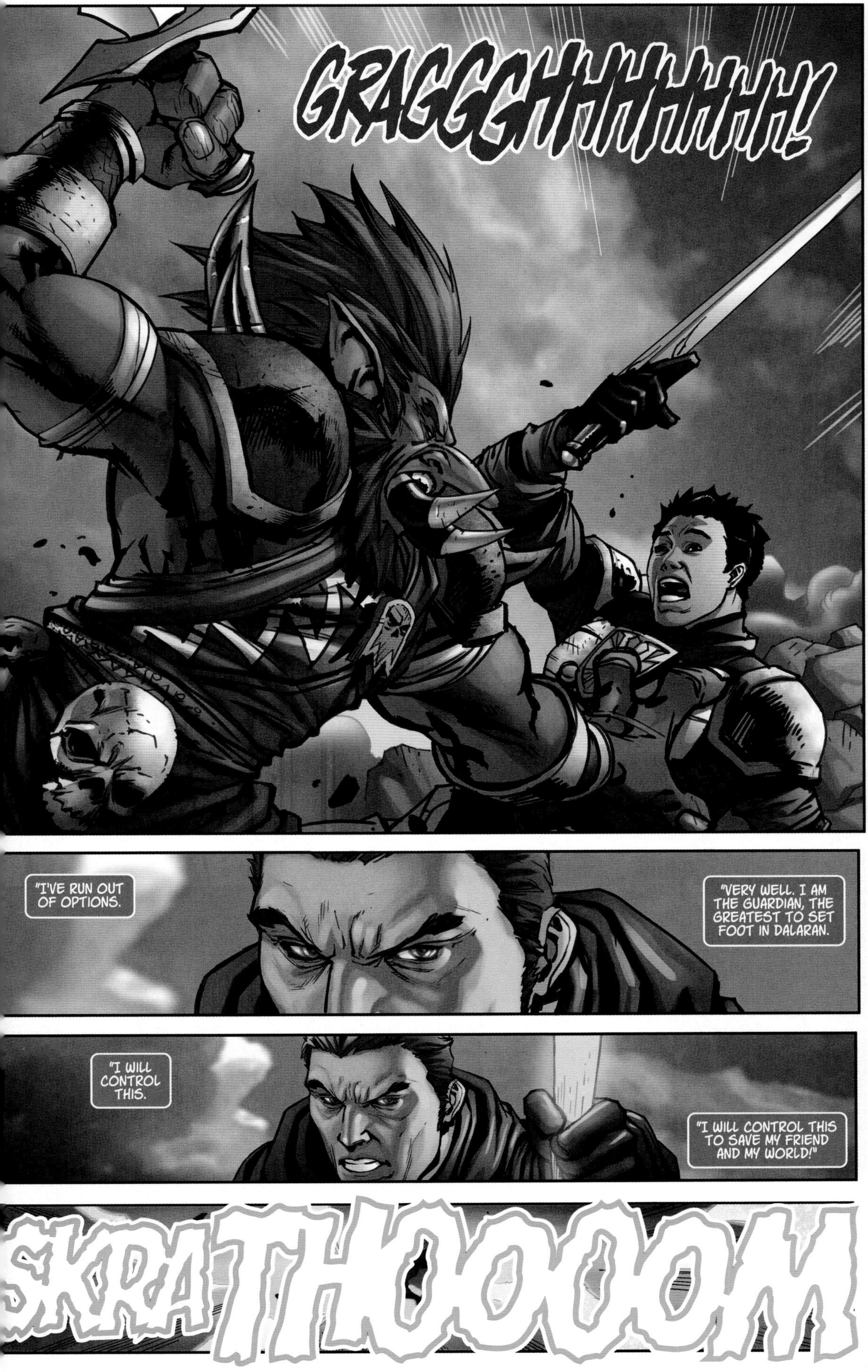
GRAGGGHHHHHHH!
"I'VE RUN OUT OF OPTIONS.
"VERY WELL. I AM THE GUARDIAN, THE GREATEST TO SET FOOT IN DALARAN.
"I WILL CONTROL THIS.
"I WILL CONTROL THIS TO SAVE MY FRIEND AND MY WORLD!"
SKRATHOOOOM

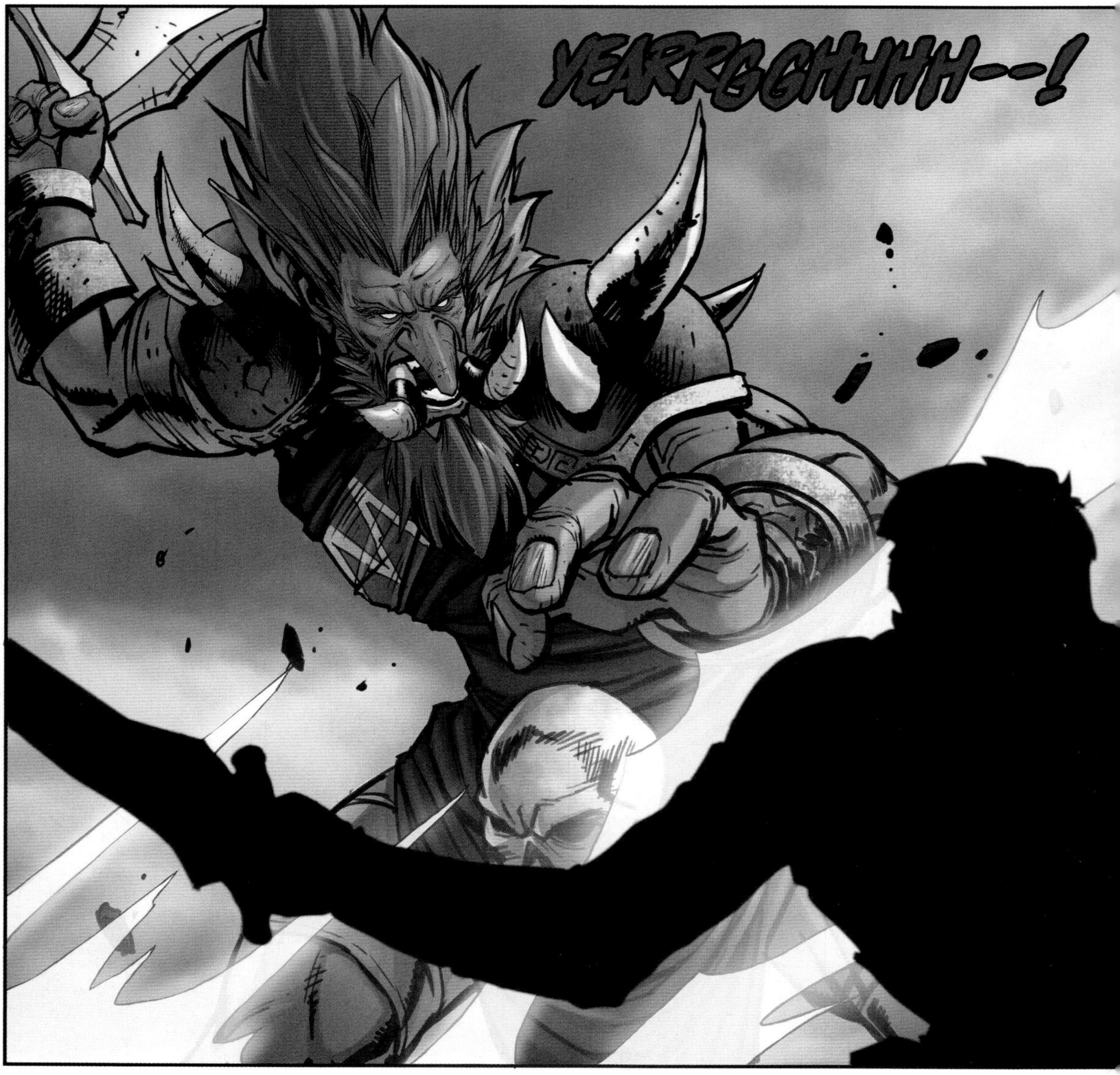
YEARRGGHHHH--!

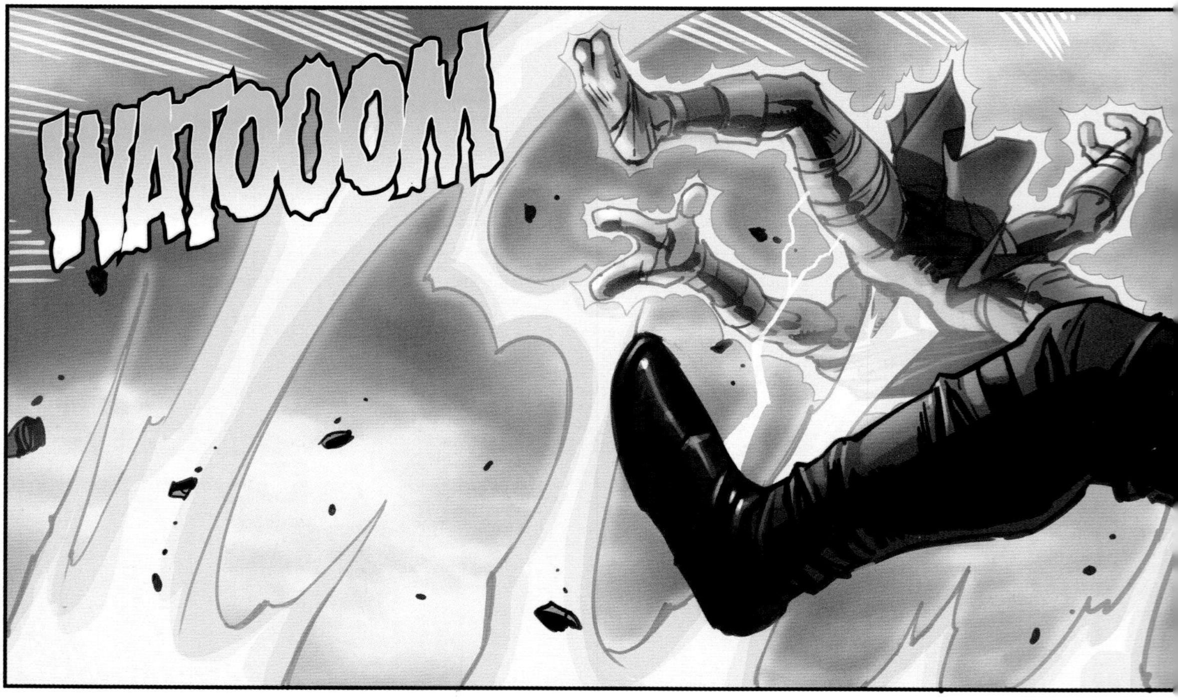
WATOOOM

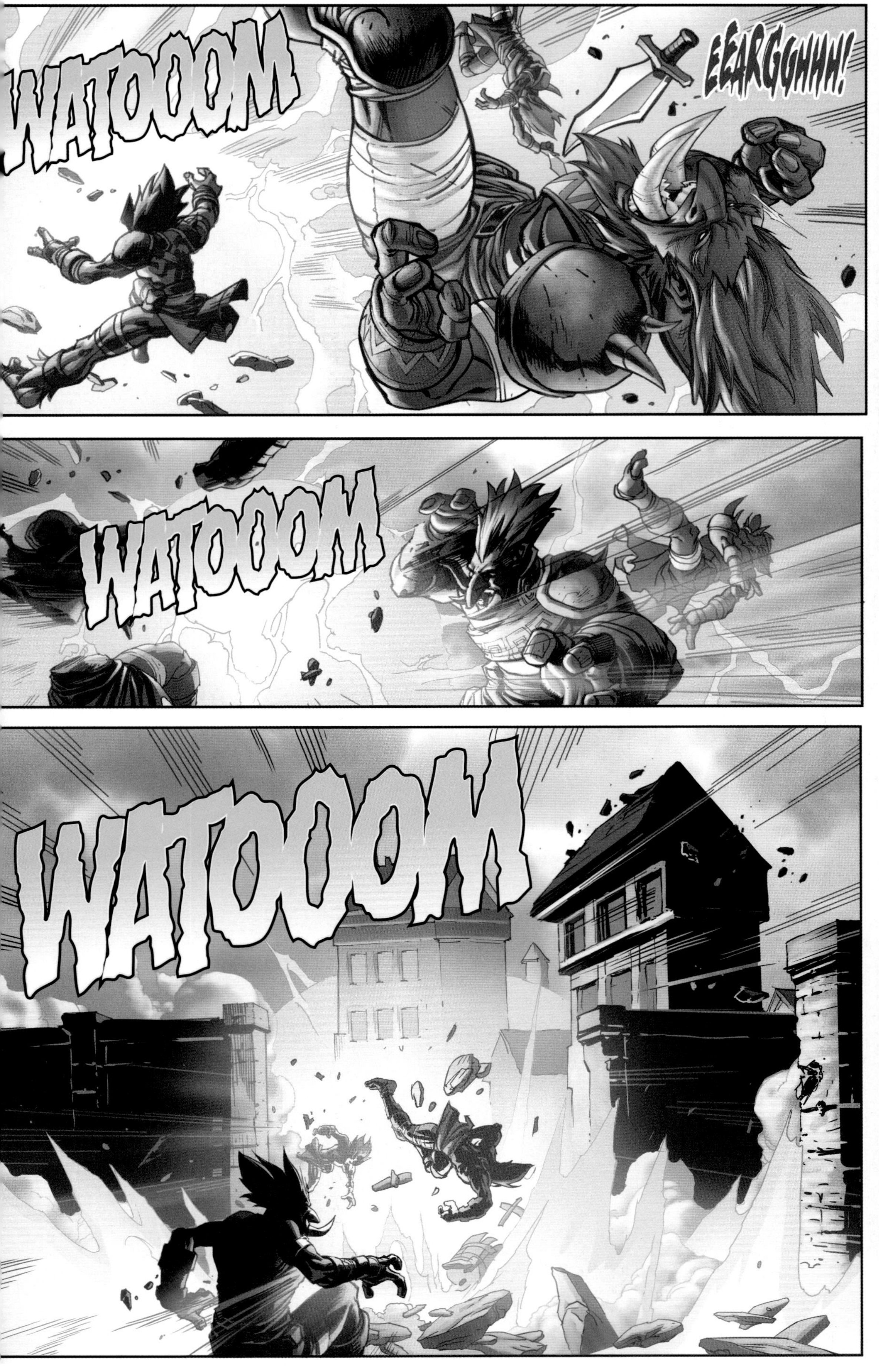
WATOOOM
EEARGGHHH!
WATOOOM
WATOOOM

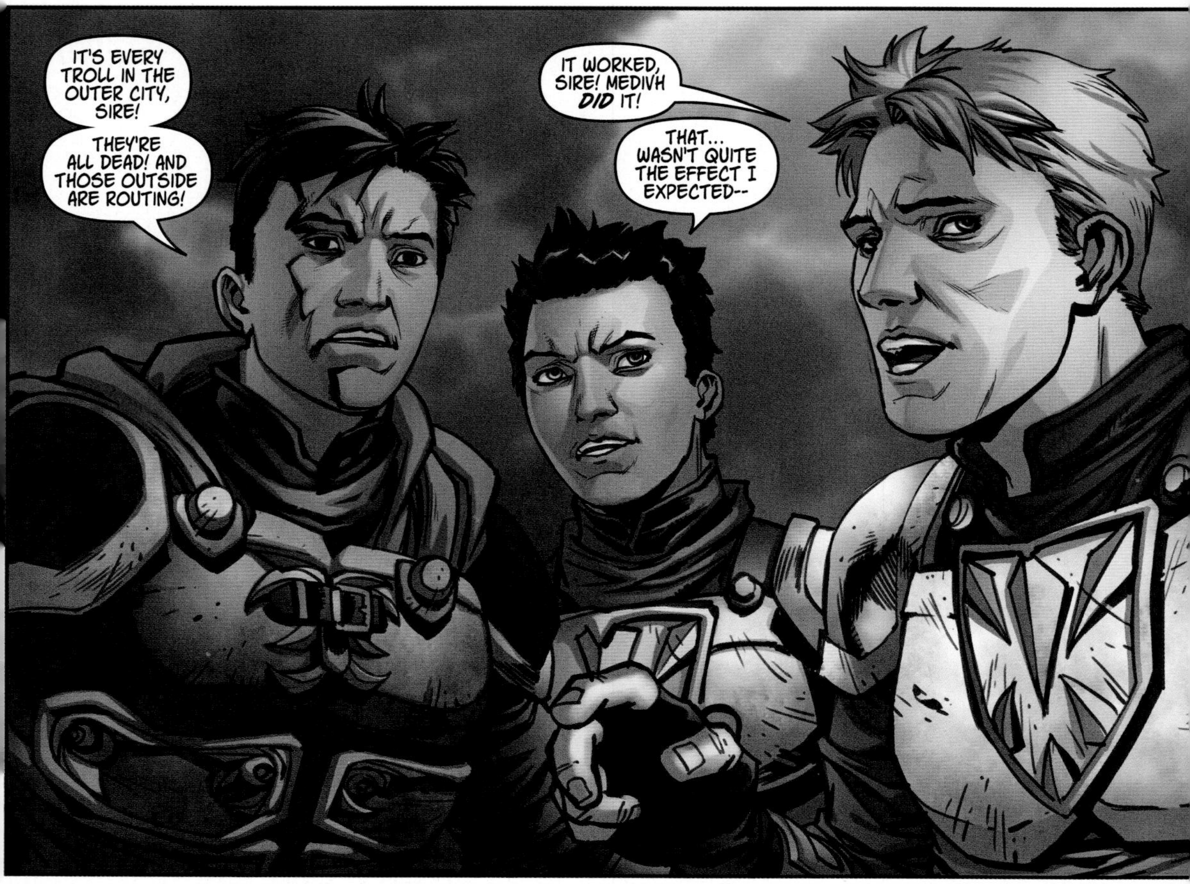
IT'S EVERY TROLL IN THE OUTER CITY, SIRE!
THEY'RE ALL DEAD! AND THOSE OUTSIDE ARE ROUTING!
IT WORKED, SIRE! MEDIVH DID IT!
THAT... WASN'T QUITE THE EFFECT I EXPECTED--
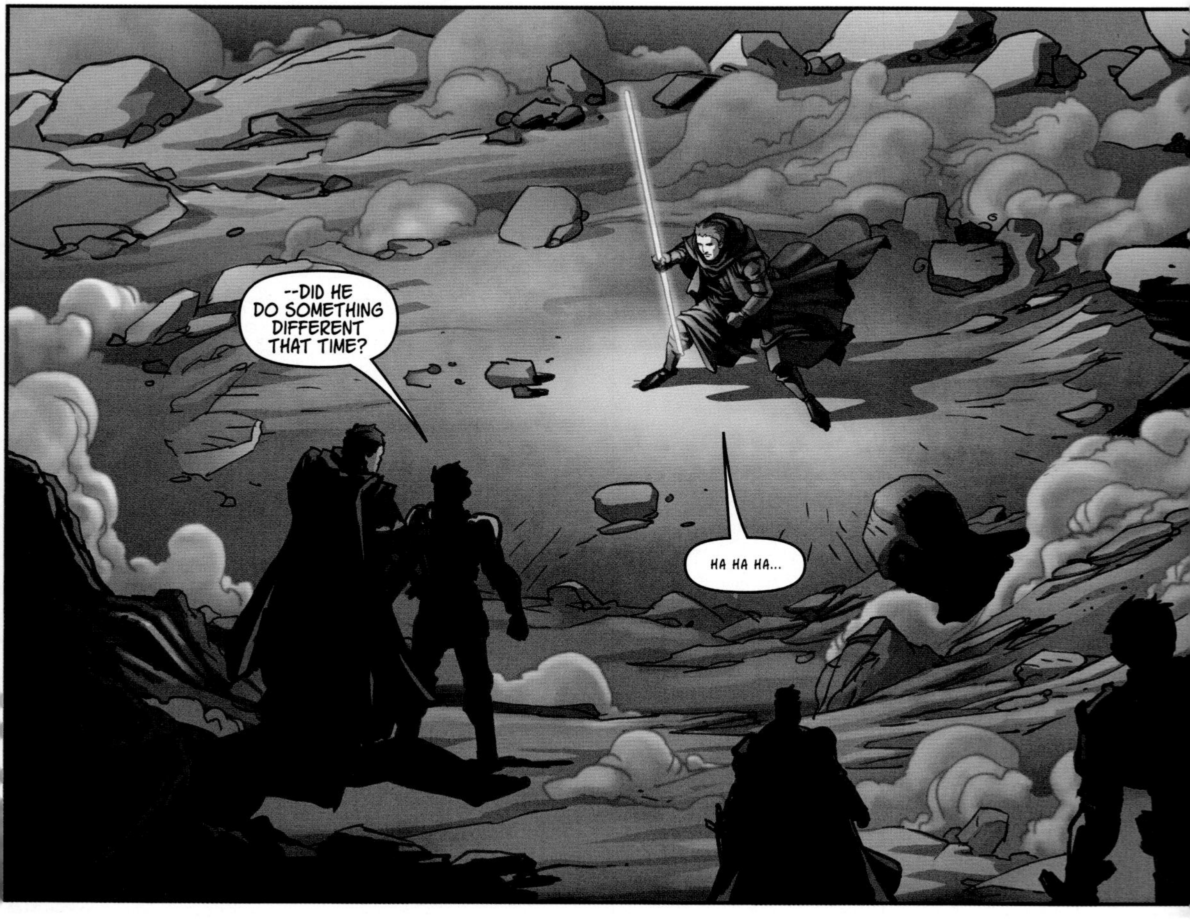
--DID HE DO SOMETHING DIFFERENT THAT TIME?
HA HA HA...

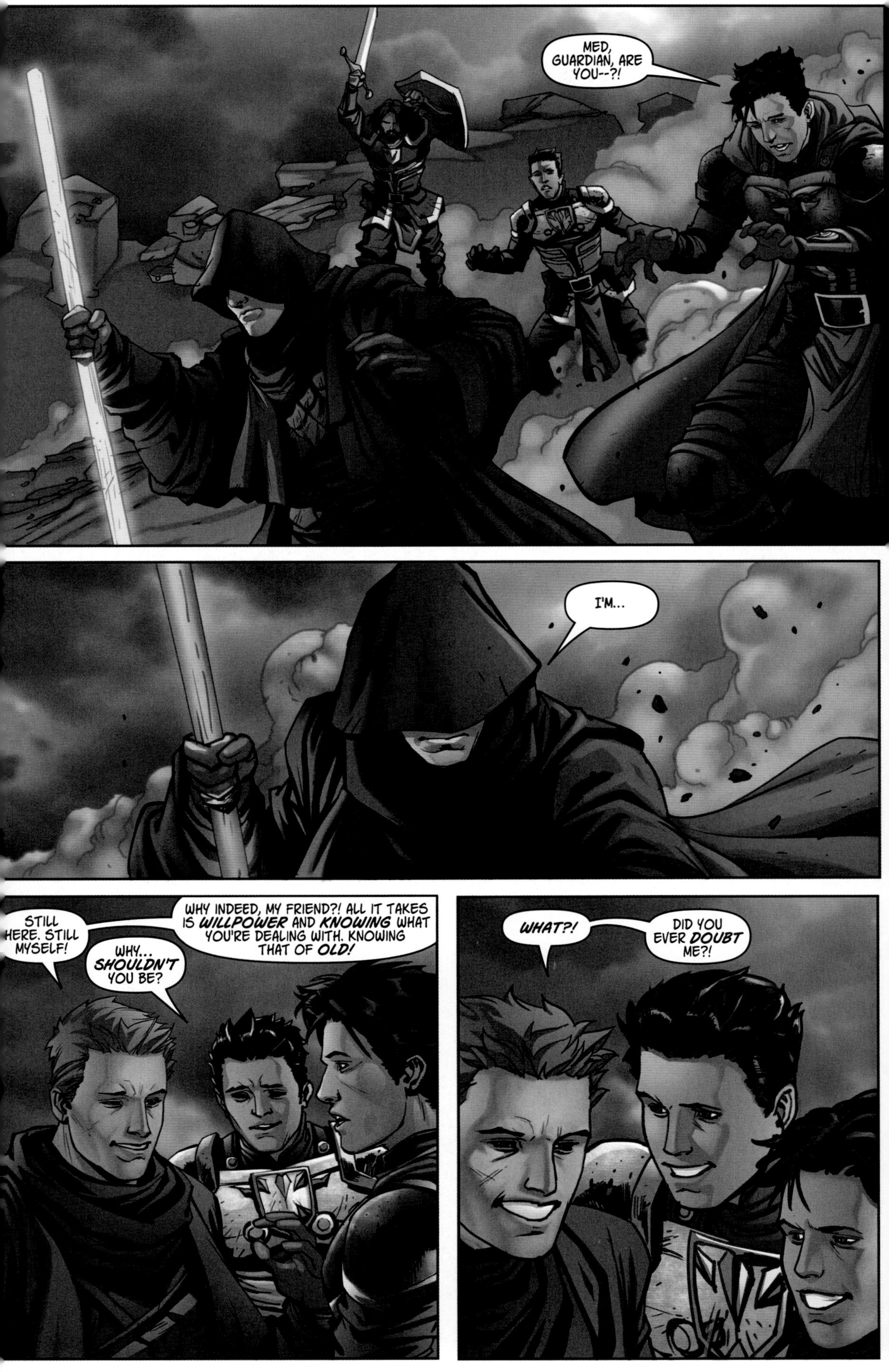
MED, GUARDIAN, ARE YOU--?!
I'M...
STILL HERE. STILL MYSELF!
WHY... SHOULDN'T YOU BE?
WHY INDEED, MY FRIEND?! ALL IT TAKES IS WILLPOWER AND KNOWING WHAT YOU'RE DEALING WITH. KNOWING THAT OF OLD!
WHAT?!
DID YOU EVER DOUBT ME?!

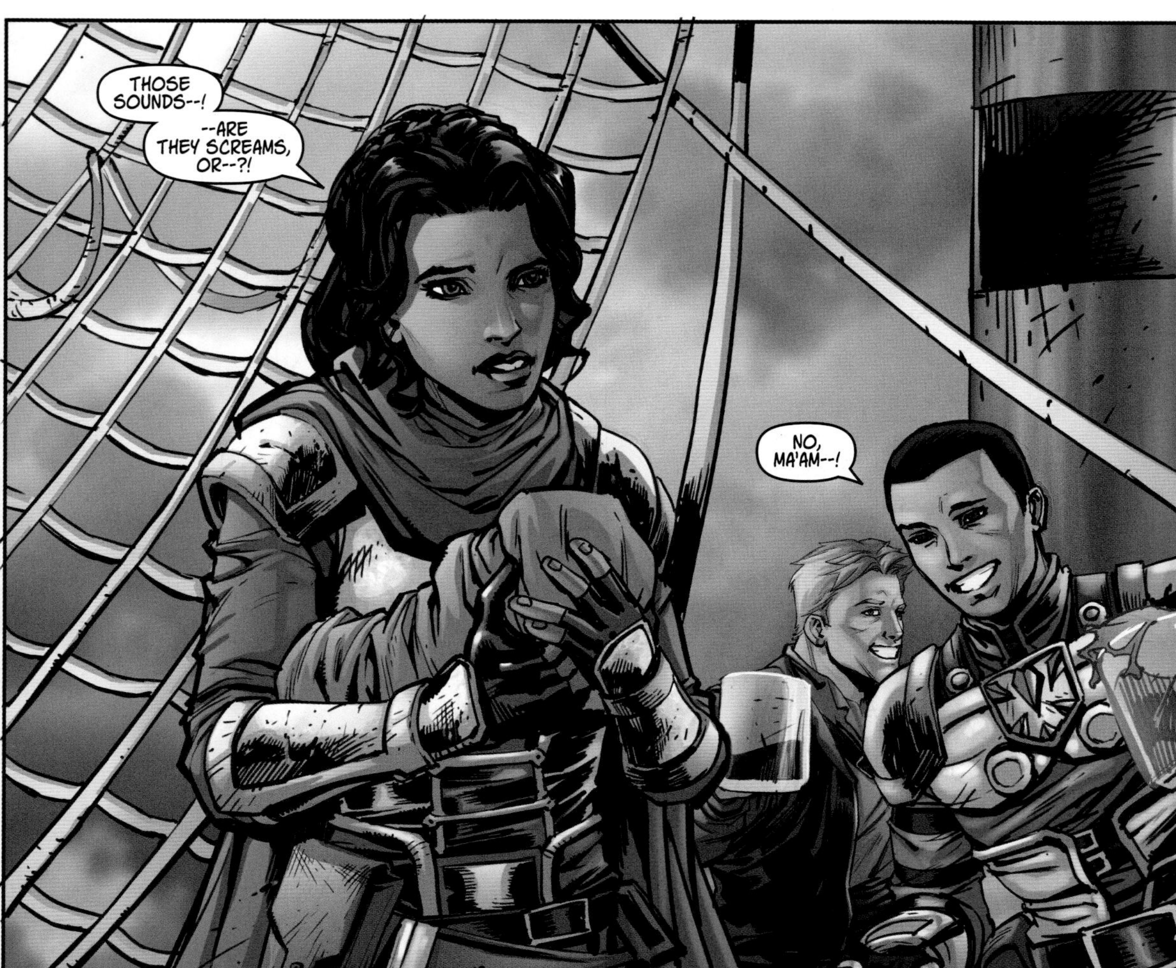
THOSE SOUNDS--!
--ARE THEY SCREAMS, OR--?!
NO, MA'AM--!

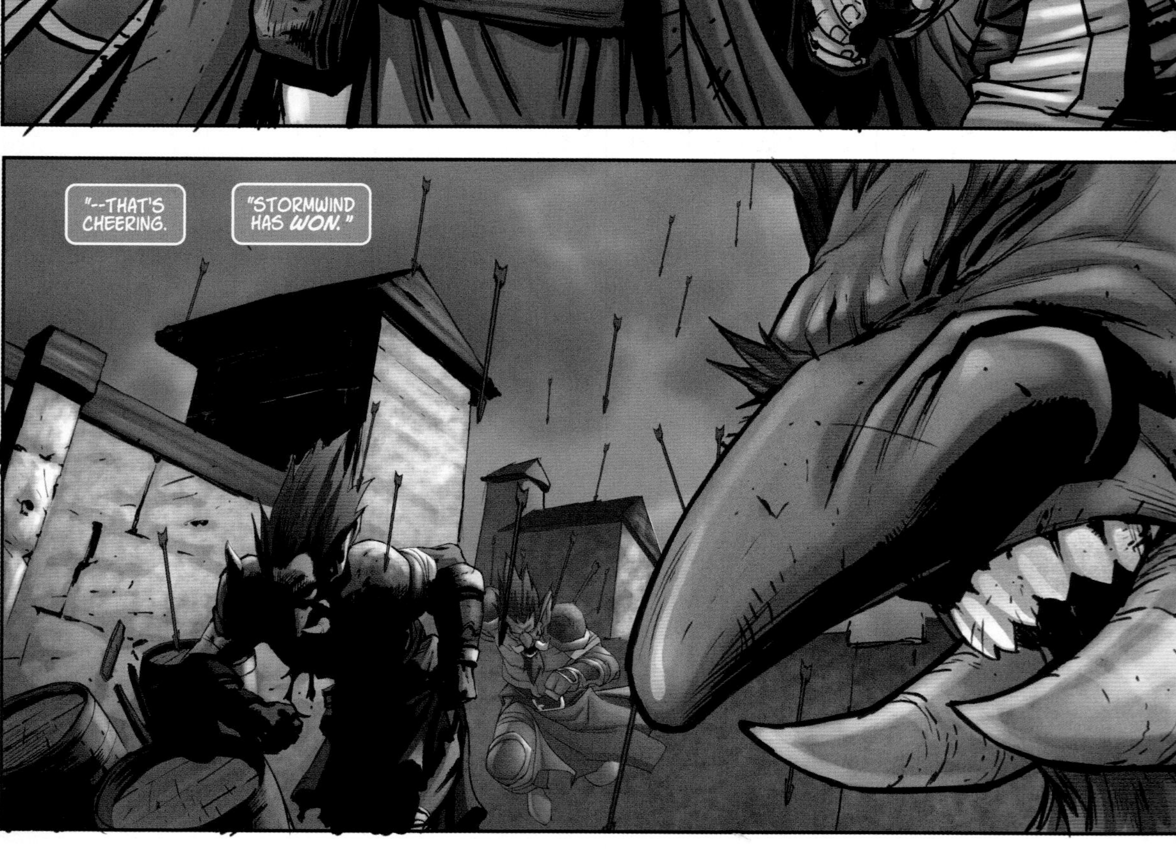
"--THAT'S CHEERING.
"STORMWIND HAS *WON.*"

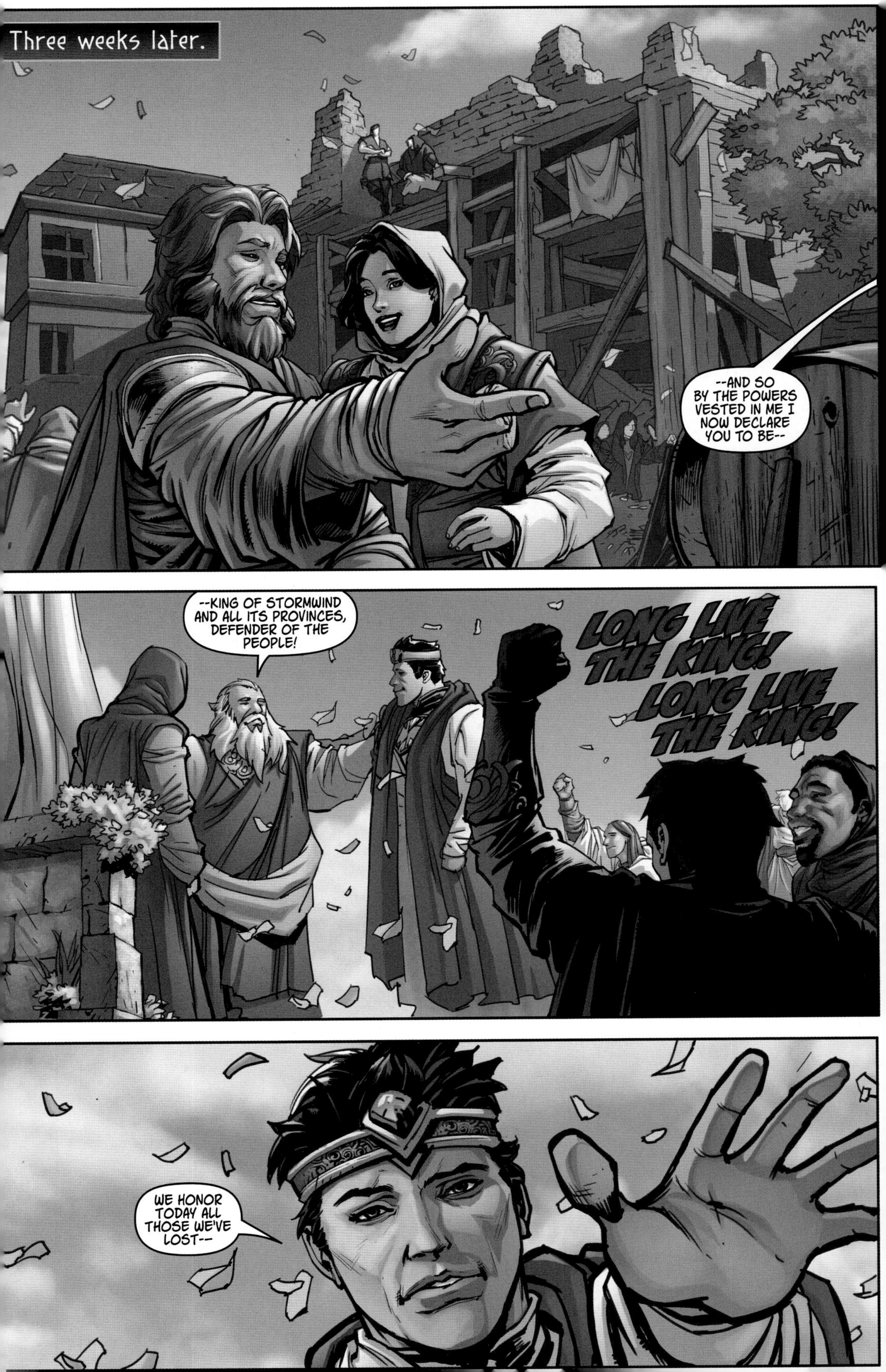
Three weeks later.
--AND SO BY THE POWERS VESTED IN ME I NOW DECLARE YOU TO BE--
--KING OF STORMWIND AND ALL ITS PROVINCES, DEFENDER OF THE PEOPLE!
LONG LIVE THE KING! LONG LIVE THE KING!
WE HONOR TODAY ALL THOSE WE'VE LOST--

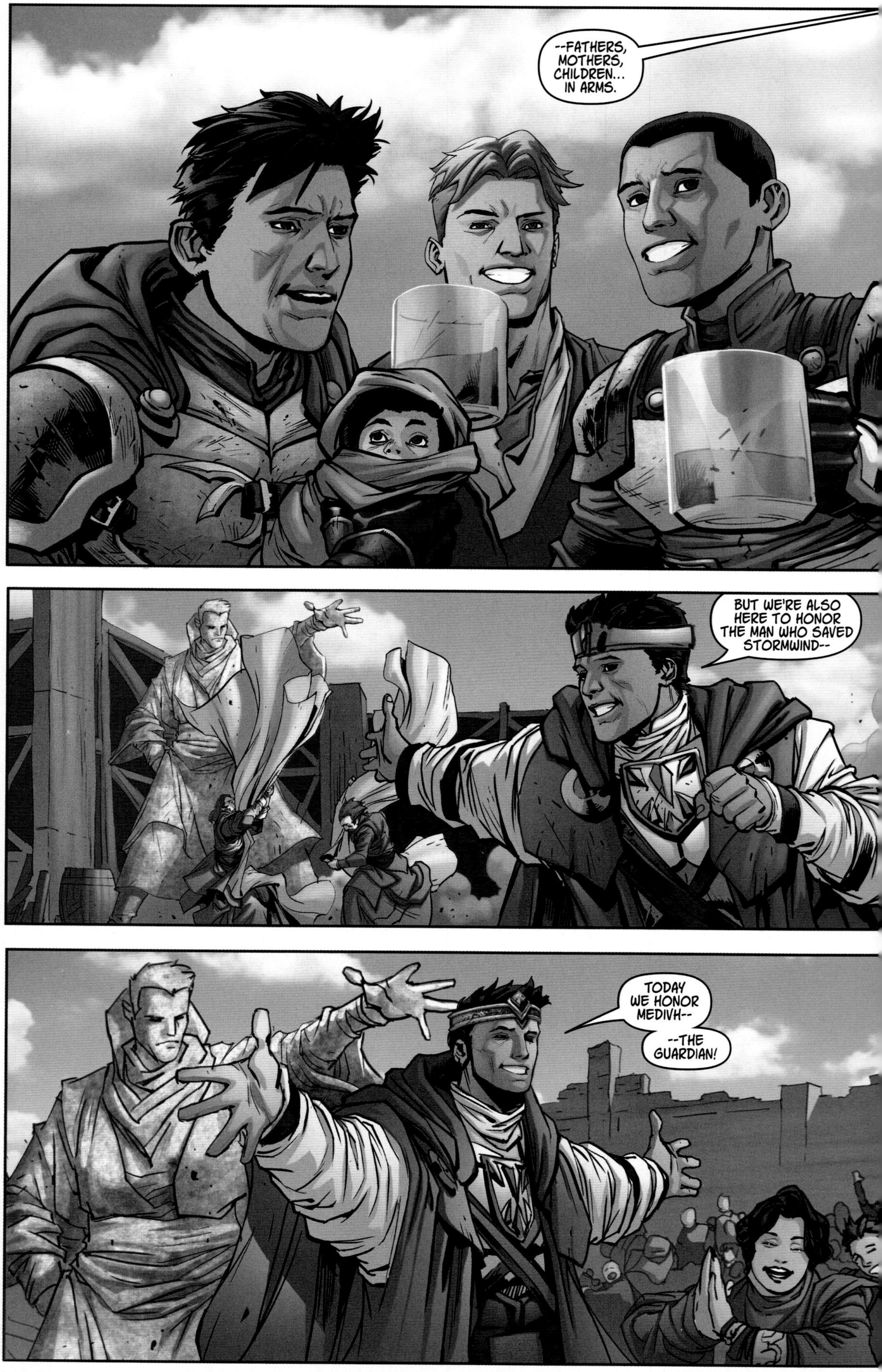
--FATHERS, MOTHERS, CHILDREN... IN ARMS.
BUT WE'RE ALSO HERE TO HONOR THE MAN WHO SAVED STORMWIND--
TODAY WE HONOR MEDIVH--
--THE GUARDIAN!

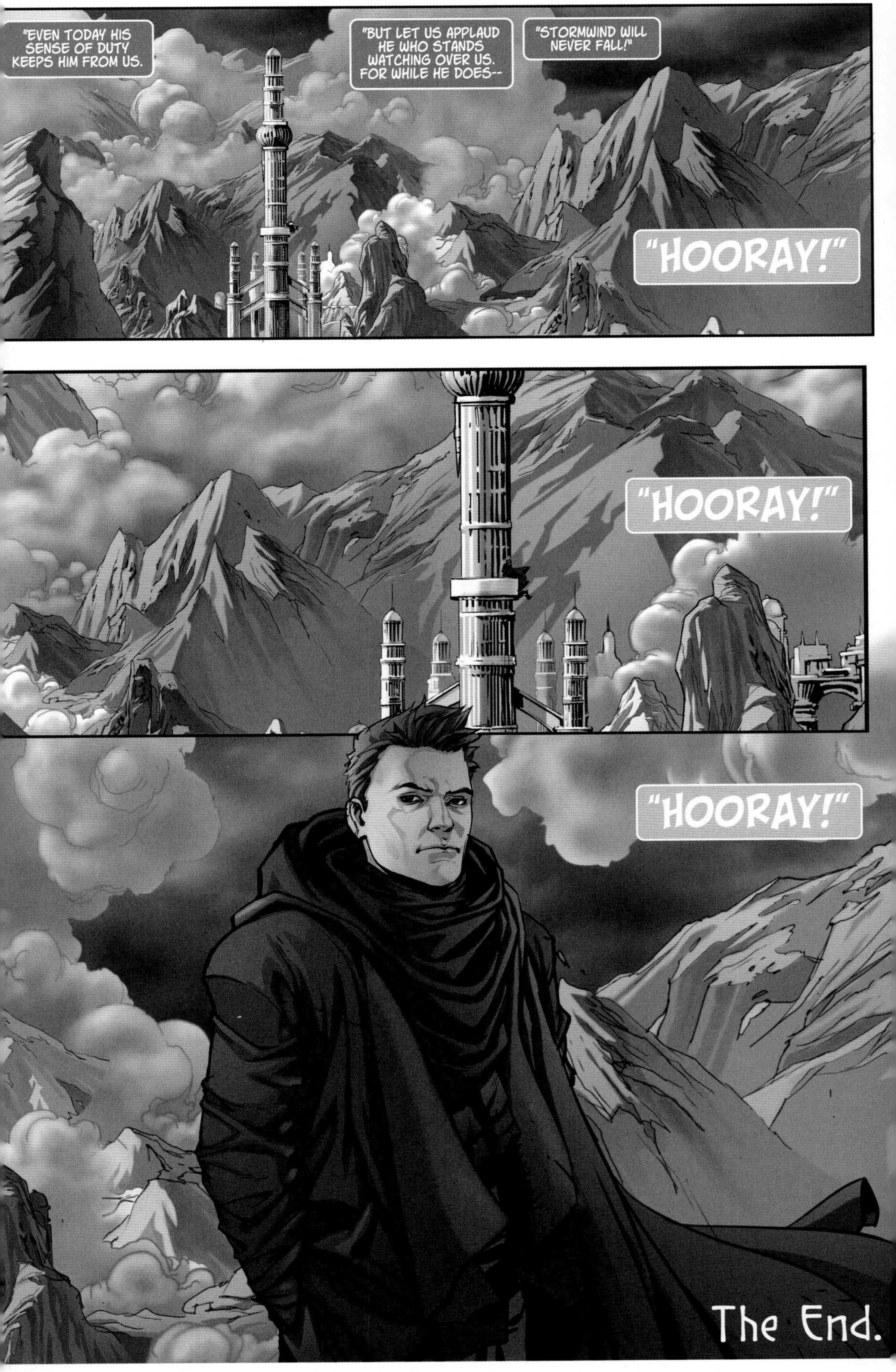
"EVEN TODAY HIS SENSE OF DUTY KEEPS HIM FROM US.
"BUT LET US APPLAUD HE WHO STANDS WATCHING OVER US. FOR WHILE HE DOES--
"STORMWIND WILL NEVER FALL!"
"HOORAY!"
"HOORAY!"
"HOORAY!"
The End.

EXTRAS

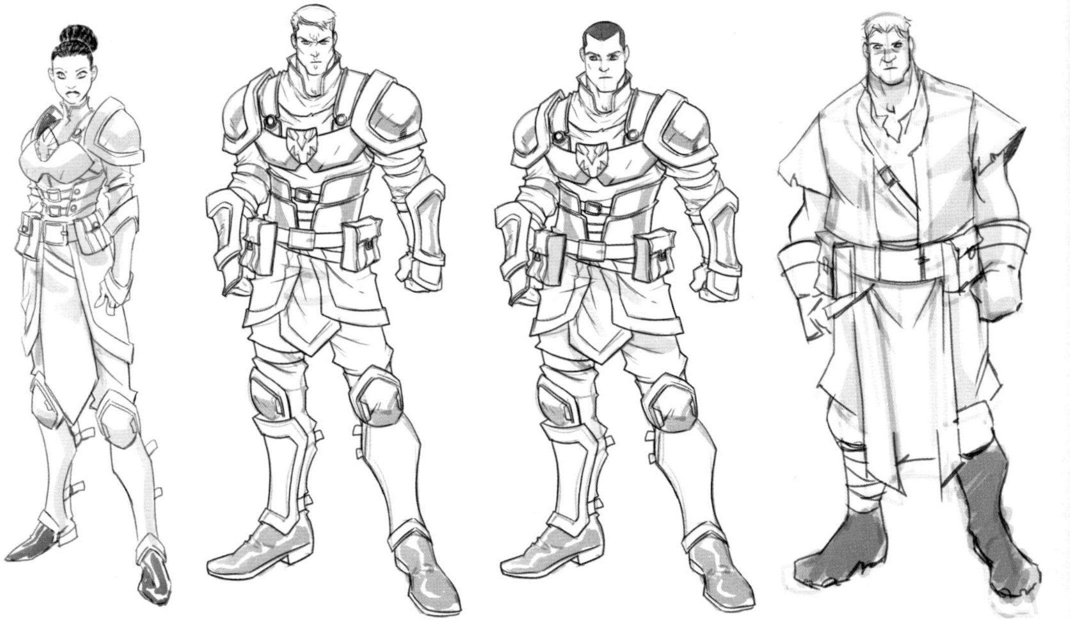

WICE HALRIK GRAGAS TYDOR

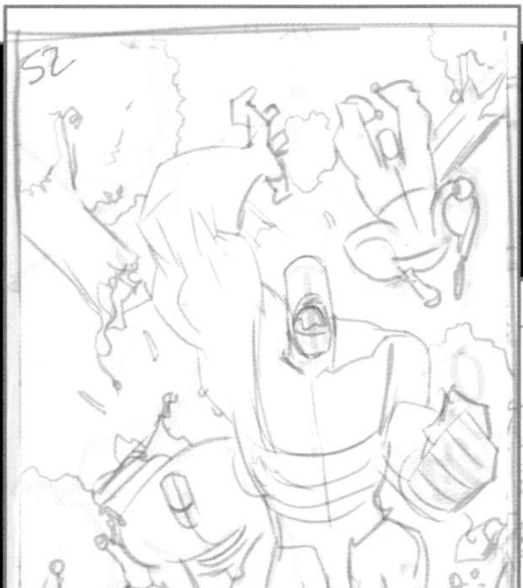

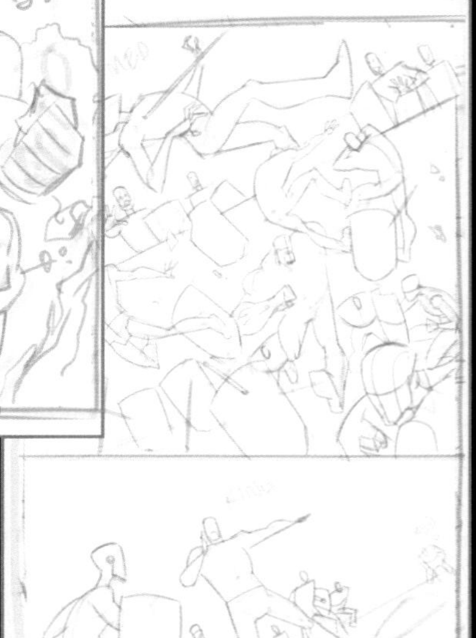

EDDIE NUNEZ

CHARACTER DESIGNS

In Chapter 3, Eddie Nunez was tasked with designing solider characters who would be secondary to the story, but immerse readers on the front lines in a battle against the Trolls.

Paul Cornell's script gave Eddie an excellent jumping-off point:

WICE is a middle-aged, experienced, black female soldier. HALRIK is a younger, but still battled-scarred male veteran. GRAGAS is young, inexperienced, scared but hiding it. Their cook, TYDOR, is a long-faced, cynical, older man.

LAYOUTS

An essential step in creating a comic book page is going from script to layout, so the writer and editors can see how the artist is designing the scripted page. Nunez's layouts brought a lot of energy to the action scenes, which dominate the third chapter.

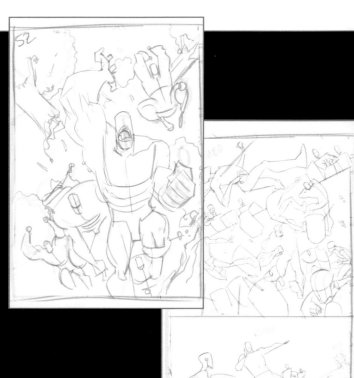

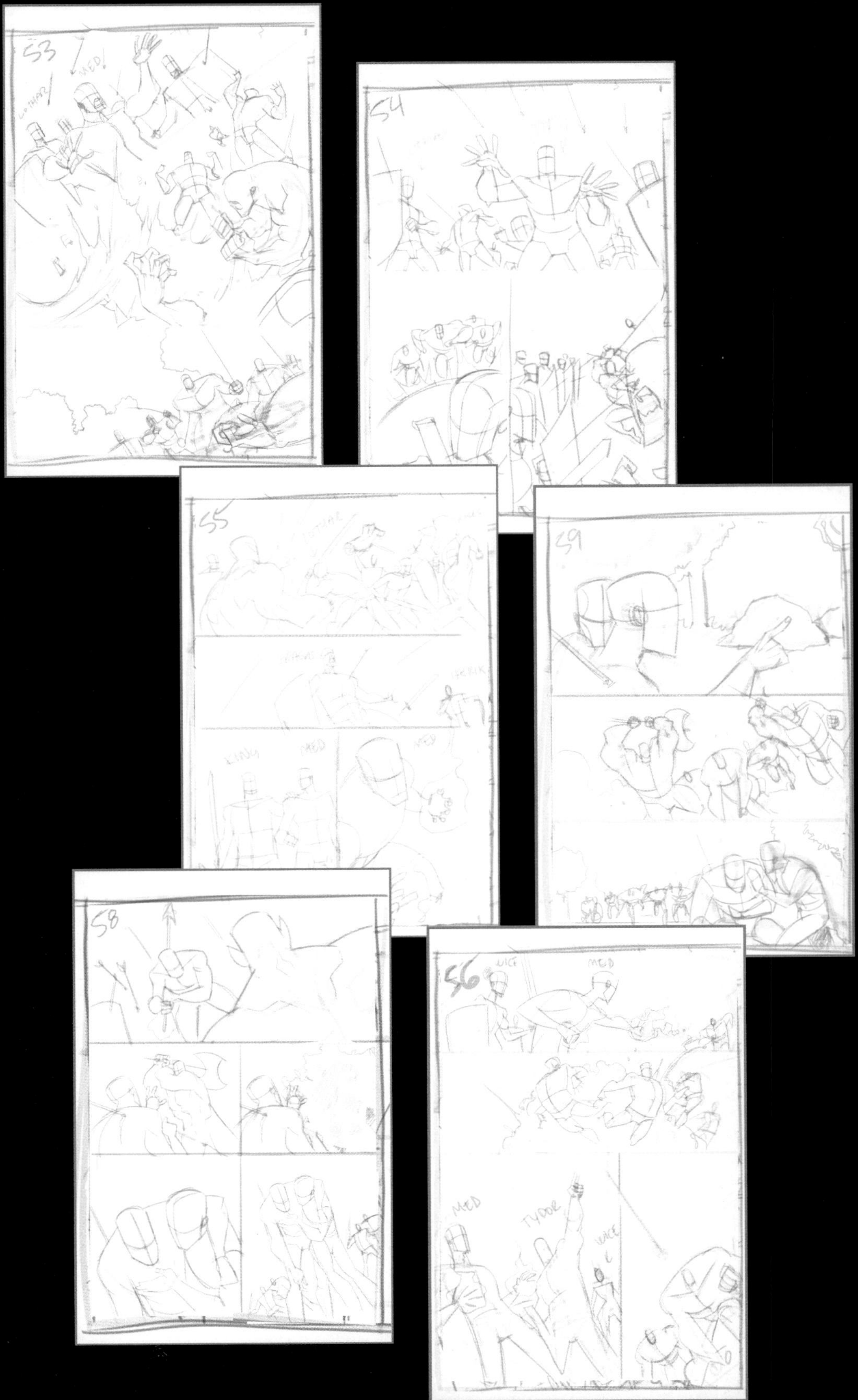

53
LOTHAR
MED
54
55
LOTHAR
KING
MED
MED
59
58
56
MED
MED
TYDOR

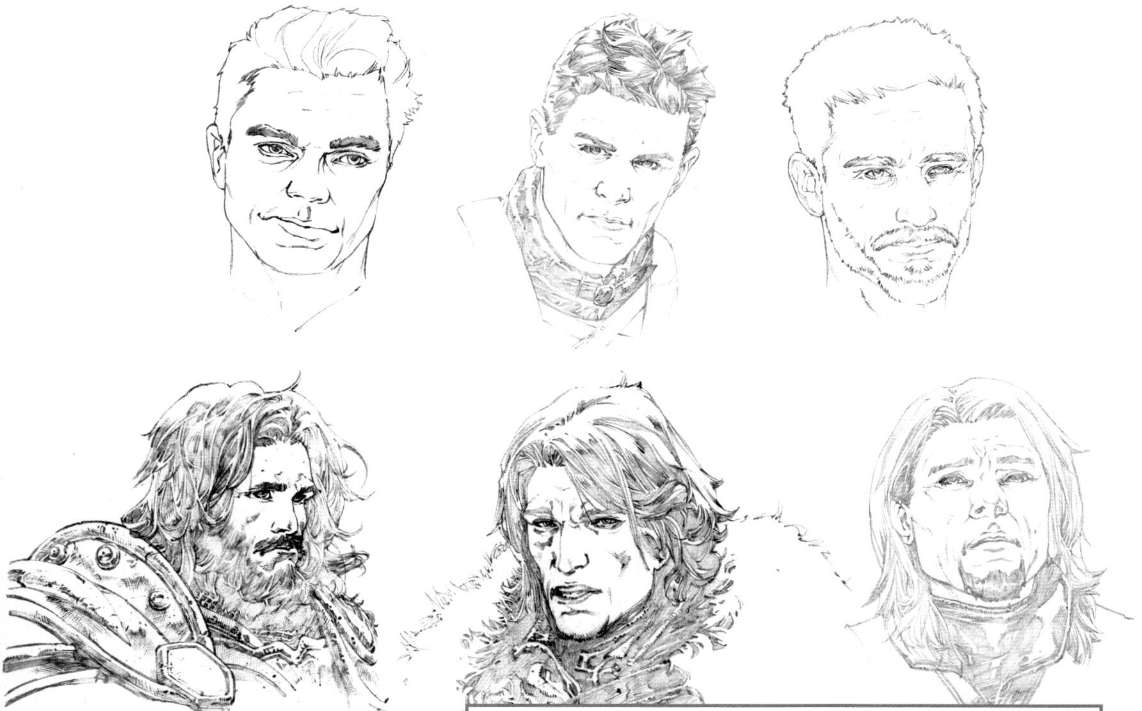

MAT BROOME

No stranger to design, Mat Broome spent some time developing the graphic novel versions of Llane, Lothar and Medivh. He was tasked with creating comic book versions of the movie characters (which differed from their in-game counterparts) and also present a younger appearance since *Bonds of Brotherhood* takes place roughly two decades before the events of the film.

The piece that ultimately became the first promotional image for the graphic novel is also featured on the back cover in a different form. This work-in-progress shows the piece half "inked," though Broome created the entire piece digitally.

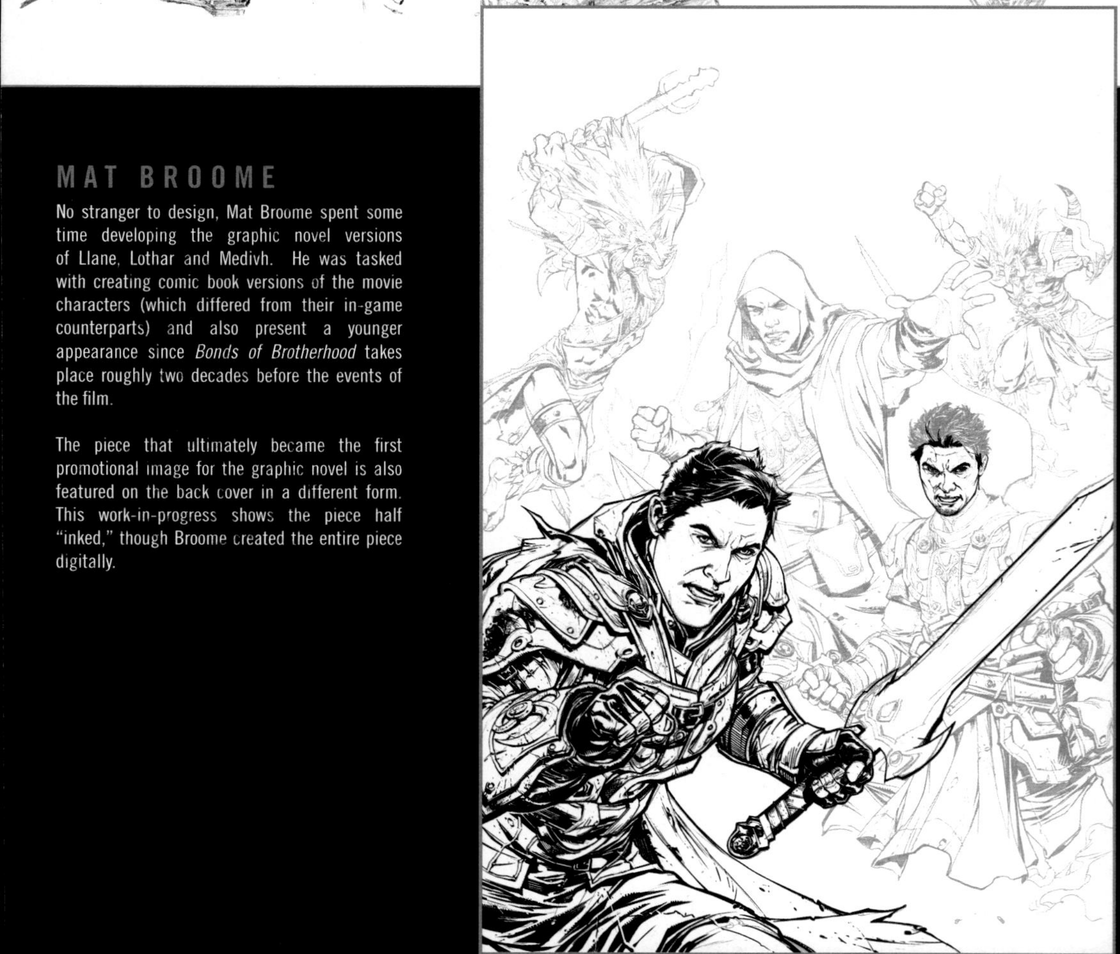

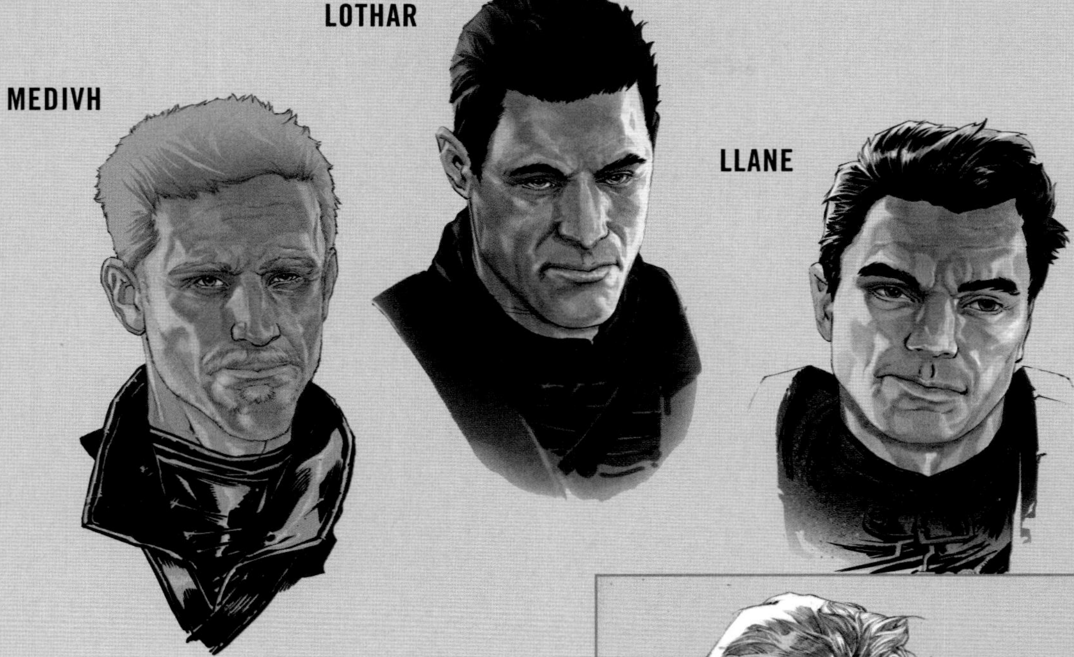
LOTHAR
MEDIVH
LLANE

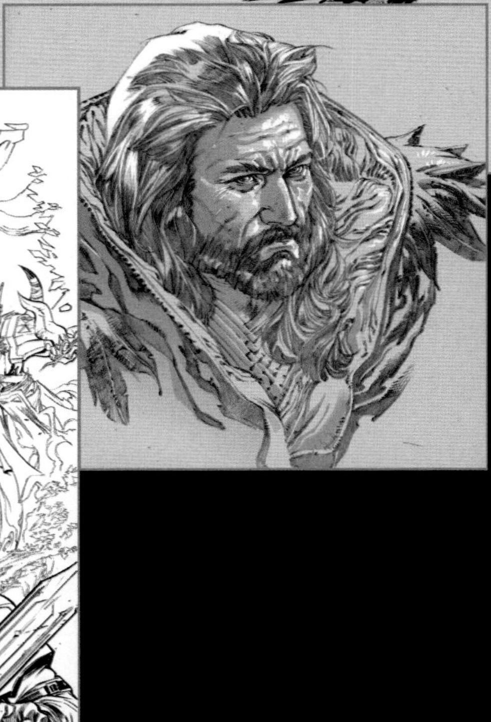

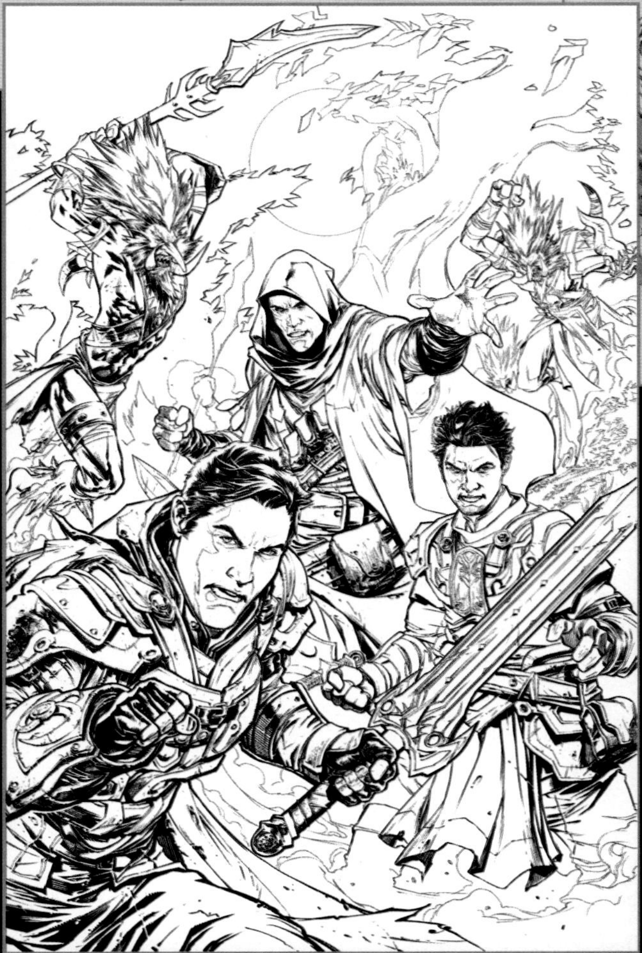

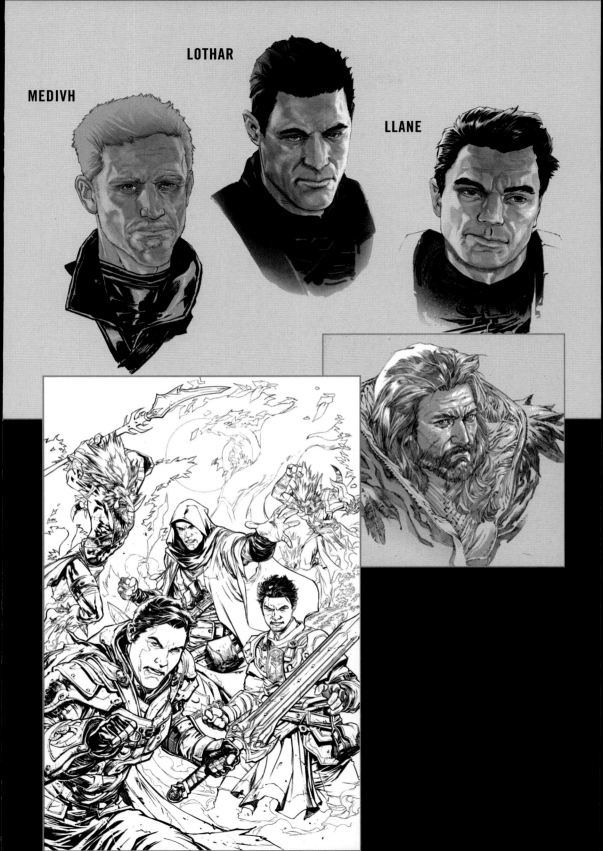

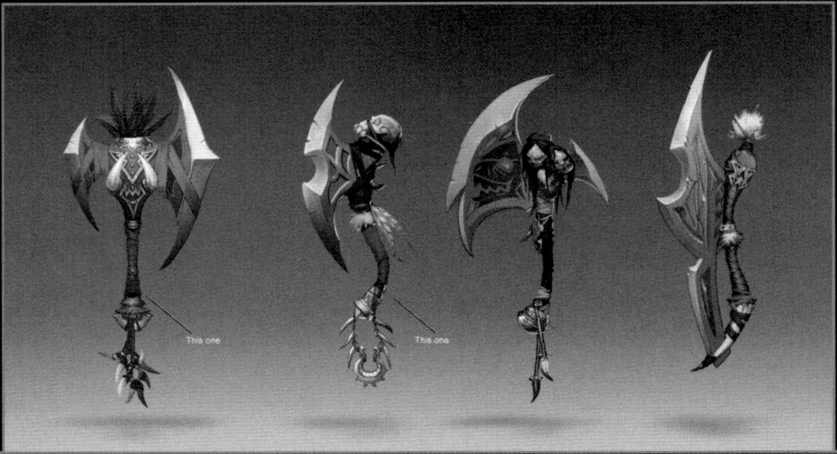
This one
This one

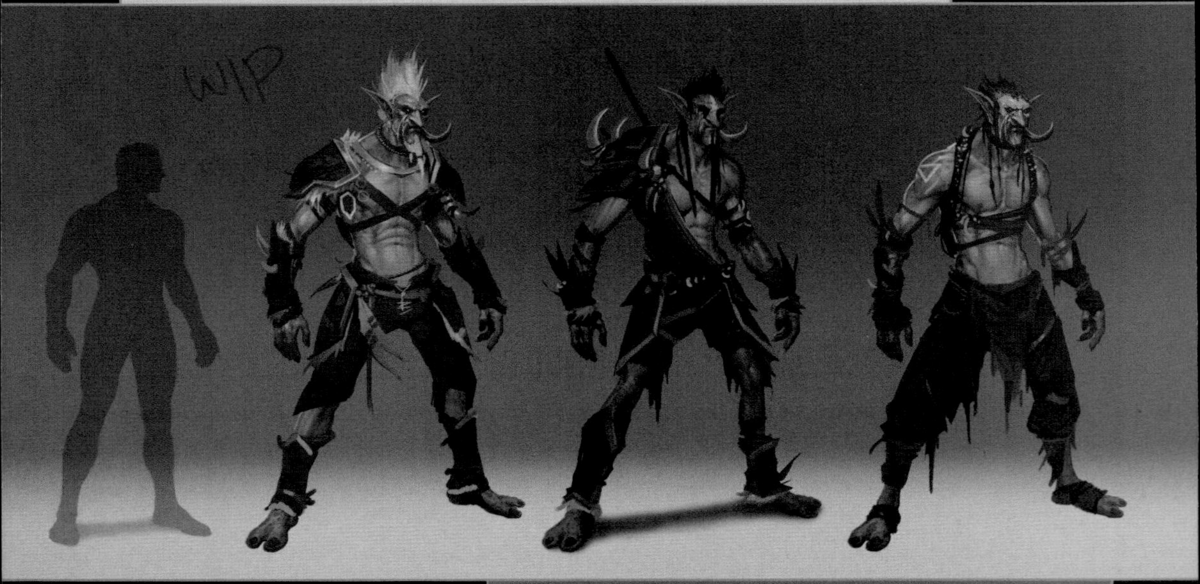
WIP

THE TROLLS

A scene featuring the Trolls was conceived and ultimately cut from the movie. Chris Metzen saw an opportunity to revive the plot in the graphic novel prequel and the comic artists were given access to the film concept art shown here, so they could illustrate Trolls in the spirit of the film design.

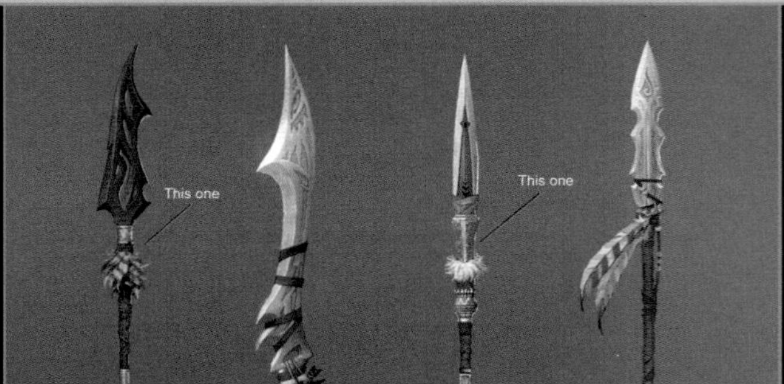
This one
This one

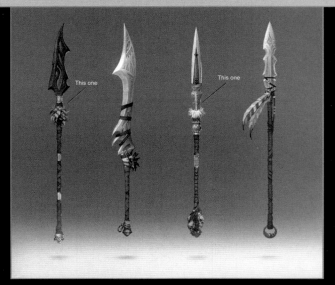

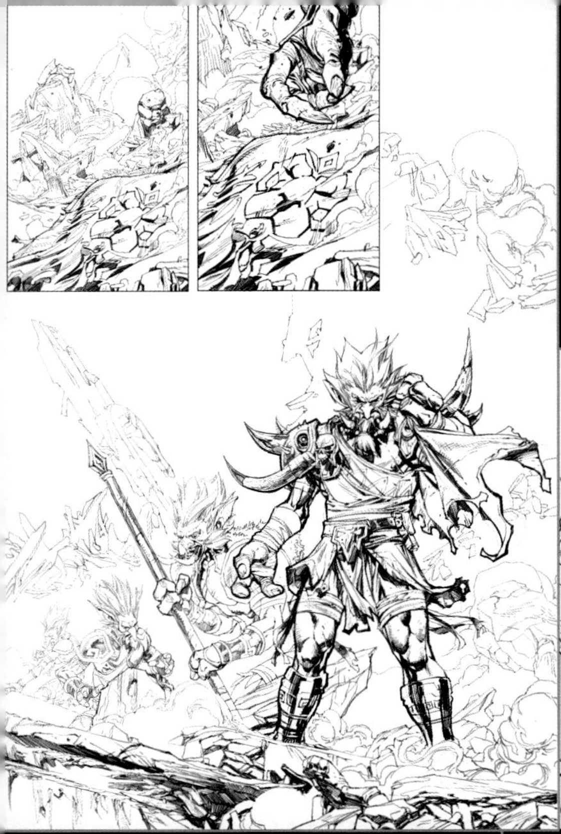

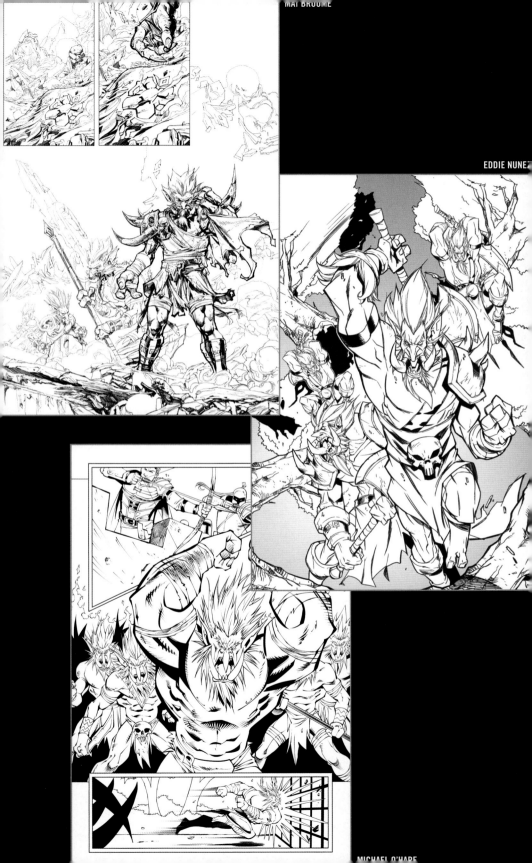

MAT BROOME

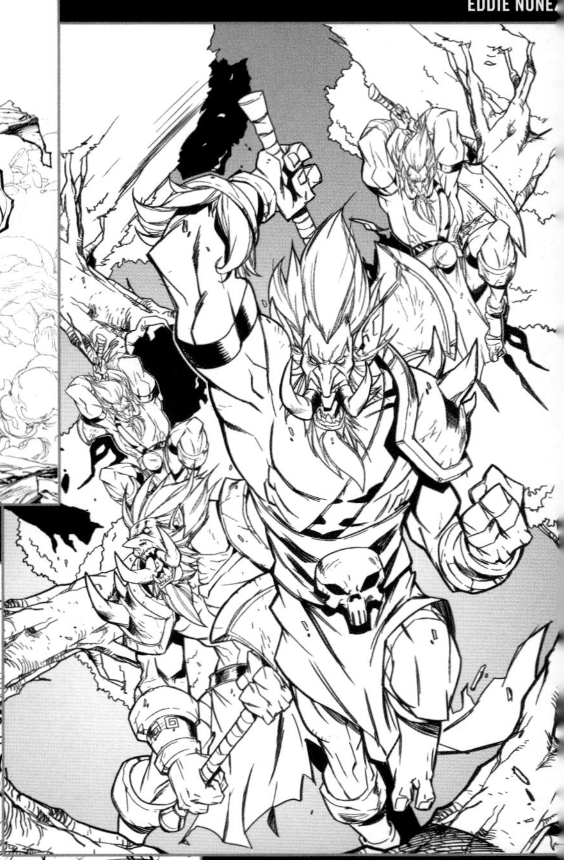

EDDIE NUNEZ

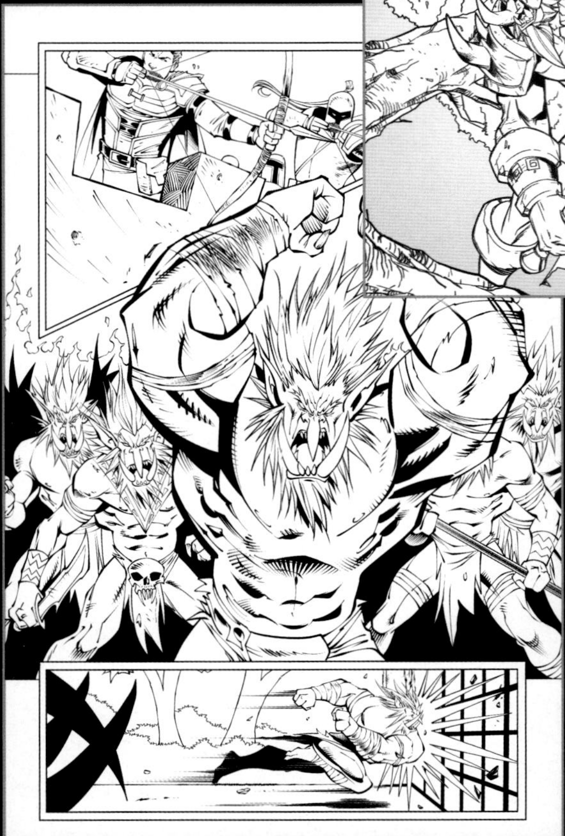

MICHAEL O'HARE

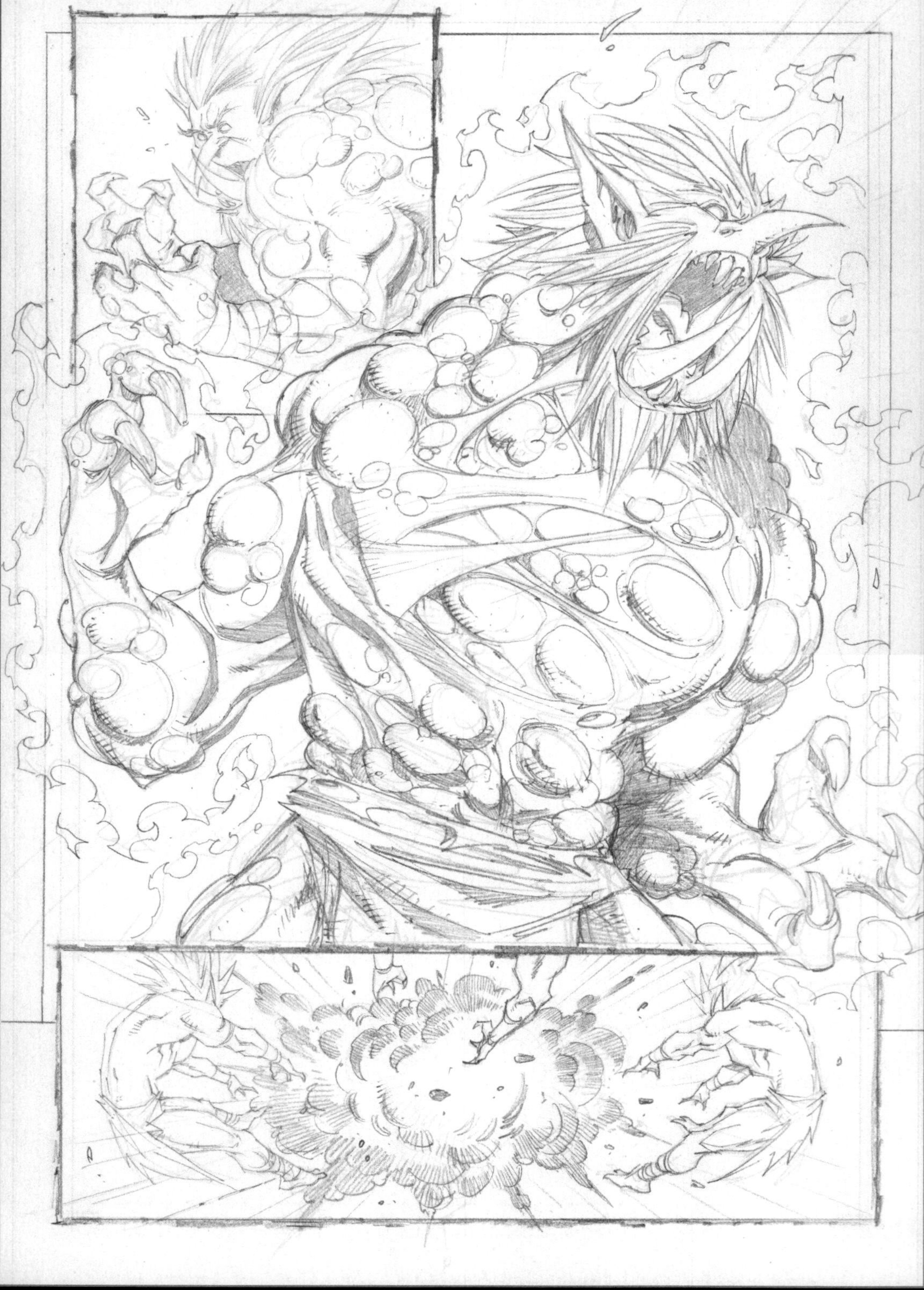

JOURNEY OF A PAGE: PENCILS

Chapter 4 artist Michael O'Hare followed the traditional process of penciling his pages by hand

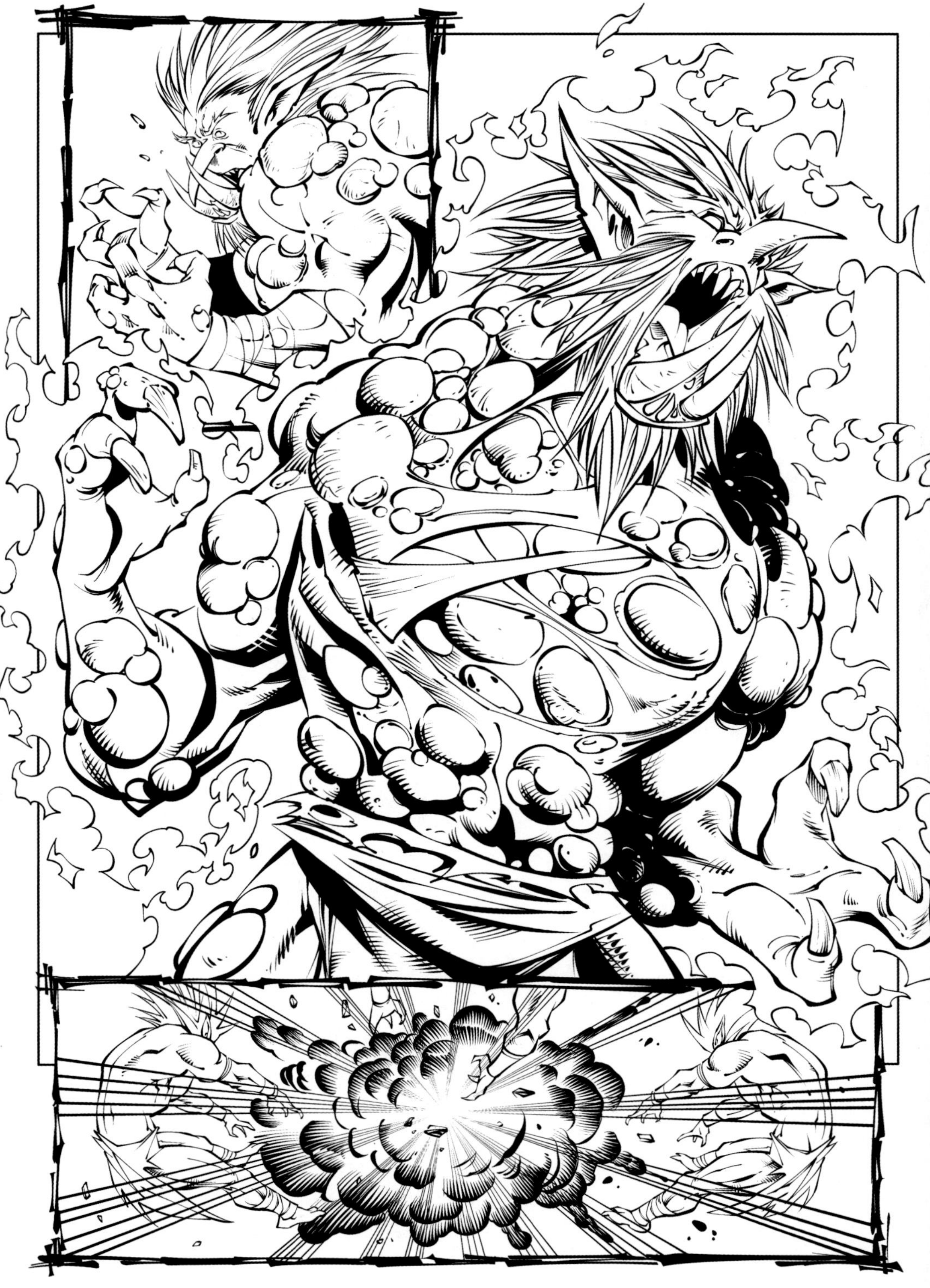

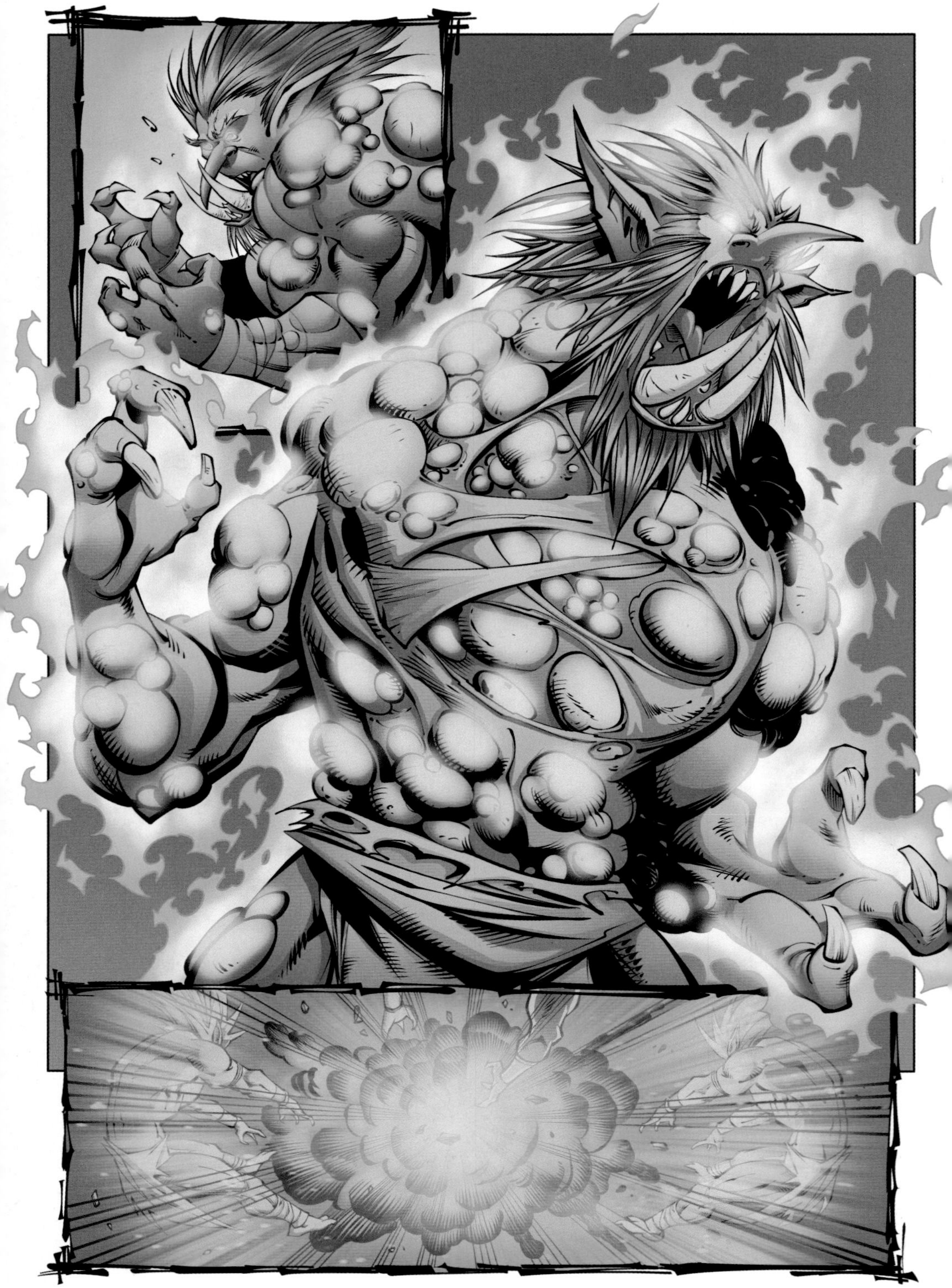

JOURNEY OF A PAGE: COLORS

Colorist Carrie Strachan completes the process by taking the digitally-inked page and coloring it, digitally. Lettering and sound effects are added last to complete the page's journey from script to final book.